D1124657

An African's Life

• • • • • • • • • • • • • •

THE BLACK ATLANTIC

General Editor: Polly Rewt, The Open University and University of Stirling

Series Advisers: Caryl Phillips, novelist; David Dabydeen, Centre for Caribbean Studies, University of Warwick; Vincent Carretta, Professor of English, University of Maryland; Angus Calder, writer

The cultural and theoretical parameters of the Black Atlantic world are explored and treated critically in this timely series. It offers students, scholars and general readers essential texts which focus on the international black experience. The broad scope of the series is innovative and ambitious, treating literary, historical, biographical, musical and visual arts subjects from an interdisciplinary and cross-cultural perspective.

The books address current debates on what constitutes the Black Atlantic, both geographically and theoretically. They include anthologized primary material and collections of seminal critical value to courses on the African diaspora and related subjects. They will also appeal more widely to a readership interested in biographical and other material that presents scholarship accessibly.

Also in the series:

Paul E. Lovejoy (editor), *Identity in the Shadow of Slavery*

Nancy Priscilla Naro, *A Slave's Place, a Master's World: Fashioning Dependency in Rural Brazil*

Alasdair Pettinger (editor), *Always Elsewhere: Travels of the Black Atlantic*

James Walvin, *Making the Black Atlantic: Britain and the African Diaspora*

AN AFRICAN'S LIFE

The Life and Times of
Olaudah Equiano,
1745–1797

JAMES WALVIN

CONTINUUM
London and New York

Continuum
Wellington House, 125 Strand, London WC2R 0BB
370 Lexington Avenue, New York, NY 10017–6503

First published by Cassell in hardback 1998.
Published in paperback 2000

British Library Cataloguing-in-Publication Data
A catalogue record for this book is available from the British Library.

Library of Congress Cataloging-in-Publication Data
Walvin, James.
  An African's Life : the life and times of Olaudah Equiano,
1745–1797 / James Walvin.
    p.   cm.—(The Black Atlantic)
    Includes bibliographical references (p.   ) and index.
    ISBN 0-304-70214-5 (hardcover)   0-8264-4704-X (paperback)
    1. Equiano, Olaudah, b. 1745. 2. Slaves—Biography. I. Title.
II. Series.
HT869E6W35 1998
305.5'67'092—dc21
[B]
                                                                98–20050
                                                                CIP

ISBN 0-304-70214-5 (hardback)
      0-8264-4704-X (paperback)

Typeset by Ben Cracknell Studios

Printed and bound in Great Britain by Biddles Ltd, Guildford and King's Lynn

CONTENTS

LIST OF PLATES

ACKNOWLEDGEMENTS

I owe particular debts to a number of colleagues. First to the late Paul Edwards who, long ago, persuaded me that Equiano was a figure to be reckoned with. Second I am indebted to Vincent Carretta for his meticulous and imaginative scholarship, which has brought together Equiano's writing in an accessible and definitive form. He has, moreover, been unfailingly generous to me, always helping with prompt replies to a range of queries. I am especially indebted to the anonymous reviewers of my original manuscript; their suggestions helped me to improve this book and saved me from some errors. I was greatly helped by comments from Norman Hampson, Jane Rendall and Edward Royle. Charles Walker my agent was, as ever, encouraging and helpful.

My views about Equiano have been informed by the comments of people at seminars in various academic gatherings: in York, at the Institute of Historical Research in London, the University of the West Indies (Jamaica), the University of Houston (with special thanks to Richard Blackett) and Emory University Atlanta. Among the libraries I have used I would like to thank the University of Maryland (Marylandia and Rare Book Collection) at College Park, the School of Oriental and African Studies (London), the Goldsmiths Collection in the University of London library, the British Library, and the Library Company of Philadelphia. I revised this book in the Humanities Research Centre of the Australian National University and would like to thank them, especially Iain McCalman, for their generosity and hospitality.

Finally I cannot fail to thank the anonymous bookseller who sold me a first edition of Equiano's *Narrative* for a mere 5 shillings in 1967. I learned everything I knew, initially, about Equiano from that prized possession.

James Walvin
February 1998

PREFACE

In 1797 an African – Olaudah Equiano – died in England. He was the most famous member of a small contemporary black community which had developed in Britain in the course of the seventeenth and eighteenth centuries on the back of the massive expansion of Atlantic slave trading. Equiano had been born around 1745 in what is now Nigeria. He was enslaved at the age of about 11 and shipped, like millions more, into the Americas, first to Barbados then to Virginia. Soon sold on, Equiano found himself working – as a slave – in England and on English ships. The youthful Equiano quickly learned to read and write (and to do arithmetic). He was converted to Christianity and, after a series of religious crises, his Christianity became his guiding light.

Returned to Montserrat in the West Indies in 1763, Equiano worked and travelled extensively in the Caribbean and North America. Wherever he sailed he conducted business in his own name. From the money he saved he was able to buy his freedom in 1766. Thereafter, much of his life was based in London, or at sea in British ships. By the early 1780s he was naturally drawn to the first English campaign against the slave trade. Then in 1787 he was employed by the British government as an agent in their ill-fated efforts to ship the black poor from London to Sierra Leone.

Equiano was now a public figure, and he decided to make his own contribution to abolition (and perhaps make some money) by publishing his autobiography – his *Narrative* (1789). For the next nine years he tirelessly promoted the book throughout Britain, and by the time of his death (1797) his efforts (and his marriage) had enabled him to accumulate a modest estate.

Equiano was famous when he died, but within twenty years he had been almost totally forgotten. In 1960 his name was revived by a number of scholars on both sides of the Atlantic. Today (1998) Equiano's autobiography is something of a bestseller and he has become established as a prominent historical and literary figure. In the process Equiano has become a heroic (sometimes a mythical) figure in West Africa, the Americas and in Europe. This book tells the story of his life and times.

INTRODUCTION: DISCOVERING EQUIANO

The seeds of this book were first sown in 1966 when I was working in the Public Records Office on research for my doctorate. Though concentrating on English radicals in the 1790s, I came across what seemed a curious fact: that one of my main interests (a Scottish shoemaker called Thomas Hardy) had an African lodger in his London home in 1792. At the time, the presence of an African in London in the 1790s seemed unusual. Odder still, Hardy mentioned that the African was writing his autobiography. I dutifully recorded the facts on my filing cards – and stashed them away, never dreaming that a generation later I would return to them. A year later, I lived next door to a city-centre bookshop in York where I stumbled across a first edition (1789) of that same African's autobiography. I bought it, simply out of curiosity, for five shillings.

By 1970 my research interests had shifted towards the history of black slavery and I had become especially curious about those slaves and ex-slaves who had been cast ashore not in the Americas (the destination for most African slaves) but in England. There was, however, no obvious historiography, no maps to what was effectively uncharted historical territory. Again, and for the third time, I came across the story of the African I had first encountered in 1966. Now I was firmly steered towards him (and other Africans) by the exhilarating friendship and advice of Paul Edwards. Edwards had already published his own editions of the African concerned – Olaudah Equiano – but, in his characteristically generous style, was insistent that others should share his ideas and his discoveries. Time spent with Paul Edwards in Edinburgh in 1971, and later, always took memorable turns. I simply could not keep up with his range of intellectual interests, nor with his zest for life (still less with his passion for wine.) But if Paul Edwards helped me in any single way, it was to persuade me of the importance of that small band of Africans who lived – and wrote – in London in the late years of the eighteenth century.

In 1971–2 I began to focus more clearly on this coterie of Africans, this time when researching the scheme to 'repatriate' London's destitute blacks to Africa in 1787–8. The most prominent African in that scheme – Equiano – was inescapable.

Moreover, by now he had dogged my historical steps, on and off, for five years. Even when, in 1973, I published a history of the English black community, my publisher chose for the dust-jacket (and without my involvement) a picture thought to be of Equiano. By then, I too had published extracts from Equiano in various anthologies about black history, but like other historians, I tended simply to abstract sections of Equiano's text, quoting and reprinting him, without too much serious criticism of the text itself. Indeed, this has been the predominant tendency among historians; to quote Equiano as unproblematic. His words are something we all agree on, and can quote, with no questions asked.

A very different tradition – of English literary criticism (where Paul Edwards was the key pioneer) – took an altogether different trajectory. Scholars, especially in North America, have turned to Equiano in their droves in recent years, and their investigations have taught us a great deal about the man. In the hands of such critics it has become clear that the initial rather bland approach of historians left something to be desired. Here, after all, is a remarkable text: an African's autobiography which was unique at the time. It is a story which tells of extraordinary events (shared by millions of Africans), beginning with boyhood enslavement in Africa and continuing through the oceanic crossing on a slave ship. Yet in places the book remains oddly silent about some of the deepest of personal psychological traumas. Equiano's story is often as striking for its omissions and silences as it is for its more obvious details. He sometimes brushes aside, skips over or minimizes, issues which closer reading suggests had a clear importance to him. To take a simple example, he was given a number of names by white people; we are even uncertain of the African name he asserted as his own. Beneath this basic fact – naming and renaming – scholars have raised the issue of a lost and recovered African identity. It is an autobiography which operates at a number of levels. It is both autobiography and polemic; a public account of one man's life. But it is also a private statement – a story – with glaring omissions, of Equiano's innermost feelings in the face of remarkable upheavals.

Some of the work of literary scholars on Equiano has left me, as a historian, uneasy about his contemporary image. I developed doubts about how Equiano has been (and is) portrayed. His autobiography offers scholars a perfect opportunity to indulge in textual analysis. Often, in the process, the man and his times have receded from view. In part, my concerns about the analysis of Equiano were a reflection of the more general trend that saw whole areas of historical reconstruction succumb to theoretical analysis and which often seemed to owe little to the historical realities as I understood them.[1] For these and other reasons, for some time past I have felt the need to write about Equiano. But I could not see how, or even why. Why write a biography, for example, when Equiano's own text seems to say everything we might want to know, and is so readily available?

Curiously, I was finally prompted to write this book by the publication of what is far and away the best edition of Equiano's autobiography. Vincent Carretta's Penguin edition is a meticulous piece of scholarship which has deservedly become the standard volume of Equiano's work. No serious scholar in the field can afford to be without it. Carretta's publication and success convinced me that there was space – and need – for a historical study of Equiano. Carretta had made available Equiano's own words to a wide and expanding readership. It seemed equally clear to me that any historical appreciation of Equiano could not even have begun without Carretta's important work; his scholarship made my own work both possible, and pressing.

There were other related forces which nudged me towards this biography. Firstly, Equiano had become established, in the USA, as an *African-American*. Anthologies of African-American writers, new editions of his autobiography, and individual scholars of all sorts and conditions repeat the claim that Equiano was African-American (i.e. North American). The more I thought about the matter, however, the clearer it seemed to me that Equiano had only tenuous links to America (unless we define the Americas in their broad hemispheric setting). He was born an African, or rather an Igbo; he lived for many years in the British West Indies, spent considerable time at sea, and was resident for long spells in England, where he made his home and began to raise a family. In what sense was he American? The simple question began to emerge: who was the real Equiano?

That question, apparently easily answered, becomes more complex when we think about two of the most durable aspects of Equiano's personality: his name and his physical image. Equiano *rarely* used the name 'Equiano'. He adopted the name only in the last decade of his life, when he had become a public, and published, figure. To his friends, his wife, in his will, in his daughters' name, in letters to the press, to and from friends and in the great majority of other references we know of, Equiano used the name 'Gustavus Vassa'. Who, then, was this man, who chose to change his name – and who is remembered today by a name he adopted late in life? Similarly, the portrait which has long been thought of as Equiano, has recently been challenged. There is, then, uncertainty about his name and about his publicly known face. Moreover there is a great deal of confusion even about his precise African identity. There are, clearly, questions to be answered, or at least to be raised.

If any one single factor persuaded me to write this book it was the feeling that many of those who had written about Equiano seemed unwilling (perhaps because they were concerned with his autobiography as a literary text) to place the man in his historical setting. Equiano was after all an African slave, plucked from his homeland in the peak years of the Atlantic slave trade, and much of his life needs to be located in the wider world of Atlantic slavery. Indeed, we can only really make sense of Equiano in that historical setting. It is *precisely* this fact that forms one of the main themes in his own book. Equiano's autobiography was written as a contribution not merely to the rising tide of British abolitionism, but as a story which spoke for millions of other African slaves who had no voice.

Anyone interested in Equiano must, of course, turn to his autobiography – and to the edition splendidly edited by Vincent Carretta. This book is not intended to deflect readers from that book, nor does it pretend to offer an alternative view. What it seeks to do is to render Equiano a little more comprehensible. What follows, then, is the story of the life of a single African in the era of the Atlantic slave trade.

Notes

1. For the most recent discussion of this and related issues see Richard J. Evans, *In Defence of History* (London, 1997).

PART ONE

FROM AFRICA TO SLAVERY

I

=1=

AFRICA REMEMBERED

Sometime around 1756, an African boy of about 11 years of age and his sister were violently seized from their home village somewhere deep in south-eastern Nigeria by a raiding party. While the adults were out of the village, two men and a woman clambered over the village walls and grabbed the two children:

> without giving us time to cry out, or make resistance, they stopped our mouths, tied our hands, and ran off with us into the nearest wood . . .[1]

It was the beginning of a nightmare experience which was to see the children dragged far from their home, separated permanently, the boy eventually sold to slave traders on the Atlantic coast and thence shipped to the Americas. We do not know what happened to his sister. It is a shocking story, recalled more than thirty years later by the African for the benefit of his British readers. His story remains one of the few personal accounts of that fundamental and traumatic experience which was the fate of millions of Africans in the era of the Atlantic slave trade.

Olaudah Equiano was born an Igbo, somewhere in the east of modern Nigeria: 'I was born in the year 1745, in a charming vale, named Essaka.' Modern scholars have not been able to locate the region precisely, and even the date is, of course, only approximate. Equiano was but one enslaved African in that enormous movement of African peoples which helped to transform the face of three continents in the course of Atlantic slavery. The Igbo people in particular provided a vast number of the slaves who were shipped across the Atlantic in the eighteenth century. Something like one and a half million Igbo people were removed from the Nigerian hinterland of the Calabar coast. About one-half of that number were enslaved in the years 1750–1807, the period covered by Equiano's life.

In this violent transfer of the Igbo people into slavery, the British were the key players; it was British ships, slavers and commercial interests which transported the bulk of those Africans into British colonies. But like all European slave-trading nations, the British operated only on the African coast and across the Atlantic. The European slaving positions on the coast were, in effect, a series of tenuous toeholds: posts, settlements, forts, transit barracoons, ad-hoc trading visits, floating off-shore positions. All this spoke to the physical difficulties (notably of ill-health) of maintaining a permanent European trading or residential presence in West Africa. Thus, though the Europeans developed a well-oiled machinery for handling Africans on the coast, they could *not* directly secure slaves from the African interior. For that they needed other Africans.

Whatever its complex origins, the internal African slave trade, which saw the enforced movement of swarms of people to the coast to feed the voracious European appetite for slaves, had by the the mid-eighteenth century become a human and economic system which reached deep into the African interior.[2] Atlantic slavery involved much more than the transport of millions of Africans from the coast to the Americas; it seeped inland from a coastline (which itself stretched from Senegambia to Angola), deep into the various interiors of that vast continent, persuading peoples of very different communities to enslave other Africans, and to move them to the coast. In return, the means of exchange for trade on the coast, the baubles of the slave trade (the goods, produce and commodities unloaded from the European ships) found their way into the African interior. Here was a trade which had fundamental and devastating consequences for Africa (reaching far beyond the obvious slave-trading regions). It served to retard the growth of population in West Africa for two centuries, it threw up new political and social systems to respond to the demand for slaves, it encouraged the use of slavery *within* Africa and generated 'a more brutal attitude towards suffering'.[3]

We now know a great deal about the Atlantic slave trade, but we know much less about the moment and the process of enslavement; that first enslavement, far from European eyes, in the African hinterland. In recent years historians have been able to reconstruct the history of the slave trade in considerable detail: the numbers involved, the nature and origins of the people enslaved and transported.[4] But the point of impact – the brutal moment of enslavement – continues to elude us. For this reason alone, Equiano's account of his own experience is critical and has been used time and again by historians to describe how Africans were enslaved. His was a personal testimony which spoke for millions of other Africans, however much the experience of others might differ quite sharply in detail.

Equiano recalled his enslavement more than thirty years after the event. He wrote as part of the abolitionist drive against the slave trade, hoping to persuade British readers that the Atlantic slave trade should be abolished. Moreover it seems clear enough, when we study his description of Africa, that he had been influenced by what he had read, in the meantime, by other commentators about Africa.[5] It has the weaknesses of any personal recollection; of memories and thoughts written down many years after the event and mediated by subsequent experiences. But his crucial traumatic enslavement remained fresh in his mind. He was, after all, eleven years old; at an age from which experiences remain clear in the adult mind. And how could time dim the memory of enslavement itself? Moreover, for years after, he continued to meet other Africans who had endured similar experiences.

Perhaps the most important of Equiano's experiences after he was removed from Africa (and one generally overlooked by scholars) was his regular contact with his 'fellow countrymen'. In the West Indies he frequently met freshly arrived Africans, describing them variously as 'natives of Eboe', 'Eboan Africans' or more simply, 'my countrymen'. Indeed, he was employed by at least two of his owners specifically as a middleman: an African who would be able to speak with and reassure African slaves stepping ashore from the slave ships. Though he was wrenched from Africa as a child, Equiano, like all Africans in the slave communities of the Americas, maintained a form of contact with his distant homeland throughout his exile via new arrivals, stumbling from the slave ships, all with their own stories and memories of Africa and of enslavement. The slave experience differed greatly, but for the Igbo people who formed the bulk of that slave army shipped by the British in the late eighteenth century, there were many experiences in common.[6] Equiano's clear memories of his homeland were periodically refreshed by his contact with new arrivals from Africa.

New Africans were expected to adapt quickly to their new environment, to learn the local patois, acquire the skills and tricks of local living (if only to avoid incurring the anger of slave-owners and drivers). If the African survived (and many did not, succumbing while in transit to a range of ailments and illnesses picked up on board ships), there followed an inevitable (and necessarily speedy) accommodation to life in the Americas. But this process did not and could not purge Africans of memories of their homelands; of their lost loved ones, their distant communities and the complexities of social customs which had shaped their African lives. Nor did it erase memories of that most traumatic of all memories: the moment of enslavement and brutal separation from family, and the searing experience of oceanic transit to the Americas. Memories of Africa may have receded, as memories tend to do, but whatever the particular experiences of the Africans who reached the Americas, Africa (or rather their particular region of Africa) remained their formative, core experience. In Equiano's case, it was Igbo. And his recollections were refreshed by periodic conversations with other Igbo people newly arrived to the Americas. What Equiano wrote over thirty years later provides a unique African insight into life and customs.

Equiano was born and reared far from the obvious influences of Europeans and their trading systems on the coast. He knew nothing even about the ocean. His home community owed a form of loyalty to what Equiano called the kingdom of Benin.[7] His own father held some kind of senior rank, an elder or chief, with appropriate facial markings to confirm his status. It was a scarring which would have come Equiano's way, had he stayed. Though a fierce polemicist against Atlantic slavery, Equiano had no qualms in describing slavery in his home community. Slavery had an accepted role in local society. Crimes – adultery by women for example – were punished by slavery. Slaves were given as wedding dowry, along with land, animals and other goods. Equiano described how local slaves lived (in their own housing, close to the family homes of their master). He also told how distant peoples, from the south-west, brought goods to local markets for sale and barter, passing through Equiano's home region accompanied by their slaves. Equiano recalled how his own people sold slaves to passing slave traders:

> but they were only prisoners of war, or such among us as had been convicted of kidnapping, or adultery, and some other crimes which we esteemed heinous. . .

In return for the slaves, Equiano's community acquired (among other things) firearms, gunpowder, hats and beads. It seems clear enough that some of this trade was exotic and had found its way, by overlapping internal trading systems, from Europeans on the coast to Equiano's homeland far from the ocean. These brief, cursory remarks tell us a great deal. Though Equiano grew up claiming to know little about the distant world of European slave traders, the influence of that trade had clearly spread to his own doorstep in the Igbo hinterland, as he was to discover to his cost. Traders from a distant region, carrying goods from even further afield, were looking for slaves for transit and sale outside the region.

Equiano's pen-portrait of his Igbo homeland sought to capture those features of local life which might interest his British readers. He described how local husbands (normally) had two wives, though womenfolk were married to a single husband. Local marriage ceremonies were preceded by elaborate rituals, culminating in bonfires, music and dancing. His people were, he wrote:

> almost a nation of dancers, musicians, and poets. Thus every great event, such as a triumphant return from battle, or other cause of public rejoicing, is celebrated in public dances, which are accompanied with songs and music suited to the occasion.[8]

No reader of Equiano's book would have been surprised to learn that music played a major role in the author's home region. Europeans had long been accustomed to the idea that Africans, in Africa, Europe and the Americas, were especially musical people. If Europeans agreed on any single aspect of black life, it was that music was part of the African personal and cultural make-up. Throughout the slave colonies of the Americas and among those small pockets of blacks living in Europe, the social life of Africans and their local-born descendants seemed to be characterized by music. They played music on a vast range of instruments, which they conjured forth from whatever materials came to hand, they danced whenever and wherever they could, and in general displayed an enthusiasm for music which seemed altogether more zestful than anything to be found in Europe. Few commentators on eighteenth-century black life could resist the temptation to talk about black musicality. Equiano's account of music-making in his homeland merely confirmed his readers' views about Africa and Africans.

Equiano tried to recall as much as he could of the social habits of his distant African childhood. He described the clothing, the materials, the jewellery, the household effects from his home of forty years earlier. In setting this African scene, he sketched a simple anthropology of the culture he remembered from childhood. Much of what he wrote was about the simple customs and artefacts of everyday life: work, cooking, food, drinking and eating habits, local produce and materials, animals and living quarters. Though apparently mundane and obvious it forms not only a unique contemporary account (however unconsciously embellished by the author's subsequent reading) but also an interesting entrée to the author's frame of mind.

What was the purpose, the significance, of describing such unexceptional items of everyday life? Was it merely a haphazard snapshot of day-to-day existence? Or was there more to it than this? Might it be an attempt to recreate a culture, a way of life which, for all its obvious differences, might impress the reader by being recognizable? By offering an image of mundane, daily routines and habits, Equiano could perhaps persuade the reader that Africa was recognizably familiar? More than that, Equiano's literary image of Africa remembered was one of bounty and fertility; a natural habitat which was 'uncommonly rich and fruitful, and produces all kinds of vegetables in great abundance'.[9] Equiano's Africa was a place which yielded much more than the human muscle power required by Europeans. The idea that Africa might offer much more than the slave trade was a claim which, in 1789, was unusual.

Equiano wrote about aspects of African cultures which were not normally presented to the reading public in so sympathetic a light. Often he employed irony to make his point, winning over the British readers by an ironic inflection and tone. But the strength of his account is rooted in more substantial issues. Here was an African's voice where none had been heard before. What Europeans knew about African religions, for example, was likely to be mythological and hostile. From the first days of European maritime exploration, African beliefs had been described in the most fanciful and lurid terms. Indeed, African patterns of worship and belief seemed so far removed from what Europeans imagined religion should be, that they were dismissed as mere superstitions; primitive, even childlike, customs and myths unworthy of serious consideration. Excepting those in Islamic regions, Africans were thought of as mere pagans; heathens whose lack of acceptable religion removed them, in European eyes, beyond the pale of civilized societies. It was this very *lack* of religion – the Africans' 'heathenism' – which Europeans used to justify enslaving them.[10] Efforts to convert Africans to Christianity were few and limited (mainly because of the physical dangers facing whites trying to live in West Africa). By the late eighteenth century the realities of African beliefs and religions remained largely beyond the ken of most Europeans. It was perhaps with this in mind that Equiano wrote of what he remembered of his native faith.

Significantly, he recalled that his people believed in 'one Creator of all things'. It might not, after all, be so far removed from the Christian idea of a single deity. People placed food and drink at the graves of dead ancestors. His people did not have special places of worship, but had priests 'or magicians', whose role was inherited by their sons and who 'were held in great reverence by the people'. These men also acted as doctors, dealing with physical as well as spiritual and mystical matters. Some of their activities reminded Equiano of customs he had seen later among slaves in the West Indies. The doctor/priests were buried, along with their implements and valuables, in presence of 'those of the same profession or tribe'.[11]

Equiano's people also had distinctive ceremonies, with blessings and offerings to mark particular times of the year (at harvests, full moons, when animals were killed) and all presided over by heads of family. They practised circumcision, and took their names from events or forebodings at the times of the birth. He wrote that his own name, Olaudah, signified 'vicissitude, or fortunate also; one favoured, and having a loud voice and well spoken'.[12] He recalled them as a clean people, with firm rituals of washing and cleaning, partly for religious purposes. A number of these habits reminded him of Jewish life, or of what he had gleaned about Jewish life from the Bible:

> of the Jews, before they reached the Land of Promise, and particularly the patriarchs, while they were yet in that pastoral state which is described in Genesis – an analogy, which alone would induce me to think that the one people had sprung from the other.[13]

This link between Africans and Jews was not as odd as it might now seem, for Equiano was drawing on a well-established debate about links; a variant of the biblical question about the descendants of Ham.[14] This debate had been revived in the late eighteenth century in the early arguments prompted by the first abolitionists. To display his scholarly credentials in all this – and to back-up his personal recollections – Equiano listed a number of contemporary biblical scholars who agreed with him. He mingled personal recollection with an engagement with literary debate.

Equiano also described the agricultural and labouring patterns of his home community. But it was a society which had to be permanently alert to the dangers of attack and slave-taking by outsiders: 'Perhaps they are incited to this by those traders who brought the European goods. . .' Though far from the coast, and from the obvious influence of European slave traders, the demand for slaves was felt deep in the interior. Though we can plot in some detail the consequences of the slave trade on the coast and across the Atlantic, Equiano provides an important insight into the way the demand for Africans had profound consequences in the African interior, far from the Europeans' immediate influences.[15]

For his part Equiano was convinced that slave-raids, and kidnapping, accounted for most of the slavery in his home region. The prisoners and captives from such raids formed the human commodities passed on by African slave traders from their interior region to the Europeans on the coast. But slaves were not used solely for export. Equiano's own community held slaves, 'but how different was their condition from that of the slaves in the West-Indies!'[16] He remembered slaves working alongside other, free members of the community, wearing similar clothes, though not allowed to eat with free people. What he described was a form of slavery more akin to serfdom in medieval Europe than the chattel slavery of the Americas. Clearly, the coastal demand for vast numbers of African slaves had profound consequences within Africa. But African slavery also had indigenous roots which predated the growth of the Atlantic trade.[17] No one, today, can doubt the seismic impact of the European demand for slaves. Equally, it is hard to deny the existence of slavery within Africa before the Europeans arrived. Put at its simplest, the Europeans did not *introduce* slavery into Africa. Equiano's account of slavery in his home region provides interesting evidence about both arguments. He assumed that the slave-raiding which troubled the region was in response to the demand for slaves elsewhere, and to the demand for imported European goods. However, he also described local, domestic slavery as an unexceptional issue; different from slavery in the Americas but nonetheless an unquestioned feature of his home environment. He did not take exception to, or denounce, slavery in his homeland. Nor did he think it inappropriate to write about it in what was essentially an anti-slavery tract.

By the time of Equiano's enslavement, the Atlantic slave trade had flourished for centuries and had *already* transformed critical areas of life in the slaving hinterlands. Whatever indigenous African slave systems had existed earlier, the arrival of Europeans on the West African coast, from the late fifteenth century onwards, tended to divert and transform them. Slave routes which had once headed north, or locally from one African community to another, were now directed along new paths towards the slave entrepôts on the Atlantic coast. Equiano was enslaved not to serve other Africans, but to be moved on, away from his homeland towards an Atlantic slave ship.

He came from a family of seven surviving children, only one of them a girl. Equiano was the youngest, and his mother's favourite. He remembered a happy childhood, being instructed at work in the fields and in soldierly activities. When adults went to work in the fields, children were coralled together, with a watch posted against strangers – a sure sign of the fear and the threat of dangers. When he was about eleven (*c.*1756) and was alone with his sister, they were seized by three strangers, two men and woman, who gagged and bound them and hurried them away. It was the beginning of a protracted nightmare. The group rushed to get clear of Equiano's native village, then travelled throughout the day, through the cover, with the children gagged and bound. After a couple of days, and to their great distress, the two children were parted. Already wrenched from his wider family, Equiano now found himself parted from a much-loved sister:

> I was left in a state of distraction not to be described. I cried and grieved continually; and for several days I did not eat any thing but what they forced into my mouth.[18]

One of slavery's great agonies was the experience of family separation. In Africa and the Americas commentators regularly told the plaintive tale of the anguish caused by the enforced parting of family members.

The loss of his family – especially the loss of his mother – recurs time and again. Throughout the book Equiano also describes his search for a father figure (among his owners/captains/teachers). His story is replete with examples of the author coming to terms with the fundamental loss resulting from enslavement; and the loss of mother and father, of sister – the sudden and unexpected wrenching from his Igbo cultural homeland.[19]

As he was moved on – he knew not where – Equiano was sold from one group to another. Everywhere he was put to work. At first he was an assistant to a man who worked as a smith (in what Equiano took to be gold). He tried to escape, but was afraid of the natural dangers in the bush – and daunted by the sheer ordeal and uncertainty of tracking back over so large a distance to his father's home. He

PLATE 1. Raiders attacking a village in Central Africa: 'It was my fate to be thus attacked, and to be carried off, when none of the grown people were nigh' (Equiano).

Source: H. H. Johnston in The Graphic, 29 September 1888. Mary Evans Picture Library.

PLATE 2.
A convoy of
captured Africans
being taken into
slavery: 'I was
now carried to
the left of the
sun's rising,
through many
different
countries. . .'
(Equiano)

*Source: Verney
Lovett Cameron,
Travels in Central
Africa (1873).
Mary Evans
Picture Library.*

crept back to his captors. After a short time, Equiano was sold again, moving onwards: 'I was carried to the left of the sun's rising'. Though travelling further and further away from his home, he was still able to understand people around him: 'The languages of different nations did not totally differ, nor were they so copious as those of the Europeans, particularly the English.'

His deepening gloom was temporarily relieved when his group met his separated sister. Brother and sister were overjoyed at this chance encounter, but it quickly ended when Equiano was sold again, travelling on to a major town, which he called Tinmah. The loss of his only sister haunted Equiano, and he found it difficult to describe her without slipping into a sentimental tone which was not typical of his writing overall. It was an event of such profound distress that words seemed inadequate to the task. By now, Equiano had begun to notice unusual features of the world around him; houses constructed differently, unfamiliar trees and crops, the unusual cowrie shell. Equiano himself was exchanged for 172 cowries. (The shells, from the Indian Ocean, had been introduced into West Africa via North Africa and were widely used as a means of exchange.[20]) Sold yet again, to a woman, Equiano was surprised when she allowed him to eat in her presence; hitherto all the slaves he had known had been obliged to eat their food elsewhere. He stayed with her for about two months, among people whose language and customs were familiar.

He was content to settle into this position but, again unexpectedly, he was once more sold, 'and hurried away even amongst the uncircumcised'.[21] It seemed to be a pattern. Just when he was becoming reconciled to his lot – however miserable it might be – he was uprooted, sold, and physically route-marched to another region. Now, many months after his initial enslavement, Equiano had entered a region where customs, language and culture were quite unfamiliar. The men were uncircumcised, and people did not wash their hands before eating. He had clearly entered a part of West Africa which fell more directly under the European sphere of trading influence: 'They cooked in iron pots, and had European cutlasses and cross bows. . .' Local people filed their teeth and scarred their faces, but what astonished him most of all was the scale of the river they were now skirting. A massive expanse of water, on which some people lived permanently in their canoes, it may have been one of the major tributaries of the Niger. Equiano now found himself travelling by water, moving down the river in daytime, and camping on the bank at night. This riverine leg of the journey was simply the latest stage of a protracted journey:

> Thus I continued to travel, sometimes by land, sometimes by water, through different countries, and various nations, till, at the end of six or seven months after I had been kidnapped, I arrived at the sea coast.[22]

He was coming to the end of his life in Africa. Like millions of others, he was never to return.

Equiano's account was of a much more benign Africa than his contemporary readers might have expected. His aim, of course, some thirty years after the event, was to describe an Africa very different from their image of the continent. It was, in part, an attempt to win his readers to the idea that Africa had virtues which went largely unrecognized in Europe. This was especially true of its commercial and economic potential. Europeans had long been accustomed to the idea that Africa yielded mainly slaves, despite a bountiful trade in other African commodities. (After all, Europeans had been initially attracted *not* by slaves, but by other commodities on the coast, notably gold.) Equiano told of the richness of the land, the plentiful supplies of foodstuffs and of tobacco, cotton and timber. It was a region which beckoned the imaginative trader, and not merely those in search of slaves.[23]

Equiano's story of Africa remembered was of a world of almost forty years earlier. Equiano was only 11 when he was enslaved and forcibly removed from his home. By the time he wrote about his homeland he was a man in his mid-forties. There were bound to be some flaws in his memory: incidents, places, events, people inaccurately recalled, wrongly attributed and mislocated. But no one was more conscious of these problems than Equiano himself: 'Such is the imperfect sketch my memory has furnished me with of the manners and customs of a people among whom I first drew my breath.'[24] Yet there is no reason to doubt the clarity of his main memories; the terror of enslavement, the wrenching from his family and sister, and the physical and mental miseries of being driven for months on end towards the Atlantic.

Equiano laid before his English readership an account of African life which was rational and sophisticated. Though it was utterly different from anything Europeans might be accustomed to, it was also quite unlike the images of irrational savagery so commonly portrayed by proponents of the slave system. For a century and more, defenders of Atlantic slavery had portrayed Africa's inhabitants as incorrigibly savage and heathen; beyond the pale of western understanding, and therefore appropriate victims for enslavement. What Equiano described, from firsthand experience, was something quite different. While not trying to hide those features alien to Europeans (facial scarring, polygamy, slavery), Equiano's image of his homeland was altogether more benign, more sympathetic than his readers might expect. In this, he also drew upon earlier writers about West Africa, but the importance of Equiano's account of his early days was that it was the account of an African. He blended the voice of experience – an unimpeachable, personal story – with details culled from later authors.

When Equiano arrived on the coast, the first thing he saw was a slave ship. It was the beginning of a new and even more terrifying ordeal, one shared with millions of other Africans. Equiano's description of what followed – the oceanic agonies of the slave trade – is the best remembered part of his book, repeated time and again by any historian lost for words to capture the unique terror of the Middle Passage (the Atlantic crossing). Equiano's account has been used so frequently because it is a unique African insight and is unsurpassed in the power of its testimony.

The recent historical search for the finer details of Equiano's African origins has not been very successful. There is disagreement about precisely where he was born and raised. It is not possible to track, with any accuracy, his various enslavements, nor to trace the exact geography of his gradual movement from his homeland to the slave ship. Doubts even remain about his name. Moreover, it is clear that his ideas about Africa were influenced by his subsequent reading, notably of the abolitionist literature of the 1780s. But there is nothing in his account which conflicts substantially with the welter of information which historians of African slavery have uncovered in recent years. For all the uncertainties – the recollections of a distant childhood by a middle-aged man – despite its obvious political gloss (it was after all an abolitionist tract), and notwithstanding its effort to portray Africa in a more benign light, Equiano's African story has a compelling authenticity and persuasiveness. It was, obviously, not offered as a scholarly account. And therein lies its strength.

Equiano offered his Africa as an honest recollection; a long-lost experience which continued to haunt him throughout the intervening years. There was, at one level, nothing special about Equiano's experience. It was endured by millions of other Africans and was to continue to blight Africa for a century more. It was a simple, factual remembrance, glossed by the occasional tug at the reader's emotions; an appeal to the humanity of a readership likely to be swayed by the abuse of childhood, family and affection between siblings. What gives Equiano's memory of Africa its strength is not its precision of recollection, nor its verifiable detail of this or that fact, but its resonance. It is a story which speaks for millions of other Africans whose voices were silenced by slavery itself. Historians have become very skilled in reconstructing the history of Atlantic slavery from the raw data of that massive commercial system. The attraction of Equiano is that he gives voice to those statistics. It is a voice of compelling strength, then as now.

Notes

1 *The Interesting Narrative of the Life of Olaudah Equiano, or Gustavus Vassa, the African written by himself*, ninth edition, 1794. This edition contains Equiano's last changes and is therefore the definitive version. All references hereafter are to the Penguin edition edited by Vincent Carretta (London, 1995), cited as *Interesting Narrative*.

2 For a good overview of the Atlantic slave trade, see John Iliffe, *Africans. The History of a Continent* (Cambridge, 1995), Ch. 7.

3 *Ibid.*, p. 127.

4 For some recent findings see David Eltis and David Richardson (eds), *Routes to Slavery* (London, 1997).

5 See Introduction by Paul Edwards, in facsimile edition of *The Interesting Narrative* (London, 1969), pp. xlvii–xlix.

6 Definitions of the Igbo people remain more uncertain than we might imagine. The regions, cultures and history of the Igbo people in all their shifting nature can best be approached through the work of Elizabeth Isichei: *The Ibo People and the Europeans* (London, 1976); *A History of the Igbo People* (London, 1976). I have also benefited from conversations with Dr Peter Yearwood on this issue.

7 Historians have, until recently, imagined that this region was relatively untouched by the eighteenth-century slave trade. Eltis and Richardson, *op.cit.*, p. 27.

8 *Interesting Narrative*, p. 34.

9 *Ibid.*, p. 37.

10 On heathenism see Winthrop D. Jordan, *White over Black* (New York, 1969).

11 *Interesting Narrative*, p. 42.

12 *Ibid.*, p. 41. In fact modern scholars have had difficulty locating this name which, some feel, has no obvious Igbo roots.

13 *Ibid.*, pp. 43–4.

14 Jordan, *op.cit.*, pp. 17–20.

15 For an account of the trade in the Igbo heartlands, see Douglas Chambers, '"My own nation"; Igbo exiles in the diaspora', in Eltis and Richardson, *op.cit.*, pp. 72–97.

16 *Interesting Narrative*, p. 40.

17 For a recent statement of this argument, see John Thornton, *Africa and Africans in the Making of the Atlantic World, 1400–1680* (Cambridge, 1992), Ch. 3.

18 *Interesting Narrative*, p. 48.

19 Paul Edwards, 'Master and Father in Equiano's *Interesting Narrative*', *Slavery and Abolition*, vol. 11, no. 2 (1990).
20 Iliffe, *op.cit.*, p. 83.
21 The account of his enslavement is in *Interesting Narrative*, pp. 46–55.
22 *Ibid.*, p. 54.
23 This argument is developed in Chapter 10 below.
24 *Interesting Narrative*, p. 43.

2

SLAVE SHIPS AND LANDFALL

Sometime around 1756 the young Equiano – confused, frightened and dispirited from months of travel and upheaval – caught sight of the British ship which would carry him across the Atlantic. He was only one of the three million Africans shipped across the Atlantic in British ships, and Equiano's ship was but one of a massive armada of such vessels used to transport African slaves. In the course of the eighteenth century more than 11,000 British ships plied their trade in human cargo, more than half of them originating from Liverpool. But there was scarcely a port worthy the name which resisted the temptation to dispatch a local vessel into the potentially lucrative Africa trade. Who today can imagine slave ships departing from Poole, Lyme Regis, from Whitehaven or Lancaster?

Outbound ships headed for Africa packed with produce and foodstuffs drawn from the length and breadth of Britain, and with goods transhipped from the furthermost points of British global trade. In the words of the Jamaican planter Edward Long, they carried 'very little that is not of British growth or manufacture', or acquired from British colonial trade.[1] By the time of Equiano's enslavement the slave trade on the African coast had long since shed its early piratical style (though that crude form of kidnapping and enslavement continued to be practised in the African interior). On the coast itself, Europeans had evolved complex and varied negotiations with African traders, power-brokers and middle men for their supplies of slaves.[2]

British slavers prowled the vast stretch of the African coast, from Senegambia to the edge of Angola, bartering their goods in return for African slaves, a handful here, a larger batch there, until the captain (himself a mix of trader and master mariner) felt ready to turn westwards, to catch the tradewinds for the slave colonies of the Americas. The early monopoly companies, which had given maritime European nations such power and global reach in the late seventeenth century, had been unequal to the task of supplying slaves in the numbers demanded by the planters in the Americas. The old system gave way to more open trading in African humanity, though it was a system which was always supervised by watchful European states, whose navies enforced national economic interests and legislation.

By the mid-eighteenth century, it was the British who ruled the waves, her international trade and colonies safeguarded by a Royal Navy whose own power waxed accordingly. Each year between 1700 and 1750, British slave traders ferried some 20,000 Africans across the Atlantic. In the next fifty years this expanded to upwards of 40,000 per year. All told, the British transported perhaps 3 million Africans during that century.[3]

Domestic British trade and manufacture thrived on the back of this Africa trade. There were, it is true, rare voices which argued that Britain's interests would be best served by developing a non-slave-based trade with West Africa and the interior,[4] but such views were simply swept aside in the course of the eighteenth century by the material bounty yielded to Britain by the Atlantic slave system. The slave trade and the slave colonies it sustained (70 per cent of all Africans were destined for the sugar islands) were, in the words of Edward Long, of 'immense importance to the grandeur and prosperity of their mother country. . .'[5]

When Equiano arrived on the African coast, he was, at 11 or 12, younger than the average slave. Before 1800, perhaps fewer than 20 per cent of slaves were children, though that proportion increased dramatically in the course of the nineteenth century.[6] European slave traders were especially keen to buy healthy young men: Africans who were likely to survive the rigours of the Atlantic crossing and command a profitable price from the planters of the Americas. The prospects looked utterly different through the dejected eyes of the enslaved Africans. Fortunately, Equiano's story provides one of the few genuine African accounts of what happened – and of how an African responded to the bruising aggression of that first contact with Europeans. As Equiano was bartered and sold, from one African group to another, he travelled ever closer to the European trading presence on the coast, gradually moving away from cultures he recognized and understood. He now encountered Africans who seemed utterly different from any he had known before:

> I was very much struck with this difference, especially when I came among a people who did not circumcise, and eat without washing their hands.

These people had acquired goods which European traders had imported as the basic currency of the slave trade. 'They cooked also in iron pots, and had European cutlasses and cross bows . . .'[7] The coastal bartering and trade on the coast had served to scatter alien goods – and tastes – in Africa. But nothing impressed Equiano more forcibly than his first sight of the ocean, and the British ship riding at anchor, awaiting its human cargo. Astonishment soon turned to terror; a terror which he was scarcely able to convey. After months of African enslavement, a new regime of horrifying indignities and threats was unleashed on all slaves newly arrived on the coast. Scrutinized, inspected in the most intimate and humiliating of fashions, Equiano, like millions of others, found himself 'immediately handled, and tossed up, to see if I were sound, by some of the crew'. Traders, sailors and surgeons tried to weed out sick Africans, and to assess the health and condition (and hence the value) of new arrivals. African slaves were, in the words of one contemporary, 'examined by us in like manner as our Brother Trade do Beasts in Smithfield'. Poked, prodded, inspected, Africans were examined for 'Countenance and Stature, a good set of Teeth, Pliancy in the Limbs and Joints, and being free of Venereal Taints'.[8] This was the first encounter which African slaves had with Europeans. It was a brutal encounter which was to set the tone for subsequent dealings between the two sides.

Equiano found himself confronted by people – the crew of the slave ship, the traders and a host of whites who hovered in and around the ship – who were unlike any other people he had met:

> Their complexions too differing so much from ours, their long hair, and the language they spoke. . .was very different from any I had ever heard. . .

Convinced that he was about to be killed, Equiano not surprisingly believed himself in 'a world of bad spirits'. Everything around him served to confirm his fate: gangs of chained Africans ('black people of every description'), a boiling furnace, and, throughout the ship, faces filled with 'dejection and sorrow'. Fearful and utterly confused, Equiano felt himself 'abandoned to despair'. He even thought he might be eaten, that deepest of fears which both sides of similar cultural encounters feared in different parts of the world in the eighteenth century.[9] Each new step he was forced to take seemed worse than the last.

While the ship lingered on the coast, the Africans were shackled together for security: in the words of one slave captain 'fastened together, two and two, by handcuffs on their wrists, and by irons on their legs'.[10] When the ship sailed, they were allowed up on deck only briefly, weather permitting, in small groups. The slave decks, infamously recorded in those cross-section sketches of inhuman packing, were, from the first, hell-holes of stable-like squalor. Equiano was thrust below:

> I was soon put down under the decks, and there I received such a salutation in my nostrils as I had never experienced in my life. . .[11]

Packed humanity, fetid air on a tropical coast, the stench of crude sanitation, all served to create a pestilential atmosphere which even hardened crew members found intolerable. Slaves were expected to relieve themselves in 'large buckets, of a conical form, being near two feet in diameter at the bottom, and only one foot at the top, and in depth about twenty-eight inches. . .'[12] Overwhelmed by 'the loathsomeness of the stench' Equiano slipped deeper and deeper into a miserable despondency. Unable to eat, listless, weary of life itself, he was placed across a windlass and severely whipped to persuade him to eat. It was an instant intro-duction to that endemic personal and communal violence which was the lubricant of the Atlantic slave system.

Inside the stinking confines of the slave ships, violence begat violence. Slaves argued and fought with each other – over food (which sometimes got scarcer as the voyage dragged on), over the latrines, over a host of irritations made worse by the dangers, squalor and sickness of the slave decks. And on top of all this there was the permanent threat of white violence. Equiano was afraid:

PLATE 3. Captain negotiating for his human cargo: 'I was immediately handled and tossed up, to see if I were sound, by some of the crew; and I was now persuaded that I had gotten into a world of bad spirits, and that they were going to kill me' (Equiano).

Source: Treating for Slaves (1798). Wilberforce House, Kingston-upon-Hull City Museums and Archives.

I should be put to death, the white people looked and acted, as I thought, in so savage a manner; for I had never seen among any people such instances of brutal cruelty; and this not only shewn towards us blacks, but also to some of the whites themselves.[13]

For the white crew, life at sea was brutal, and often short (especially if they lingered for long on the African coast). Wayward sailors were put in irons and flogged, though such punitive treatment rarely deflected them from violating the slaves. Sexual assaults, sometimes 'of such brutal excesses, as disgrace human nature', were common on the slave ships.[14] Equiano witnessed one white man 'flogged so unmercifully with a large rope near the foremast, that he died in consequence on it...' In this violent environment, where human and physical outrages of the most appalling kind were the stuff of everyday shipboard life, slaves were as fearful as they were sick and depressed. The more Equiano saw of the crew's violence, the more afraid he grew of them. This shipboard culture of violence was in place even before the ships left the African coast.[15] Of course, writing in 1789, Equiano (like other abolitionists) was keen to highlight such violence, knowing it would outrage his readership.

When the slave captain felt he had enough slaves packed below, or when he had lingered long enough (balancing risks to his crew versus possible future slave purchases), the ship headed into the Atlantic, hoping for a speedy, trouble-free passage. For the Africans, life's considerable agonies were made even worse as their maritime prison pitched and rolled its way to landfall in the slave colonies, upwards of two months to the west. The Africans were now confined more or less permanantly below decks, largely for security. On Equiano's ship in 1756, 'now that the whole ship's cargo was confined together, it became absolutely pestilential'. Though historians have in recent years produced an abundance of detail about the Atlantic crossing (statistics about numbers, timing, deaths, disease, sex ratios), Equiano's recollections provide flesh to these statistical bones. The slaves were stifled, and 'so crowded that each had scarcely room to turn himself'. Sickness was everywhere. Like most contemporaries, Equiano thought it was spread by 'miasma' (by the foul, polluted atmosphere). The slaves' chains rubbed and chafed. The stench, especially from 'the necessary tubs' was inescapable and horrible. 'The shrieks of the women, and the groans of the dying' created 'a scene of horror almost inconceivable'.[16]

At sea, the Africans might remain shackled below for days – even weeks – on end. In the grim squalor of their confines, dysentery ('the bloody flux') began to take its toll; the dying still chained, in their distress, to the living. Slave traders' logs tabulated, in impersonal detail, the Africans' sufferings. In June 1751, only five years before Equiano was enslaved, the Liverpool captain John Newton recorded:

This morning buryed a woman slave (No 47). Know not what to say she died of for she has not been properly alive since she first came on board.

The last of Newton's ten African fatalities died – of dysentery – one day before the crew caught sight of land in the Caribbean.[17]

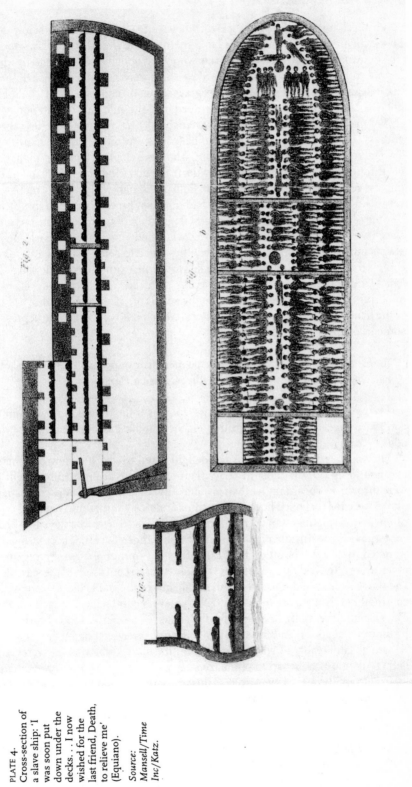

Fig. 2.

Fig. 1.

Fig. 3.

PLATE 4.
Cross-section of
a slave ship: 'I
was soon put
down under the
decks. . . I now
wished for the
last friend, Death,
to relieve me'
(Equiano).

*Source:
Mansell/Time
Inc/Katz.*

Physical ailments spread quickly from slave to slave in the filth below decks. So too did despair. The slavers had to remain alert to the threat of slave suicides: 'the crew used to watch us very closely who were not chained down to the decks, lest we should leap into the water. . .' Slave ships were rigged with encircling nets, to catch any African intent on a watery grave. Equiano confessed that 'could I have got over the nettings, I would have jumped over the side, but I could not. . .'[18]

For the African slave, the long nightmarish Atlantic crossing must have seemed endless. Understandably, some took the obvious way out when the chance arose. Two of Equiano's 'wearied countrymen, who were chained together' managed to get through the safety nets, 'preferring death to such a life of misery', and jumped into the sea, followed by a third African. Equiano remarked that 'many more would very soon have done the same, if they had not been prevented by the ship's crew'.

One of the Africans was rescued, and flogged for his pains. All the remaining slaves were battened down below. Slaves who tried – and failed – to escape were always punished, yet such vigorous penalties failed to deter distressed slaves who could no longer tolerate the conditions. Time and again the Atlantic slave ships lost Africans overboard. The desperate, the disturbed, the dispirited, seized any opportunity to launch themselves into the sea. It often seemed the only solution to the living hell of the slave ships. Other slaves slipped into catatonic depression, some into shrieking madness:[19]

In this manner we continued to undergo more hardships than I can now relate; hardships which are inseparable from this accursed trade.[20]

Even stripped of its abolitionist gloss, there is little in Equiano's account that contradicts recent historical research on the Middle Passage, and much which adds to it.

Life was often made worse by the delight taken by sadistic crew members in compounding the Africans' miseries. Left-over scraps from freshly caught fish were thrown overboard rather than given to Equiano and his hungry companions. Slaves were fed on boiled horse beans, yams and rice – sometimes beef and pork – often with a 'slabber-sauce' made from palm oil. Slaves disliked the beans, sometimes throwing such food at each other in anger. Weather permitting, they were fed twice a day but their food came from a communal bowl serving groups of ten slaves. Individual spoons were soon lost in the confusion of the slave decks and the Africans fed themselves by hand, all amidst the stable-like squalor of their confinement. Not surprisingly, the slaves soon succumbed to stomach ailments. The sick and the weak, unable to feed themselves properly, slipped further and further into a gloomy indifference (often despite force-feeding by the crew).

The ghastly reality of what happened on the slave ships was no secret. Long before abolitionists began to publicize such evidence in the mid-1780s, tens of thousands of Europeans were privy to this grim information, notably of course the sailors, traders, merchants, planters and the rest whose livelihood was so intimately linked to the Atlantic slave trade. Something like one third of a million Britons were involved in the slave trade in the course of the seventeenth and eighteenth centuries.[21]

To compound the physical horrors and personal fears, Equiano like millions more, found himself in an alien world. The very nature of the ships (their sails, anchor, navigational aids), the crew's ability to move the vessel through the waters, to bring it to a halt, the wonders of the deep (flying fish landing on the deck), all seemed to Equiano more magical than real.[22] Little could he have realized, in 1756, that this world of oceanic travel would soon become his own, as he made his career as a professional mariner (both enslaved and free).

For the survivors of the Atlantic crossing, landfall must have seemed a mixed blessing. The terrors of the last few weeks were quickly replaced by new alarms and worries. Equiano's ship made landfall in Barbados, the most easterly of the Caribbean islands. When the crew first caught sight of the island, 'the whites on board gave a great shout and made many signs of joy to us'. We can only guess what went through the Africans' minds: relief that the horrors of the crossing were coming to an end, apprehension about the future? In Equiano's enigmatic words, 'We did not know what to think of this.'[23]

By the time Equiano first saw Barbados, that small, compact island had already surrendered its sugar-producing primacy to Jamaica. But for the best part of a century Barbados had been a by-word for the prosperity yielded by slave-grown sugar. Its high ground was dominated by hundreds of windmills (for crushing the cane), its best lands controlled by an elite of successful planters, whose wealth was secured by battalions of African slaves and their local-born descendants. As early as 1660, Barbados was home to 20,000 slaves; ten years later the figure was 40,000. Though the Atlantic slave ships generally carried more men than women, from an early date Barbados developed a balance between the sexes, and by 1715 women outnumbered men on the island. But in Barbados, as elsewhere, Africans died in horrifying numbers soon after arrival. Of the 180,000 Africans imported into Barbados between 1700 and 1760, about 50,000 died within the first three years.[24] Among the survivors was Olaudah Equiano.

Then (and since) no one doubted that 'The labour of the negroes is the principal foundation of riches from the plantations.'[25] Though slaves toiled at myriad tasks, in time infiltrating themselves into every nook and cranny of the local economy, their prime importance lay in sugar production. Some 70 per cent of all Africans transported to the Americas were destined, initially at least, for the sugar fields. And just as their sweat transformed the physical face of the islands, imposing an ordered, rational agriculture on a luxuriant wilderness, so too did their produce (sugar) transform the habits, economies and diets of the western world.[26] By 1700 England was importing 50,000 hogsheads of sugar a year; fifty years later the figure had doubled. By 1775 the British West Indies produced 100,000 tons of sugar.

By the mid-eighteenth century the British were addicted to sugar. It sweetened their drinks and was an integral part of their daily social routines. It stood at the centre of their fashionable domestic routines. Sugar was heaped into coffee in the nation's coffee houses and was a key ingredient in a host of contemporary drinks and recipes. Late-eighteenth-century British social life was unimaginable without the sweet produce of slave labour. Slaves also produced that lubricant of life in the Royal Navy – rum.

For the backbreaking work of sugar production, planters wanted healthy Africans. But the Atlantic crossing (and the preceding traumas in Africa) wrought untold physical damage on the slaves. At landfall the slave traders were forced to make their human cargoes look more presentable – and sellable. They tried to make the weak look strong, the depressed less miserable, seeking to hide the various, manifold human frailties and ailments among the Africans. Cleaned, rubbed down with oil to give the skin a healthier gloss, even bunged-up if afflicted by gastric troubles, slaves thus endured another round of public, intimate humiliations – and all in preparation for a lifetime's bondage.

On landing, Africans were sold in a variety of ways, but whatever the method they were, again, terrified by what was happening to them. Once Equiano's ship had docked in Bridgetown, local merchants and traders streamed on board. The Africans were divided into small groups for close inspection, tested for their strength and health, and returned below to the slave decks. Equiano's shipmates were once more deeply alarmed, fearing again that they might be eaten: 'there was much dread and trembling among us and nothing but bitter cries to be heard all the night from these apprehensions'.

To ease their worries, experienced slaves from Barbados were sent on board 'to pacify us'. (In later life Equiano had a similar role as intermediary with newly arrived Africans.) The Africans were told that they were to be set to work on shore, 'where we should see many of our country people...' When, finally, the slaves were marched on shore, 'there came among us Africans of all languages'. Slave communities throughout the Americas – especially those dependent on supplies of Africans – varied enormously. Slaves came from a host of different African regions, cultures and languages, and though certain groups predominated, new arrivals needed help from resident slaves who spoke their own language. It was vital for African slaves to pick up the local patois quickly in order to understand what was required of them. Incomprehension and ignorance was all too readily construed as wilful refusal or slavish resistance by white masters and mistresses.

Even the reassurances of experienced local slaves could not always allay newcomers' fears, most especially in the tumult of the slave sales. Equiano found himself in a group marched to a merchant's yard in Bridgetown, 'where we were all pent up together like so many sheep in a fold, without regard to sex or age'. A few days later, the formal sale began 'after the usual manner'. Equiano's account of being sold has been quoted many times, but it bears repitition, if only to convey the slaves' confusion at this alarming turn of events. At a given signal, potential buyers rushed into the merchant's yard, grabbing those Africans they had previously inspected and chosen:

> The noise and clamour with which this attended, and the eagerness visible in the countenances of the buyers, serve not a little to increase the apprehensions of the terrified Africans...

All bonds of friendship, camaraderie and family were destroyed in the confused and violent lunges of the buyers. Among Equiano's peers 'there were several brothers, who, in the sale, were sold in different lots...' In Africa, on the African coast, at landfall and later throughout the slave colonies (especially in the USA in the nineteenth century) such family break-ups remain among the most distressing of slave stories. From one slave society to another, contemporary accounts echo with the grief of separated loved ones; leaving for different Barbados plantations in Equiano's presence in 1756 or for the US frontier a century later. As his shipmate brothers were separated Equiano recorded, 'it was very moving on this occasion to see and hear their cries at parting'. Thirty years on Equiano made the most of this upheaval, playing on the conscience of his readers, appealing to people of sensibility that the break-up of the slave family was an unnecessarily cruel twist for people already damned by the European drive for luxury and profit. It was, he claimed, 'a new refinement in cruelty, which, while it has no advantage to atone for it, thus aggravates distress, and adds fresh horrors even to the wretchedness of slavery'.[27] Even now, two centuries later, it is hard to disagree with him.

Not all Africans found a ready buyer. The most unfortunate – the sick, the lame, the dying – held few attractions for purchasers who expected a return on their human investments. By the time of Equiano's arrival, slavers could rarely guarantee that all their Africans would find an immediate buyer. Slavers often had to move on to another colony, hoping to off-load the miserable remnants of their cargoes. Equiano was in Barbados for only a few weeks when he found himself lumped together with 'some few more slaves that were not saleable amongst the rest, from very much fretting, [and] were shipped off in a sloop for North America'.

As they sailed north, heading for that other major slave economy, Virginia, their treatment improved: 'we had plenty of rice and fat pork'. Equiano and his companions were 'landed up a river a good way from the sea'.[28] They were presumably somewhere along the meandering network of water systems which drain into the massive expanse of Chesapeake Bay. The settled lands around the edges of this river system formed the centre of the tobacco industry.

As early as 1620 tobacco had established itself as the region's crucial export crop (after earlier unsuccessful experiments with other commodities). By the late 1630s more than one million pounds of tobacco were exported from the Chesapeake each year. By 1670 the figure had grown to 20 million pounds. Gradually, African slaves began to replace the pioneering European (mainly Irish and Scottish) indentured labour. In the eighty years after 1690 perhaps 100,000 slaves had been imported, mainly from Africa. But unlike slaves in the Caribbean, the enslaved black population of the Chesapeake soon began to reproduce itself. Only two years after Equiano arrived in Virginia an Englishman remarked that slave numbers were 'upon the whole nearly equal, if not superior, to that of the white man; and they propagate and increase even faster'.[29] By then, the region exported some 200 million pounds of tobacco.[30] Equiano arrived, then, at the apogee of the Chesapeake's slave-based tobacco prosperity.

When Equiano looked around his new North American home, a region dominated increasingly by local-born slaves, he saw few fellow Africans but he found 'not one soul who could talk to me'. He was in a slave community increasingly dominated by second- and third-generation slaves, many of whom were local and acculturated to the demands and institutions of local European life, most notably in the languages they spoke.

Slave-owners had long since learned not to expect too much too soon of their new African slaves. Most (if not all) new African slaves were unwell, miserable, unable or unwilling to embark on physically demanding tasks in their early days in the Americas. Planters therefore tried to introduce them to simple, less demanding agricultural routines. Thirty years before, when Job ben Solomon, an Islamic slave, had landed in the Chesapeake, he was put to tobacco cultivation, but rapidly slid into ill-health, 'so that his Master was obliged to put him to tend cattle'.[31] Such precautions (though successful in this case) failed to head off a high death-rate among newly arrived Africans; one in four died within the first year in the Chesapeake.[32]

Equiano followed a well-worn path. Turned over to 'weeding grass, and gathering stones in a plantation', he soon found himself alone, his various ship-mates dispersed to different locations, 'and only myself was left'. Not surprisingly, he declared himself 'exceedingly miserable, and thought myself worse off than any of the rest of my companions; for they could talk to each other, but I had no person to speak to that I could understand'.

Most slave-owners in Virginia, in the period of Equiano's arrival, owned only a handful of slaves; five or less.[33] Inevitably, this had major repercussions for the nature of local slave life. Isolation and loneliness could only have compounded whatever miseries and afflictions Africans carried into the New World. Equiano, stranded in Virginia – unable even to converse with other slaves – began 'grieving and pining, and wishing for death, rather than any thing else'.[34] Time and again – in Africa, on the slave ship and now in 1757 in Virginia – Equiano (still only a boy) thought of dying. How many others shared his gloomy thoughts? Of course death often provided a quick release for enslaved Africans; so many were too far gone in their physical decline, too debilitated by their oceanic sufferings, to recover their strength and health. If Equiano was typical, it seems likely that many would have welcomed such a premature release from life's unimaginable and apparently endless sufferings.

For all his miseries and isolation, Equiano's new home prompted that intellectual curiosity which was to remain a striking characteristic throughout his life. He recalled details of everyday life in his new environment in terms of bemused confusion. He was (as he had been on the ship) in an utterly alien world, where people around him behaved and conducted their lives in a completely unfamiliar and unexpected fashion. The simplest of Virginian/European customs and artefacts seemed odd. In his Virginian master's house two objects disturbed him and seemed to provide evidence of the white man's magic. The noise of the clock ('a watch which hung on the chimney') frightened him and he thought it might somehow relay his activities to the master. Even more alarming was a picture on the wall, 'which appeared constantly to look at me'. Equiano thought that this picture 'might be some way the whites had to keep their great men when they died and offer them libations as we used to do our friendly spirits'.

Such artefacts, along with other indications, such as their mastery of navigation and seafaring, struck Equiano as proof of the whites' remarkable abilities: 'these people were all made of wonders'.[35] These were also signs of a confused boy, astonished by the white man's world.[36]

Yet these people 'of wonders' were the same who had transported him, and untold shiploads of fellow Africans, from their homelands to the very edges of European settlement in the Americas. For the next quarter of a century Equiano was to toil, in various humble capacities, for the betterment of his white owners and masters. He was also able to elevate himself, bit by bit, from a sick and miserable African boy – an isolated, lonely slave in Virginia – to a mature individual of some material substance and intellectual attainment. But it was to be a long haul.

Notes

1 Edward Long, *The History of Jamaica*, 3 vols (London, 1774), vol. I, p. 491.
2 For the most recent study of the trade, see David Eltis and David Richardson (eds), *Routes to Slavery* (London, 1997).
3 David Richardson, 'Liverpool and the English Slave Trade', in *TransAtlantic Slave Trade: Against Human Dignity*, ed. Anthony Tibbles (London, HMSO, 1994), pp. 71–3.
4 Malachy Postlewayt, *The Universal Dictionary of Trade and Commerce* (London, 1757), p. 25.
5 Long, *op.cit.*, vol. I, p. 494.
6 Joseph Miller, *Ways of Death: Merchant Capitalism and the Angola Slave Trade* (London, 1988), pp. 387–9; Paul Lovejoy, 'The Impact of the Atlantic Slave Trade on Africa', *Journal of African History*, 30 (1989), pp. 385–6.
7 *Interesting Narrative*, p. 53.
8 John Atkins, *A Voyage to Guinea, Brasil and the West Indies* (London, 1735), p. 179.
9 *Interesting Narrative*, pp. 55–6.
10 Alexander Falconbridge, *An Account of the Slave Trade on the Coast of Africa* (London, 1788), p. 19.
11 *Interesting Narrative*, p. 56.
12 Falconbridge, *op.cit.*, p. 20.
13 *Interesting Narrative*, pp. 56–7.
14 Falconbridge, *op.cit.*, p. 24.
15 *Interesting Narrative*, p. 57.
16 *Ibid.*, p. 58.
17 *The Journal of a Slave Trader (John Newton), 1750–1754*, ed. Bernard Martin and Martin Spurrell (London, 1962); entry for 12 June 1751, p. 56.
18 *Interesting Narrative*, p. 56.
19 Falconbridge, *op. cit.*, pp. 30–2.
20 *Interesting Narrative*, p. 59.
21 P. D. Morgan, 'British encounters with Africans and African-Americans', in Bernard Bailyn and Philip D. Morgan (eds), *Strangers within the Realm. Cultural Margins of the First British Empire* (Chapel Hill, 1991), p. 160.
22 *Interesting Narrative*, pp. 57–9.
23 *Ibid.*, p. 60.
24 Hilary Beckles, *Natural Rebels: A Social History of Enslaved Women in Barbados* (London, 1989), p. 39.
25 Quoted in David Watts, *The West Indies* (Cambridge, 1987), p. 284.
26 James Walvin, *Fruits of Empire: Exotic Produce and Western Taste, 1600–1800* (London, 1997).
27 *Interesting Narrative*, pp. 60–1.
28 *Ibid.*, p. 62.
29 Quoted in Alan Kulikoff, *Tobacco and Slaves* (Chapel Hill, 1986), p. 73.
30 James Walvin, *Black Ivory* (London, 1992), p. 9.
31 P. D. Curtin (ed.), *Africa Remembered* (Madison, 1967), p. 41.
32 Kulikoff, *op.cit.*, pp. 326–8.
33 Walvin, *Black Ivory*, p. 71.
34 *Interesting Narrative*, p. 62.
35 *Ibid.*, p. 63.
36 Paul Edwards, 'Equiano and his Captains', in Anna Rutherford (ed.), *Commonwealth* (Aarhus, 1971), pp. 20–1.

PART TWO

VARIETIES OF SLAVERY

=== 3 ===

A SLAVE AT SEA

Landfall did not herald the end of the Africans' travels. Most were moved on, after sale, to other destinations; to plantations on the island, to another island, some still further to other distant colonies. Just when they must have thought life had settled down, they were again uprooted. Equiano was no exception. He had been in Virginia no more than a month (the longest period he spent in North America) when he was shifted once more. Sometime in 1756 an English sailor, Michael Henry Pascal, on a business trip to Virginia, visited Equiano's owner.[1] Pascal was clearly impressed by the young African, and promptly bought him as his own slave, for a price of £30–40. We do not know why the young man was sold, but the transaction simply confirms the capricious twists and turns in the life of an African slave. At a moment's notice, slaves were bought and exchanged and transported to remote places; cast abroad, they knew not where, for reasons they could not grasp, by people they did not know. Destined as a gift for his new owner's cousins in England, Equiano once more found himself on board a ship, but this one loaded with tobacco and bound for England.

Equiano was surprised by his treatment (he was well fed and generally well cared for) but confused about his fate, a confusion worsened by his lack of English and by the crew maliciously feeding him false information. As the *Industrious Bee* crossed the Atlantic, Pascal renamed his African, calling him Gustavus Vasa – to the irritation of the African, who insisted that he remain known as Jacob (a name he had been given earlier). The matter was resolved by a flurry of blows and Equiano finally gave in, accepting the name 'by which I have been known ever since'.[1] In fact, Equiano was given a variety of names by different white people. After 1756, however, and perhaps tiring of the bewildering and regular change of names, Equiano did not use his African name in public until he published his autobiography in 1789, preferring instead to use the name he accepted, with such great reluctance, at the age of about 12 in mid-Atlantic. This renaming process involved more than a change of name. It involved, from the slave-owner's viewpoint, a stripping of African identity.[2] But how did the Africans react; how did they reshape an identity of their own from the welter of names bestowed on them by outsiders? Equiano called himself Gustavus Vassa throughout most of his life, but he consciously promoted his African name in the last decade: the years in fact when he openly asserted his identity as an African.

As the *Industrious Bee* closed on England, after an unusually long Atlantic crossing, provisions began to run short and food was rationed. Some of the crew joked that they planned to eat Equiano, reviving those basic terrors which had haunted him a year earlier when he had first been thrust into the slave ship on the African coast. Even the captain, Pascal, joked that 'the black people were good to eat'. At moments of tension on board ship – a man overboard, a storm – Equiano feared for his safety, though not from natural forces. He worried that the white crew would sacrifice him to appease the 'Ruler of the seas'. His fears were magnified through not fully understanding what was said to him, but finally a new friend, Richard Baker, and the captain put his mind at rest.

Equiano took great comfort from this new friendship. Richard Baker was a young man (aged 15 or 16) with whom he could share his worries and pleasures. Baker, a well-educated youth, clearly took to Equiano, instructed him in life on board ship, and later generally helped him. Baker was to die at sea, in Greece, two years later, but Equiano continued to hold him in fond esteem for the rest of his life, describing him as:

> a man superior to prejudice; and who was not ashamed to notice, to associate with, and to be the friend and instructor of one who was ignorant, a stranger, of a different complexion, and a slave!

This seems to have been the first kind and humane treatment Equiano enjoyed outside Africa – and he never forgot the young American's friendship.

Other men, notably Daniel Queen, also helped Equiano and proved influential in the life of a young boy bereft of the authority figures from his own cultural background. And they seem to have been important in shaping Equiano's balanced view of white people in general. For a man whose woes were a direct result of European actions, Equiano showed no obvious hostility to white people, choosing instead his friends and enemies by their behaviour, not their ethnicity.

The *Industrious Bee* made landfall at Falmouth. Food poured on board for the hungry crew, and Equiano joined in the 'feasting, almost without ending'. Not surprisingly, he was amazed by the commonplace sights of an eighteenth-century English town, his bewilderment compounded by the snow which covered the town and the ship. Even more amazed was his reaction to the first church service he attended in Falmouth (though we do not know what prompted him to attend church in the first place). He fired off a series of questions about the service he had just seen, but was confused by the answers he received. He confessed to being impressed by what he learned of this newfound God, and of the whites' cultural traits ('at their not sacrificing, or making any offerings') which differed so much from his own African customs.[3] Equiano's description of his encounter with Christianity during his first days in England acted as a symbolic drawing of his readers' attention to the enlightening revelation of England itself. In many ways, Equiano's book was the diary of a soul: an account of an African's discovery of God. And it began on arrival in England.

In Falmouth he lodged with his master at a house where the family quickly took a great fancy to him.[4] This experience was repeated shortly afterwards, when Equiano travelled on to Guernsey (his ship was part-owned by a Guernsey merchant). Lodging again with a local family, Equiano began, for the first time, to think about his colour, nudged that way by those around him. A daughter of the house had a rosy appearance when washed; try as he might Equiano could not produce the same effect on his own face, 'and I now began to be mortified at the difference in our complexions'.[5] He claimed that he was glad that local people, unlike his own people, did not mark their faces with scars. He seems to have begun to question some of his African cultural habits, and to see the virtue of European customs. Slowly, Equiano had begun that process of accommodating himself to his new environment; accepting as normal, as credible (even desirable) European cultural traits which were, at first, utterly incomprehensible and sometimes fearful.

In the summer of 1756[6] Equiano was summoned to join his master, Pascal, now appointed to a Royal Navy ship, the *Roebuck*. He joined the crowded and heavily armed warship at the Nore, no longer feeling 'those apprehensions and alarms' which had surfaced when he first mixed with Europeans. No longer a stranger, less ill at ease in a European environment, he was altogether more at peace with himself. But he was also keen to persuade his readers that he had begun, in his early days in England, to appreciate the benefits of English life:

> My griefs too... were now wearing away; and I soon enjoyed myself pretty well, and felt tolerably easy in my present situation.

For one thing, life was easier because there were young boys of his own age on board: 'we were always together, and a great part of our time was spent in play'.[7] The boys were sometimes forced to box with each other, for the entertainment and gambling of men on board. There were traditionally large numbers of young boys on British warships – sometimes as young as six, seven or eight.[8] Indeed, many of the most famous of eighteenth-century naval heroes had joined the Navy as children. Officers were reared up from a young age in the skills and disciplines of seafaring, learning their trade the hard way and, in the process, missing out on what we might expect of normal childhood.

Equiano now began to see a very different world, through the eyes and experiences of the Royal Navy, as he sailed between many of the points of international conflict in the Seven Years War (1756–63), experiencing at first-hand the dangers and the horrors of naval life in wartime. His ship flitted from one spot to another: off-shore France, ferrying people from Holland, transporting troops from Scotland and the Orkneys, and spending time in various English ports. Finally Equiano was put ashore in London, 'the place I had long desired exceedingly to see'. He did not have time to see very much, however, because he fell seriously ill with smallpox (the great scourge of slave communities in the Americas). He recovered in time to join his master, briefly, on board his new command, the *Preston*, a man-of-war of fifty guns, before they were both transferred to the *Royal George*, a massive warship destined for Turkey. Equiano stepped aboard what seemed to be a floating town, filled with crew and with 'men, women, and children, of every denomination', with its own shops and vendors. But this too proved a mere transit point, for Equiano's master was again moved on, this time to the *Namur* at Spithead, the flagship of a major expedition destined for North America. Their expedition sailed for some days in the company of a convoy commanded by Admiral Cornish bound for the East Indies, before parting company and heading for destinations in distant parts of the British empire.

Equiano's fleet (after being blown off course to Tenerife) finally arrived in Halifax, where they were joined by an expanding armada of warships and transports. The assembled fleet then sailed for Cape Breton in Nova Scotia, with Equiano on board the same ship as General Wolfe, whom he described as 'highly esteemed and beloved by all the men'.[9] (Equiano had his own reason to like Wolfe, for he had saved him from a flogging.) Their aim was an attack on Louisbourg, a settlement of 3,000 souls and the largest garrison in French Canada. This was part of a massive British onslaught on French positions across North America in an attempt to dislodge them from the continent.[10] At Louisbourg Equiano experienced his first military engagement, with all its associated horrors, though his description of the fighting and the fatalities were oddly matter of fact and cool: 'I had that day in my hand the scalp of an Indian king, who was killed in the engagement: the scalp had been taken off by an Highlander.' (Europeans had picked up the habit of scalping dead enemies from North American Indians.)[11]

For two months the British laid seige to the French fleet, and to the garrison in Louisbourg. When it finally fell to the British, Equiano was able to enjoy himself on shore, watching with great curiosity as senior officers from both sides wined and dined each other, the British fleet festooned in full regalia to celebrate what was a major victory in the global struggle against the French empire. With British control established, the bulk of the fleet returned to England, but not before further skirmishings with French vessels in the Channel on the last leg home. When his ship put into Portsmouth for a refit, late in 1758, Equiano travelled to London with his master.

Equiano was now back in the country he had first visited more than three years before. For much of the interim he had been at sea, and was now a seasoned sailor, long accustomed to the terrors of the deep and of warfare, and no longer afraid of their dangers. Life as a sailor in wartime seemed not to frighten him nearly as much as his first terrifying encounter with Europeans, when he had been sold and thrust into the hold of a slave ship. He had now lost his fear of the Europeans, helped by his improved grasp of English. 'I could now speak English tolerably well, and I perfectly understood every thing that was said.' He had become thoroughly acculturated. He felt 'almost an Englishman'. More than that, he not only felt 'quite easy with these new countrymen, but relished their society and manners'.

Casting aside his initial worries that white people might merely be evil spirits, Equiano had come to think of them 'as men superior to us; and therefore I had the stronger desire to resemble them; to imbibe their spirit, and imitate their manners'. Here was a young African in the process of reinventing himself; acquiring those qualities of refinement and cultivation which might make him acceptable to his new compatriots. It was a conscious process: 'I therefore embraced every occasion of improvement. . .' The most important first step was the need to read and write.

Literacy had become a critical element in the European definition of 'enlightenment' and 'civilization'. In the course of the seventeenth and eighteenth centuries, and as educated Europeans took growing pride in their collective civilized attainments, literacy came to be seen as a distinguishing characteristic of civilization itself. To come from an illiterate society was proof of a person's position at the bottom of the human pile. It thus became a crude justification for slavery itself. Along with 'heathenism', the illiteracy of African cultures provided a justification for enslavement, and, perverse as it now seems, slavery was viewed as the means of translating the slave to a higher culture. As slavery in the colonies matured, as local societies became ever more complex and sophisticated, it was inevitable that literacy would grow among the slaves. Some slaves *needed* to be literate to undertake their various tasks. Slave-holders, and their local political systems, discouraged the growth of slave literacy (and slave learning in general), for it seemed too closely tied to the rise of black ambition and, in places, to black resistance.[12] But it proved an impossible task. In white communities on both sides of the Atlantic, where literacy was on the rise – where the printed (popular) word proliferated in books, tracts, broadsheets and newspapers[13] – how could the appetite for print and reading be obstructed at the artificial boundaries of race or slavery?

Equiano was a perfect case in point. He confessed, 'I had long wished to be able to read and write; and for this purpose I took every opportunity to gain instruction, but had made as yet very little progress.' On his first voyages, Equiano had been bemused when he had seen sailors reading. Not able to understand the mechanics of the skill, Equiano often picked up a book, and 'talked to it, and then put my ears to it, when alone, in hopes it would answer me; and I have been very much concerned when I found it remained silent.'[14] The belief in the 'talking book' became a prominent theme in early African-American writing, and had been established as early as 1772 by James Gronniosaw in his own African memoir, thus founding a tradition which was repeated by five black authors, including Equiano, between 1770 and 1815.[15]

On returning to London in 1758 Pascal sent Equiano to work as a servant for two sisters named Guerin. The women furthered his education by sending him to school. Other servants in the house told Equiano that he could never go to heaven unless he was baptized, so he promptly raised the issue with the elder of the Guerin sisters, who agreed to let him be baptized. Overcoming the initial objection of his owner, Equiano was baptized in February 1759 at St Margaret's, Westminster.[16] Equiano was gradually transforming himself from a humble African slave to a man of rounded European accomplishments. The baptism of a slave, however, involved more than simple acceptance into the Christian church. It had, for a long time, caused social and legal friction. Did baptism confer freedom on the slave? Planters in the West Indies were notoriously resistant to allowing their slaves to become Christian, though the situation was obviously different in England. In Equiano's case, baptism seems not to have proved as troublesome to his owner as it did for many other English slave-holders.

At his baptism, the priest gave Equiano a book. It was perhaps his first, but thereafter books were to accompany him, on sea and land, for the rest of his life.

When he returned to sea, in the early 1760s, Equiano's interest in self-improvement continued unabated. It was, however, bound up with a much broader ambition. He wanted to be free and to earn some money 'to enable me to get a good education; for I always had a great desire to be able at least to read and write'. Life at sea curiously afforded plenty of opportunities for such improvement. On board the *Aetna* in 1762, for example, the captain's clerk taught him to write 'and gave me a smattering of arithmetic as far as the rule of three'. He was also greatly helped by an older, educated sailor, Daniel Queen who 'took very great pains to instruct me in many things': how to shave and cut other sailors' hair 'and also to read in the Bible, explaining many passages to me, which I did not comprehend'. Equiano became so close to Queen that other sailors used to call him by the same name; 'they also styled me the black Christian'.[17] Again, Equiano forged an important relationship with an older man who, almost like a father-figure, took the young African under his wing.

The best-remembered pleasures and pastimes of sailors in the cramped confusion of eighteenth-century ships (especially the warships) tended to be gambling and music-making. Although 'the least noticed of all recreations at sea', reading was also commonplace. We have lots of evidence of sailors reading in their hammocks and of substantial proportions of ordinary sailors signing petitions for this issue or that; of young officers being urged to read particular books to improve their career prospects.[18] Equiano was not unusual, then, in carrying books in his sea chest. Gradually he became a literate sailor – though still enslaved – and one who was able to handle business calculations, who was keen to read (especially the Bible) in his spare time, and useful to any master or employer in the varied literate tasks needed in and around the business of shipping and transporting goods. Equiano read widely and his *Narrative* is filled with literary references (not always accurate), but he began, as so many did, with close attention to the Bible.

In early 1759 Equiano was still in London, but the enjoyment he derived from formal school instruction, and the informal lessons from the Guerin sisters, was not to last. That spring he was ordered back on board his master's ship, the *Namur*, now at Spithead, refitted and ready to rejoin the action against the French as part of a major fleet bound for the Mediterranean. Loaded with presents from the sisters, and with cautions of good behaviour ringing in his ears, the 14-year-old Equiano rejoined his ship.

There followed a period of deep disappointments. He discovered that his close friend and former shipmate, Richard Baker, was dead (his possessions were later passed on to Equiano). His early years had been marked by several losses – of parents and siblings, especially of a much-loved sister, and now he lost a friend for whom he had developed a close affection. Newly aroused hopes that he might, by an amazing twist of circumstance, once again meet the sister with whom he had been enslaved, were dashed when he discovered that the woman, though very similar to his sister, was 'of another nation'.[19]

Equiano had always been curious about the peculiarities of life around him; even the public executions in London, and the grotesque punishments doled out to men at sea. For an African, of course, everything he saw was foreign, but his career at sea on board English ships gave him an English viewpoint, and his reflections on the sights and customs of other countries were mediated through English eyes. Equiano visited Spain, the south of France and Gibraltar and wrote of the strangeness of Mediterranean habits as any Englishman might have done. He also described the confusion, noise and destruction of war at sea, the periods of relaxation on land, and the turmoil of hurried preparations to meet the French enemy – peppering his narrative with quotes (and misquotes) from classical English texts.

In August 1759 Equiano was with the English fleet which engaged the French as they tried to break out of the Mediterranean. Equiano found himself in a fierce, destructive sea battle. His own ship was at the centre of the action for much of the time and Equiano found himself 'frequently stunned with the thundering of the great guns'. It was a bloody conflict, though Equiano's description of the bloodshed had a curious phraseology: the guns 'hurried many of my companions into awful eternity'.[20] Throughout the battle, Equiano was on the middle deck, fetching powder for the guns: 'and here I was a witness of the dreadful fate of many of my companions, who, in the twinkling of an eye, were dashed in pieces, and launched into eternity.'

Despite the swirling shot and splinters, Equiano escaped unscathed. It was a dangerous position; as Equiano and his gun mate ran the length of the ship they were always exposed to in-coming fire. In handling the powder (from rotten boxes) they also ran the risk of causing devastating accidents to their own ship. Pondering desperately which would be the least dangerous moment to dash for fresh powder, Equiano realized that such choices were pointless. He persuaded himself that 'there was a time allotted for me to die as well as to be born', and simply got on with the tasks at hand, consoling himself with the thought that he would be able to regale his London friends with stories of the battle 'when I should return to London'.[21]

After much confusion, the French line broke, the British taking a number of prizes and the rest of the French fleet fleeing as best they could. The French flagship, the *Ocean*, blew up ('the midnight seemed turned into day by the blaze, which was attended with a noise louder and more terrible than thunder'). Equiano's own vessel, the *Namur*, was so badly damaged that the Admiral had to transfer to another ship. In addition to the dead and wounded crew, the ship 'was almost torn to pieces', and carpenters from other ships were drafted in to make her seaworthy, able to sail with the prizes to England. *En route*, Equiano's owner, recovered from wounds received in the engagement, was made captain of the fireship *Aetna*. Equiano was transferred with him as his steward.

Equiano enjoyed his new post. He was well treated and had enough time on his hands 'to improve myself in reading and writing. The latter I had learned a little before I left the *Namur*, as there was a school on board.'[22] This is hardly surprising since boys serving as servants to the officers, might make up 6 to 10 per cent of the ship's complement. All needed training and educating for their future seafaring careers.[23] Sometimes Equiano met other Africans. Back in England in 1760–61, for example, Equiano found himself based on the Isle of Wight, 'this delightful island' where he found 'the inhabitants very civil'. There he made friends with another black slave 'a black boy about my own size', who dashed over to greet Equiano when he had caught sight 'of one of his own countrymen'. Equiano was taken aback by the effusiveness of the greeting: the stranger 'caught hold of me in his arms as if I had been his brother, though we had never seen each other before'. They quickly became friends and saw a great deal of each other until, in March 1761, Equiano's ship was ordered to join another fleet destined for an attack on Belle-Isle, off Brittany.

As he once again sailed into the uncertainties of military conflict – still, at the age of 16, very young – Equiano pondered the nature of providence and the workings of the Almighty. Looking back, as he wrote the *Narrative* in 1789, Equiano brought to bear his sophisticated grasp of Christian theology to explain the accidents and quirks of his early life. Each and every escape from danger, by himself or others, needed explanation. And the explanation for everything was divine. A fellow crewman, John Mondle, 'a man of very indifferent morals', was saved from certain death in a collision at sea *en route* to Belle-Isle through realizing the error of his own ways and awakening to the Lord. Mondle had wandered away from his berth, in a state of spiritual agitation, at the very moment the ship was struck, at that precise spot, by another British warship.[24] Such incidents, and other capricious/fortuitous acts of circumstance, prompted Equiano to think of the Lord's doings. Life at sea was full of dangers – quite apart from warfare itself – and Equiano recited a string of near-misses: accidents which should have been fatal but from which the victim walked away unharmed. He himself had once fallen from the upper-deck down into the hold, 'and all who saw me fall called out I was killed; but I received not the least injury.' In this and similar incidents Equiano 'could very plainly trace the hand of God, without whose permission a sparrow cannot fall.' He turned ever more surely to the Lord, 'and to call daily on his holy name with fear and reverence', hoping that the Lord would 'implant the seeds of piety in me'.[25] Such incidents were clear signs, in Equiano's view, of predestination.

Equiano had his own narrow escapes from death and injury when he found himself back in action against the French at Belle-Isle, in a protracted battle which, again, resulted in a British victory. As the naval war dragged on, Equiano's ship saw plenty of action, blockading the French fleet in Rochefort, later sailing to Spain and Bayonne on different missions, before finally returning to Portsmouth in the summer of 1762. After a further trip to Guernsey, and with talk of peace in the air, Equiano's ship was ordered to London to be paid off at the end of 1762. 'We received this news with loud huzzas, and every other demonstration of gladness; and nothing but mirth could be seen through every part of the ship.'

Throughout these turmoils at sea, Equiano's life had reflected the experiences of tens of thousands of men caught up in the global conflict between the French and British empires. It was a war fought on both sides of the Atlantic and as far away as India. The end result was success for the British, the Peace of Paris granting them major territorial rewards, notably in North America and the Caribbean. For their part, the crew on Equiano's ship had had enough; they headed for demobilization in London in good heart and spirits. Equiano, however, wanted much more than a return to normal civilian life. He was, after all, still a slave. He had had opportunities on shore to run away. But how could an isolated African survive in alien environments? We do not know how many blacks serving on British naval ships were slaves, but Equiano's experience suggests that whatever the formal position of the Admiralty, the navy accommodated slaves alongside free men (and impressed men) in the ranks.

The young African wanted to be free. He had had more than his share of remarkable experiences and was still, in 1762, only 18. He had flirted with death on a number of occasions (his days of longing for death were now behind him), he had become ever more accustomed to the alien British world, and had found, in Christianity, a secure home and solace for his manifold tribulations. But he remained a slave, a status and a role which increasingly irked him, not least because it stood in sharp contrast to his aspirations and his attainments. He wanted to be free and to work for himself.

He had, as we have seen, already acquired the rudiments of literacy on board ship and in London. At the same time, Equiano had already shown those entrepreneurial instincts which were to flourish in later years. On ship he had accumulated cash – from games of chance and, more revealingly, from shaving and hairdressing the crew. These were the acquisitive habits which were to transform his later life.

Equiano looked forward to the end of the war with more relish than most. Although he had not been formally manumitted, nor promised his legal freedom, Equiano had come to believe that he was entitled to his liberty. Other crewmen assured him that, once the ship had been paid off, the young African would be as free as the next man, and that no one had a right to retain him. Moreover Equiano had been won over to the idea that he was free by the consideration and care which his owner, Captain Pascal, had shown to him; 'he even paid attention to my morals'. He had learned not to tell lies, nor to deceive his master, believing that, if he did, 'God would not love me'. Because of Pascal's general display of fondness towards him, Equiano 'never once supposed, in all my dreams of freedom, that he would think of detaining me any longer than I wished'.[26]

He was to be horribly disabused.

Equiano approached London in the full expectation of stepping ashore a free man for the first time since he was enslaved in Africa seven years before. But when his vessel anchored off Deptford on 10 December 1762 Equiano was unexpectedly bundled into the ship's barge, forced to leave behind all his prized possessions. Pascal accused him of preparing to run away. Equiano was dumbstruck, unable even to answer – though he asked to be allowed 'to go for my books and chest of clothes'. Pleading that he was a free man, and that the law was on his side, Equiano's arguments were brusquely swept aside by a captain keen to hand him over, as quickly as possible, to a new owner. The rest of the crew were equally surprised by this unhappy turn of events, siding with Equiano and showing Pascal their disapproval of Equiano's threatened re-enslavement. But it was all to no avail. As their boat fell down to Gravesend on the ebb tide, they came alongside the *Charming Sally*, whose captain, James Doran, was about to leave for the West Indies. The helpless young African was pushed into Doran's cabin and told, 'you are now my slave.' Equiano's protestations of freedom – that he had faithfully served Pascal for years and that Pascal had kept all his pay and all his prize money – made no impression, nor did his plea that he was a baptized Christian. Captain Doran cut short the discussion, complaining that Equiano 'talked too much English' and saying he had a method for silencing him. As memories of the slave ship flooded back, Equiano fell silent, but not before telling his captors that, though he might be unable to secure his rights on earth, 'I hoped I should hereafter in Heaven'. He quit the cabin 'filled with resentment and sorrow'. Pascal left the ship, even taking Equiano's coat with him (though the African had managed to hide nine guineas on his person).

After all the tribulations and dangers of the last few years, the permanent dangers of life at sea, the risks to life and limb from military engagements, despite all his efforts at self-improvement, despite his unquestioned attainments – his chest of books and his cash earned from independent enterprise and hard work – Equiano found himself, at the end of 1762, a slave once more. He was a slave to another Englishman and had been bought and sold, enslaved again, on the Thames in London.

For five years, between the age of about 12 and 18, Equiano had worked mainly at sea and in the Royal Navy. Throughout those years of major conflict his slave status scarcely affected the range of work he had undertaken both at sea and on land. He had worked as a steward, servant, hairdresser, as a combat powder-carrier and more besides. He was still owned, however, by Captain Pascal. From the moment of his purchase in Virginia in 1757 to his resale in London in 1762, and despite his own hopes and aspirations, Equiano remained the private property of an Englishman. As he watched Pascal and his men depart for their own ship, leaving him alone again, a slave in the company of a crew of total strangers, Equiano wrote how he 'threw myself on the deck, with a heart ready to burst with sorrow and anguish'.[27]

It was of course a fate shared, in various forms, by millions of fellow Africans. Yet in its suffering and anxiety it was an utterly personal distress. Nor did it seem to have an end in sight. What he could not have known was that he was in good company on the Thames. There were other Africans enslaved in the heart of London, whose situation was as miserable as Equiano's.

Notes

1 *Interesting Narrative*, p. 64.
2 Orlando Patterson, *Slavery and Social Death* (Cambridge, MA, 1982), pp. 54–6.
3 *Interesting Narrative*, pp. 67–8.
4 *Ibid.*, p. 68.
5 *Ibid.*, p. 69.
6 Equiano says 1757; see Carretta's comments, *ibid.*, p. 255, n. 146.
7 *Ibid.*, p. 70.
8 N.A.M. Rodger, *The Wooden World, An Anatomy of the Georgian Navy* (London, 1986), p. 27.
9 *Interesting Narrative*, p. 73.
10 A.N. Porter, *Atlas of British Overseas Expansion* (London, 1991), p. 40.
11 *Interesting Narrative*, pp. 73–4; James Axtell, 'The unkindest cut, or who invented scalping?' in *The European and the Indian* (New York, 1981).
12 Henry Louis Gates Jr, Nellie Y. McKay *et al.* (eds), *The Norton Anthology of African American Literature* (New York, 1997), p. xxix.
13 David Vincent, *Literacy and Popular Culture. England, 1750–1914* (Cambridge, 1993).
14 *Interesting Narrative*, p. 68.
15 *Norton Anthology*, p. xxviii. But see especially Carretta in *Interesting Narrative*, pp. 254–5, n. 143; also Vincent Carretta, *Unchained Voices* (Kentucky, 1996), p. 53, n. 1.
16 *Interesting Narrative*, p. 78.
17 *Ibid.*, pp. 91–2. The ship's log lists the man as Daniel Quin (*ibid.*, p. 266, n. 260).
18 Rodger, *op. cit.*, pp. 45–6.

19 *Interesting Narrative*, pp. 79–80.
20 *Ibid.*, pp. 82–3.
21 *Ibid.*, pp. 83–4.
22 *Ibid.*, pp. 84–5.
23 Rodger, *op. cit.*, pp. 27–8.
24 The man's name was actually Mundall. Carretta, *Interesting Narrative*, p. 263, n. 226.
25 *Interesting Narrative*, pp. 87–8.
26 *Ibid.*, p. 92.
27 *Ibid.*, p. 94.

4

ENGLAND, SLAVES AND FREEDOM

Late in 1762, after spending the best part of the past two years at sea, Equiano looked forward with relish to life in London. For some time past, he had actively prepared himself for a new life. He had made great efforts to be educated. He could read and write, and understood basic arithmetic (thanks to instruction by other sailors). He read the Bible regularly, again encouraged by a shipmate, and had been known on board his ship as 'the black Christian'.[1] More significantly, when he had been baptized three years before, in February 1759, at St Margaret's Church, Westminster (under the name Gustavus Vassa), he believed himself henceforth to be a free man. Like many other slaves, he was to be sadly disillusioned.

When the re-enslaved and bitterly disappointed Equiano found himself, in December 1762, sold to Captain James Doran of the *Charming Sally* and bound for the West Indies, he pleaded that he was a free man: 'I have been baptised; and by the laws of the land no man has a right to sell me.'[2] His experience was, in fact, just one of many similar instances (to be repeated for much of the eighteenth century) of blacks' inability to resist kidnapping close to the water's edge in British ports. His outrage was all the more acute because he was convinced that baptism had freed him. It was a widespread belief which derived largely from one of the peculiarities of slavery in the British West Indies.

Planters in the British Caribbean had, from the early days, refused to admit slaves to local Protestant churches. In slave-owning eyes, slaves were pagan brutes, beyond the pale of civilized life. In the words of the Barbados Assembly in 1681, the slaves' 'Savage Brutishness renders them wholly uncapable' of conversion to Christianity. Shortly after, the Jamaican Assembly took a more sympathetic line, urging the baptism of those slaves whom planters 'can make sensible of a Deity and the Christian Faith'. But they were clear that baptism did *not* bestow freedom.[3] At the heart of this debate lay one of the basic justifications for African enslavement: that Africans were heathen, living outside the reach of Christian civilization, for whom slavery was no hardship or misery. Though it was a key issue in the development of chattel slavery in the Protestant Americas, it also had unforseen consequences for Europe.

From the early arrival of Africans in England, their religion (or apparent lack of one) was a sensitive issue. The 1601 Elizabethan Proclamation, ordering the expulsion of early black settlers in England, was linked to their heathenism. Not only did they cause resentment, and consume local foodstuff (at a time of shortage), but also 'most of them are infidels, having no understanding of Christ or his Gospel'.[4]

In the course of the eighteenth century, however, as more and more blacks arrived in England, many of those working as domestics in prosperous homes were converted and baptized. Parish records across the face of England document black baptisms (and, of course, marriages and deaths). Black baptisms took place in all corners of Christian Britain, from the most humble and remote of local parish churches, through to the nation's great cathedrals. The parish registers of Bedfordshire, for example, are dotted with black baptisms from the late seventeenth century onwards.[5] A similar story unfolded in York, the second centre of English Christendom. As early as 1687 a black ('John Moore the Blackamoore') was even made a freeman of the city of York – at a cost of £4.[6] In May 1777, Benjamin Moor, 'the son of James Moor, a Black Man living on Little River, north of Charles Town in South Carolina', was baptized in York Minster. Later that same year, a 'negro servant belonging to Mr Hutton', thought to be 17 years old, was also baptized in York Minster.[7] Recent research on a clutch of London parishes, for the years 1780–1811, has revealed details of 159 black baptisms (the great majority of which were of young men.)[8] For his part, Equiano had been nudged towards Christianity by sailors, by white domestics he had worked and lived with, and by his employers.[9]

Black baptism was, then, unexceptional in eighteenth-century England. The critical question remains, however: did baptism bestow freedom? Though a number of seventeenth-century legal cases had suggested that the 'heathenism' of imported blacks confirmed their bondage, the West India lobby was particuarly anxious to clarify the matter; they were unwilling to bring slaves to England if the slave could secure freedom by baptism (or even by stepping ashore in a free land). The matter seemed to have been decided by a ruling of law officers in 1729: the famous Yorke–Talbot judgment. In reply to a petition from West Indian interests, the Attorney and Soliciter General asserted that slaves were *not* freed by simply landing in England. Moreover they ruled that 'baptism doth not bestow freedom on him, nor make any alteration in his temporal condition in these kingdoms'. This judgment was confirmed twenty years later by Yorke (now Lord Chancellor Hardwicke). Popular mythology, however, remained wedded to the idea that baptism conferred freedom.[10]

In 1762 Equiano had fallen victim to *English* slavery. It was not the slavery which thrived in the Americas (though that too had ensnared him earlier), but was a peculiar institution which existed in England itself. However vaunted the

English pride in the freedoms secured in the Revolution of the previous century, slavery existed in England throughout the seventeenth and eighteenth centuries. And it was, as Equiano had so painfully discovered, a consequence of the Atlantic slave system.

On the eve of the European incursions into the Americas, slavery had declined across Europe. However, European settlers in the New World quickly evolved forms of slavery they had dismantled at home and some, notably black chattel slavery, they had never used.[11] Slavery in England had long since disappeared, but the rise of the slave colonies saw the transplantation of an alien slavery *back* into English (and British) life.[12] It was a simple – and inevitable – process, but its consequences were enormous. Men returned from a career in (or even a visit to) the slave colonies in the company of enslaved domestics. Some vessels involved in slave trading (and there were some 11,000 of them in the course of the eighteenth century) returned to British waters with slaves on board. The numbers were always small (why bring costly slaves to Britain when they were more valued in the Americas?) In time, however, black slaves came to form a noticeable presence, their numbers sometimes augmented by larger groups, notably after the British defeat in the American War in 1783 and the flight of loyalists and their slaves. Historians continue to argue about the numbers involved,[13] but there can be no dispute about the basic fact: for the best part of two centuries, perhaps even longer, black slaves were to be found in England.

Many were African, some of them brought direct from Africa, though most, like Equiano, arrived in England via the Americas. Others had been born in the slave colonies. Their story can be told via a number of historical sources, most revealingly perhaps via the advertisements for slave sales, or the the return of runaways which dot contemporary prints and newspapers. Many such notices appeared in the London press – understandably, since both slavery and the press were more developed in the capital:

> A Negro boy about 12 years of age, that speaks English, is to be sold. Enquire of Mr Step (?) Rayner, a Watchmaker, at the sign of the Dial, without Bishopgate.[14]

Another advertisement offered for sale:

> A Black boy, twelve years of age, fit to wait on a gentleman, to be disposed of at Denis's Coffee House in Finch Lane, near the Royal Exchange.[15]

More starkly, in 1728 readers of the *Daily Journal* were told:

> To be sold, a negro boy aged eleven years. Enquire at the Virginia Coffee House in Threadneedle Street.[16]

Because a slave was property – part of the material estate of their owner – they were disposed of like other forms of goods and chattels. When John Rice was hanged for forgery at Tyburn in 1763, 'his effects were sold by auction, and among the rest his negro boy'.[17] Eight years later, the *Stamford Mercury* recorded that 'at a recent sale of a gentleman's effects at Richmond a negro boy was put up, and sold for £32'.[18]

Other major slave ports had their own (more modest) slave sales in the local press. In Liverpool, a local advertisement offered for sale:

at George's Coffee House, betwixt the hours of six and eight o'clock, a very fine negro girl, about eight years of age; very healthy, and hath been some time from the coast.[19]

We catch the occasional detailed glimpse of English slaves (their physical appearance and characteristics) simply because they *were* slaves. In Bristol, the local postmaster offered two guineas and expenses, in 1715, for the return of 'Captain Stephen Courtney's negro aged about 20 'having three or four marks on each temple and the same on each cheek'.[20] A Scottish slave sale offered, 'A NEGRO WOMAN, named Peggy, about nineteen years of age. . . speaks good English; an exceedingly good housewench, and washer and dresser; and is very tender and careful of children. She has a young child a NEGRO BOY, about a year old, which will be disposed of with the mother.'[21] Black slaves became so commonly available in Britain that in 1769 Catherine the Great sent an agent to purchase 'a number of the finest, best-made black boys, in order to be sent to St Petersburgh, as attendants on her Russian Majesty'.[22]

This ad hoc process of small-scale black (mainly domestic) migration to England inevitably created legal problems. In English courts, local slavery confronted traditions which were contrary to the habits of the Americas. Perhaps *the* most important consequence of the seventeenth-century revolution was the defence of individual liberties guaranteed by the *Habeas Corpus* Act of 1679. Though designed for a different purpose, this Act was to have major implications for the history of slavery in England. But what did slaves, like Equiano, know about the law? What practical help could they secure from a legal system which tended to support the interests of the slave-owning class? After all, the prosperity which flowed from the Atlantic slave system was plain for all to see. And slavery seemed indivisible; an Atlantic system which bound together three continents. When legal conflicts emerged it was soon clear to English judges that decisions about slavery *in England* could easily prove to be the solvent of the broader slave-based prosperity. Any decision which denounced slavery in England might have consequential effects on slavery in other parts of Britain's Atlantic empire.[23] Though English slave cases might seem particular – local – they could easily lead to an unravelling of the entire fabric of British Atlantic slavery.

There were, moreover, people who wanted slavery to thrive in England. The West India lobby, for example, sought to secure their hold over slaves in England by a variety of tactics. They actively publicized those legal pronouncements which supported their position and which confirmed the right to hold slaves in England. They sought to prevent black baptisms, if only because the popular belief that baptism conferred freedom simply refused to go away. But efforts to prevent the spread of black Christianity were counter-productive; they alienated outsiders and, in any case, failed to work.

Black slaves turned to the only practical way out. They ran away. It was, of course, impossible for Equiano to escape from re-enslavement in 1762. He was in that most vulnerable of positions – already on board a ship and with no direct access to friends or refuge on shore. Others were luckier. Again, we know about

Granville Sharp

PLATE 5. Granville Sharp, abolitionist; engraving, 1794. Scholar and reformer, he was a founder of the society for the abolition of the slave trade.

Source: Mary Evans Picture Library.

such runaways both from the legal consequences of their escapes, and from the regular newspaper advertisements seeking their return. In 1696 the *London Gazette* carried the following:

> Run away from Captain John Brooke of Barford near Salisbury, about the middle of August last, a middle-sized Negro Man, named Humphrey, aged about 30, in a dark brown Cloath Coat with hair Buttons.

In 1768, the *Liverpool Chronicle* advertised for the return of:

> A Fine Negroe Boy, of about 4 feet 5 inches high. Of a sober, tractable, humane Disposition, Eleven or Twelve Years of Age, talks English very well, and can Dress Hair in a tollerable way.[24]

But where could they run *to*? Some were lucky and found a comfortable refuge. Ignatius Sancho, whose posthumous letters made him the most famous African in London in the early 1780s, ran away from domestic work with domineering sisters, and escaped to work in the more sympathetic household of the Duke of Montagu.[25] But other black fugitives clearly had greater trouble. Some must have stood out in a crowd, their physique, markings (i.e. especially any facial markings) and clothing making them hard to ignore:

> Run away from his Master about a Fortnight since, a lusty Negroe Boy about 18 years of Age, full of pockholes, had a Silver Collar about his Neck engrav'd Capt. Tho. Mitchel's Negroe, living in Griffiths Street in Shadwell.[26]

From the mid-1760s, however, runaways in London acquired an important defender. Granville Sharp was a man who both cared for their physical well-being and was keen to promote their claims to freedom, both through the courts and among the politically influential. Sharp was to prove a critical figure in the history of English slavery. Later, Equiano and other Africans formed an important alliance with Sharp to defend black interests in England.

Sharp had discovered the plight of London's blacks by accident. Born in 1735 into a northern ecclesiastical family, Sharp had served his business apprenticeship in London before taking up a post in a government department. He was an industrious, serious young man, devoted to his Bible and his siblings, taking pleasure in the family's weekend travels and in their collective music-making. But his life – and his subsequent reputation – were to change for ever in 1765. He bumped into a young black, Jonathan Strong, who had been severely beaten by his master, David Lisle, a Barbadian planter. Sharp took the wounded man to his brother, a doctor, who tended him and supervised his recovery. Two years later, the erstwhile master met the now-healthy Strong, and promptly had him kidnapped and prepared for transportation to Barbados. When alerted, Sharp was galvanized into action, persuading a local magistrate to have Strong released. It was a turning point for both men. Strong had, narrowly, avoided Equiano's fate of three years earlier in being shipped back to West Indian slavery, and Sharp resolved to press on with the defence of England's blacks.[27] Sharp's discussions with lawyers, however, revealed that English law might favour the slave-owners, though there was an ambiguity that he resolved to exploit.

From 1767 onwards Sharp began to educate himself in the law, studying past cases, precedents and judgments in the search for the principle of universal freedom in England. His personal view, based on a close textual analysis of the law, was that the infamous 1729 York–Talbot judgment (that slavery was tolerated in England, and that slaves could be returned to the islands against their wishes) was legally flawed. He distributed copies of his argument among lawyers and this had the effect of dissuading Strong's putative owners from claiming damages against Sharp for having prised their slave from their possession. Jonathan Strong, however, did not enjoy his English liberty for long; he died a few years later aged only 25.

Granville Sharp was now determined to clinch his argument and overthrow the Yorke–Talbot judgment; to establish the general principle that enforced repatriation from England was illegal. Thus in 1769 he wrote his major tract, *A Representation of the Injustice and Dangerous Tendency of Tolerating Slavery: or of Admitting the Least Claim of Private Property in the Persons of Men, in England* (1769). Were his argument to be accepted, the law would not tolerate slavery in England *or* the enforced removal of people out of England. It was a principle which threatened the slave lobby, and indeed anyone who wished to employ or transport people as slaves. More than that, however, it formed the kernel of a more broadly based argument. It might only be a matter of time before the denunciation of slavery as an uncivilized, inhuman – and illegal – institution rippled outwards, from English usage and acceptance, to the slave colonies themselves. If slavery were immoral and illegal *in England*, what justification could be offered for the English slave trade; for the transportation of tens of thousands of Africans in English ships in conditions which defied belief? Clearly, Sharp's intention was simpler and more limited – to protect threatened blacks in England. But the *consequences* of what he did were potentially enormous – and the West India lobby knew it.

Sharp effectively set in train a two-pronged defence of the black community in England. Firstly he offered them a legal defence by establishing that English law was their defender, not their enemy. It was to take a whole generation before that battle was finally won, but Sharp's actions marked a break with a contrary tradition which stretched back more than a century, namely the use of English courts to give legal succour and comfort, not to the slaves, but to the slave-owners. Secondly, Granville Sharp offered practical comfort to blacks who found themselves threatened by arbitrary arrest and kidnapping. He and his growing band of friends were not always successful. What mattered, however, was that here was a man blacks *knew* they could turn to for practical assistance. Sharp's reputation soon spread. Not surprisingly, Equiano later knocked on Sharp's door when he needed a sympathetic English friend.

Blacks in London quickly learned that they had a friend in Granville Sharp. One such was John Hylas, a free black whose wife Mary – still a slave – had been shipped back to Barbados against her (and John's) wishes in 1766. Sharp organized John's legal case against Mary's owners (who were ordered to return her and to pay John a derisory 1 shilling damages). Yet such cases failed to deter slave-owners from shipping blacks abroad. In 1770 Sharp was again called in, at the last moment, to prevent another former slave, Thomas Lewis, being shipped back to Jamaica. It was a close-run thing; the offending captain had sailed from Gravesend bound for the Downs, but contrary winds delayed departure, giving Sharp time to have a last-minute writ of habeas corpus served on the captain. Sharp then took prompt legal proceedings on behalf of Lewis, hoping to secure a general judgment which would prevent subsequent cases of kidnapping and transportation. The case came before Lord Chief Justice Mansfield in 1771; he was deeply reluctant to make so general a point of law, and merely said, piously, 'I would have all the masters think them free, and all Negroes think they were not, because then they would both behave better.'[28]

It was a hesitant performance by the Lord Chief Justice, which angered Granville Sharp, who was now more than ever determined to clinch a lasting legal judgment on behalf of blacks in England.

Sharp's campaign came to a focus in the person of James Somerset, who had arrived in England from Boston to serve his Scottish master Charles Stewart. Somerset had, like so many others, simply run away, only to be recaptured and imprisoned on the *Ann and Mary*, captained by John Knowles and bound for Jamaica. A writ of habeas corpus was issued and the case began in February 1772. Angered by the actions of Lord Mansfield in the preliminary hearing, Sharp determined to mastermind the case, organizing and financing sympathetic counsel, Francis Hargrave, who had already worked out a strong case against slavery in earlier discussions with Sharp. The case hinged, once again, on the contradictions in English law; did it, or did it not, sanction the enforced repatriation of blacks from England against their wishes? Mansfield, reluctant as ever to be involved in a decision fraught with so many implications, tried to persuade the parties to settle the matter out of court. That, however, was precisely what Sharp did not want. What Sharp and his colleagues wanted was a clear-cut judgment.

The case moved through eight hearings from February to early summer 1772. Lord Mansfield regularly hinted at the consequences ('many thousands of pounds would be lost to the owners by setting them free'). But West Indian planters (backing the slave-owners) and Granville Sharp for the abolitionists, were not about to budge. Throughout the proceedings the outcome remained unclear, not least because of the Lord Chief Justice's procrastinations. But the various delays through which the case stumbled served to heighten public interest in the issue. When judgment was finally delivered, on 22 June 1772, it took place before a packed Westminster Hall. Reporters from the capital's major newspapers, slave-owners, and a large gathering of blacks, crowded the gallery. According to one report, a 'great number of Blacks were in Westminster Hall yesterday, to hear the determination of the case, and went away greatly pleased'.

When Mansfield made his judgment, the blacks in the court

> bowed with profound respect to the Judges, and shaking each other by the hand, congratulated themselves upon their recovery of the rights of human nature, and their happy lot that permitted them to breathe the free air of England. . .[29]

Although Mansfield's precise words have remained a subject of historical debate, his judgment effectively ended any legal pretence that slavery could be maintained in England. The common law was held not to support slavery, and slaves could not be removed from England against their wishes. Newspapers and contemporary commentators – and the blacks themselves – all greeted the decision as a triumph for the black cause. There remained, of course, the practicalities; how could a poor black, like Equiano in 1762, secure the necessary assistance and legal help when confronted by a swift and organized kidnap attempt? Their only hope lay in having a friend close by who might be able to raise the alarm and bring in suitable help. Equiano and others – how many we will never know – were unlucky.

There were, it is true, a number of cases where blacks were held as slaves *after* 1772. Slaves and slave cases periodically flitted in and out of the public gaze. Between 1772 and 1784 there were at least 15 cases where masters tried to assert their legal right over slaves in English courts. But in no single case was their right upheld. In effect – and whatever the confusion about Mansfield's words in 1772 – slavery had been outlawed in England.

Blacks continued to face personal threats, of course – whatever the law decreed. In 1790, for example, Hannah More told Horace Walpole the story of a terrified young black woman, who was dragged from a hiding place in Bristol and forced on board a ship bound for the West Indies. At the last minute, when the ship had to return to port, local Quakers secured her freedom. Hannah More confessed that, had she known about the incident in time, she would have raised money from among her friends to buy the girl's freedom.[30] Even when not enslaved or destined for the slave colonies, blacks long remained exposed to arbitrary arrest and maltreatment, exposed by their colour, and by the hostility to it, to whatever punishment seemed fit for their shortcomings. Occasionally such kidnapping came to the public attention. Even then, the press reports often betrayed a sneering cynicism towards the aggrieved black.[31]

In the years after the Somerset case, there is little evidence of slavery in England. The instances recorded are few – and not on the scale (frequency or infamy) of those of the 1760s and 1770s. Something had indeed changed. Yet these were the years when slavery in the British Caribbean reached its apogee. The years of the late eighteenth century saw the Caribbean disgorging slave-based prosperity as never before. Yet slavery in England seemed to fade away, driven into ill-usage not so much by legal decisions as by a changing social and political climate. Active in that changing climate was the work and influence of a small band of Africans, the best-remembered of whom would be Olaudah Equiano. Who would have imagined in 1762, as Equiano sailed for the West Indies, kidnapped and re-enslaved, that twenty years later he would return to London to become the most famous, and the most influential, African of his generation? At the end of 1762, however, Equiano was in considerable despair: 'Thus, at the moment I expected all my toils to end, was I plunged, as I supposed, in a new slavery: in comparison of which all my service hitherto had been perfect freedom.'[32] He thought his miserable state was God's punishment for his earlier thoughts of earthly pleasures on arrival in London. He felt 'that the Lord was able to disappoint me in all things'. As his ship headed for the miseries of the slave islands, Equiano passed through a crisis of faith, beseeching his Lord not to forget or abandon him, rising from his turmoil, hoping 'that the Lord *would appear* for my deliverance'. In the event, Equiano (as always) was to be the author of his own fate.

Notes

1 *Interesting Narrative*, p. 92.
2 *Ibid.*, pp. 93–4.
3 Richard Dunn, *Sugar and Slaves: The Rise of the Planter Class in the English West Indies, 1624–1713* (London, 1972), pp. 249–50.
4 P. L. Hughes and J. F. Larkin (eds), *Tudor Royal Proclamations* (New Haven, 1969), pp. 221–2.
5 Baptisms of blacks in F. G. Emmison (ed.), *Bedfordshire Parish Registers*, 1682 (vol. III); 1773 (vol. IV); 1766 (vol. V); 1661 (vol. VIII); 1710 (vol. X); 1735 (vol. XII); 1774 (vol. XIX); 1758 (vol. XXXIV); 1736/7 (vol. XXXVII).
6 1 October 1687, *Chamberlain's Accounts, 1680–1687*, vol. 27; 29 September 1687, *City of York, House Book, 1663–1688*, vol. 38. Both in City of York Archives.
7 *Yorkshire Archaeological and Topographical Journal, 1879–1880*, vol. VI, p. 393; 203.
8 Norma Myers, *Reconstructing the Black Past: Blacks in Britain, 1780–1830* (London, 1996), pp. 31–2; 121–2.
9 *Interesting Narrative*, p. 78.
10 Peter Fryer, *Staying Power* (London, 1984), pp. 114–15.
11 Robin Blackburn, *The Making of New World Slavery: From the Baroque to the Modern, 1492–1800* (London, 1997).
12 We need to be alert to the distinction between British and English practice in these cases, primarily because of the differences between English and Scottish law.
13 For the latest figures see Myers, *op.cit.*
14 J. Ashton, *Social Life in the Reign of Queen Anne. Taken from Original Sources* (London, 1883; reprinted Detroit, 1968), p. 63.
15 From the *Tatler* (1709). In *The Quarterly Review*, vol. 55 (1855), p. 209.
16 *Ibid.*, p. 210.
17 *Notes and Queries*, V (1858), p. 375.
18 *Ibid.*, VI, p. 267.
19 *Liverpool and Slavery, by a Genuine 'Dicky Sam'* (Liverpool, 1884; reprinted 1969), p. 9.
20 J. W. Damer Powell, *Bristol Privateers and Ships of War* (Bristol, 1930), p. 126.
21 *Scot's Magazine*, vol. 28, (1766), p. 445.
22 *Notes and Queries*, VI (1852), p. 411.
23 Seymour Drescher, *Capitalism and Antislavery* (London, 1986), p. 32.
24 F. O. Shyllon, *Black People in Britain, 1555–1833* (Oxford, 1977), p. 13.
25 Reyahn King *et al.*, *Ignatius Sancho: An African Man of Letters* (London, 1997).
26 Ashton, *Social Life*, pp. 62–3.
27 For the latest account see Gretchen Gerzina, *Black England: Life before Emancipation* (London, 1995).
28 These cases are covered in Peter Fryer, *Staying Power*, pp. 118–20. But the definitive analysis of the case is William R. Cotter, 'The Somerset Case and the Abolition of Slavery in England', *History*, vol. 79, no. 255 (1994). See also William M. Wiecek, 'Somerset: Lord Mansfield and the Legitimacy of Slavery in the Anglo-American World', *University of Chicago Law Review*, vol. 42 (1974).
29 *The Morning Chronicle and London Advertizer*, 24 June 1772, 2b.
30 W. S. Lewis *et al.* (eds), *Horace Walpole Correspondence* (Oxford, 1961), vol. 31, pp. 340; 350.
31 See the story of the black lover, press-ganged because of his love affair with a married white woman; *The Times*, 11–12 February 1794.
32 *Interesting Narrative*, p. 95.

= 5 =

WEST INDIAN
SLAVERY

The debate about the legal niceties of slavery meant nothing to Equiano in the last days of 1762, as he found himself on board the *Charming Sally* bound for the West Indies. The ship called briefly at Portsmouth to wait for the gathering convoy of vessels. There Equiano tried to escape, paying a guinea to another sailor to supply him with a boat, but the sailor cheated him and kept the money (to the disgust of other sailors on board). Like other blacks before and afterwards, Equiano found it hard to rely on others; accomplices might simply betray or cheat a slave planning to escape. Yet there were some who tried to help. True to their promise, some sailors from Equiano's old ship travelled to Portsmouth to help him, and a female acquaintance in Portsmouth contacted him with offers of help. But before anything could be arranged, on the last day of 1762, the command vessel ordered Equiano's ship to weigh anchor. As they slipped down the channel and into a new year, England – Equiano's 'wished-for land' – disappeared from view. He fell again into that mood of bitter despair which had marked his departure from London: 'I reproached my fate, and wished I had never been born. I was ready to curse the tide that bore us, the gale that wafted my prison, and even the ship that conducted us. . .' Equiano knew what awaited him in the Americas for he had already tasted the bitterness of slave life there – 'and I called on death to relieve me from the horrors I felt and dreaded, that I might find in that place'.[1]

The convoy enjoyed a smooth, swift Atlantic crossing (apart from an accidental collision between the lead vessel and a brig – which sank without trace). On 13 February the look-out caught sight of their destination – the tiny island of Montserrat. It is a teardrop-shaped, mountainous, volcanic island, which had been dramatically transformed by the invading Europeans. The land had been comprehensively deforested, replanted with sugar cane, its native flora substantially replaced by imported crops. The pioneering labour force, mainly Irish indentured labourers, had given way (after the arrival of sugar) to African slaves and by the time Equiano arrived at the island in 1763 his fellow Africans and their local-born descendants outnumbered whites by something like ten to one.[2] If Equiano enjoyed any good luck, it was in not being forced, on arrival, to join the field slaves who toiled to tap the island's agricultural bounty. He was, after all, an experienced and literate sailor, and was used in port in Montserrat in the loading and off-loading of goods. But that too was hard, back-breaking and difficult work, made worse by the climate and weather. Equiano had become accustomed to the European climate; now he had to toil in the tropics.[3] As he settled into his life as a West Indian slave, Equiano clearly continued to rail against his fate, fearing all the time that there was worse to come.

It came, in May 1763, when he was sold yet again, to Robert King, a Philadelphia-based Quaker, who was also one of Montserrat's leading merchants. It remains an unexplained curiosity why a Quaker should buy a slave in 1763, at a time when the Society of Friends had already taken firm steps to prevent members from holding slaves.[4] Equiano had hoped to sail back to England in May 1763 on the returning vessel, now loaded with produce from Montserrat. But it was obvious to the captain that Equiano would simply disappear on arrival back in London; melt away into that growing and receptive black community and be lost forever to his erstwhile slave-owner. More than that, it was obvious that Equiano had friends in England (some of whom had rallied to him in Portsmouth), who were prepared to help him secure his freedom. Captain Doran confessed to Equiano that 'he could not venture to take me to London, for he was sure that when I came there I would leave him'.

Thus it was that Equiano was passed on – sold (albeit with a glowing testimonial to his industry and character) – to Robert King. Captain Doran described Equiano as 'a very deserving boy', and King bought him, in Equiano's words 'on account of my good character'.[5] Such praise, and assurances that he was now employed by 'the very best master in the whole island', did little to soothe Equiano's tearful anger. He was now aged 18/19, yet his troubles seemed endless. No matter how hard he worked, how much he saved (and he was robbed of his money, yet again, by sailors in Montserrat), no matter how much he proved himself to his owners and masters, he found himself passed on, like loose change, from one set of hands to another. He was a young man of fiercely independent outlook and aspirations, one, moreover, destined throughout his childhood for high status and rank in his African community. Born into a family which promised him esteem, Equiano now found himself the mere bauble of other men's interests and fancies. The sheer helplessness of his position clearly frustrated him enormously. Not surprisingly, this latest blow once more plunged him into tears of frustration, and produced anguished pleas for a return to England. But it was not to be – for the time being at least.

Having failed to persuade Captain Doran or Robert King to let him join the returning vessel for London, a miserable Equiano went down to the waterside and watched it depart for England. He 'looked at her with a very wishful and aching heart, and followed her with my eyes until she was totally out of sight.' The misery of his fate weighed heavy, and Equiano confessed: 'I was so bowed down with grief that I could not hold up my head for many months.' But he was blessed – in however small a fashion – by having a decent master. Robert King, 'possessed a most amiable disposition and temper, and was very charitable and humane.'[6]

In the violent, uncertain world of West Indian slavery, where a slave's fate depended on an owner's whim and caprice, to have such an owner was no mean benefit. King sought to extract the best from his slaves, not by harsh control but by good treatment. His solution to recalcitrant slaves was simple:

> If any of his slaves behaved amiss, he did not beat or use them ill, but parted with them. This made them afraid of disobliging him; and as he treated his slaves better than any other man on the island, so he was better and more faithfully served by them in return. . .[6]

Equiano responded well to King's slave management, even though initially he was unhappy and (interesting that he should make the remark) 'moneyless'. For his part, King quickly discovered the truth of Equiano's testimonial: that Equiano was no ordinary slave. Equiano told King that he knew something about seamanship, 'could shave and dress hair pretty well; and I could refine wines'. More crucially perhaps, Equiano admitted that 'I could write, and understood arithmetic tolerably well as far as the Rule of Three'. Here was a slave whom King could train and use in his varied business activities, working alongside his six clerks, in the unloading and loading of the regular vessels which ferried King's trade between the West Indies and his home base in Philadelphia.

Seaborne trade in the West Indian islands involved more than the obvious, direct shipping routes between the main ports of Europe, Africa and the Americas. Fleets of small coastal and riverine craft, from crude rowing boats and barges to large sailing vessels, flitted between different parts of the islands, delivering and retrieving goods and produce from isolated beaches and rivers, from remote inland properties and secluded riverside jetties. Shifting the islands' basic produce – notably sugar and rum – often involved an arduous (and sometimes dangerous) transfer from land, onto small vessels and thence to the large ships bound for Europe. Equiano proved himself adept at handling smaller vessels, and in the sugar season (which ran from January to the end of July) he toiled for upwards of sixteen hours a day ('slaved' was the word he used). For this he was paid 'fifteen pence sterling per day to live on, though sometimes only ten pence'. Slaves doing similar work for other masters were often paid considerably less.[7] But why pay slaves in the first place?

Plantation slaves had most of their physical needs provided for by their owners in return for an unremitting application to the routines of plantation labour. But there were also other kinds of slavery. Jobbing gangs for instance were common: gangs of slaves rented out by their owners for profit, or used for specific work on the plantation, or for whatever work their employer might demand. In Jamaica (the largest and most important of all the late-eighteenth-century British sugar islands), there were about 20,000 slaves employed in jobbing gangs (in 1832).[8] It seems likely though that there was a smaller *proportion* of jobbing slaves in Montserrat when Equiano lived there.[9] Such slaves were given a daily allowance – their pay – and expected to keep themselves like any other labourer. But unlike other labourers, they had little control over their pay levels and merely had to accept what was offered. Equiano knew of other slaves ('poor souls' he called them), who received 'never more than nine-pence a day'. Owners hired them out for a profit, often paying minimal wages, to guarantee a profit for themselves from the deal. Robert King sometimes had to feed slaves he had hired from other slave owners, finding that the slaves' allowance was inadequate to feed themselves properly. Time and again, Equiano reported that slaves' low wages – or late payment (even non-payment) caused friction and sometimes violence between jobbing slaves and their owners.

Enterprising jobbing slaves might, with effort and good luck, save some of their earnings. But even when they made the most of their labours and their talents – as Equiano did throughout his life – they were in constant danger of robbery and theft by white people. Slave possessions (cash or property) were regularly seized by whites, who claimed the right to remove property from slaves who were *themselves* property, and who therefore had no right to ownership. Equiano was frequently cheated in this way. A fellow jobbing slave in Montserrat, who had saved enough to buy a boat (with which he traded independently), had the boat seized by none other than the island's governor, and was powerless to seek redress. (Later this same slave made his way to England where Equiano saw him on a number of occasions.)[10] Not surprisingly, when slave efforts at self-improvement were rewarded by such coarse violations, slaves were driven to despair. An ever-deeper chasm opened between black and white. In anger and frustration, some slaves simply ran away, only to face inevitable harsh ill-treatment when recaptured.

Despite such abuses, it is clear enough that the economy of the slave islands could not function properly unless slaves were granted important areas of independence; independence to cultivate and trade on their own, to nurture their own plots, to care for their own families, and to improve themselves as best they could. Slave-owners *needed* slaves to operate on their own in order to get the best of the slave system itself; slavery worked best when key areas of the local economy granted slaves a latitude which was in effect the lubricant of slavery itself.[11] Yet in a society dominated by the view that slaves were the economic and social playthings of the whites, slave independence sometimes confronted individual white hostility. Equiano's life in Montserrat was peppered with such incidents. Whites sometimes refused to trade their sugar and rum to Equiano when he travelled alone to distant properties, and his owner was obliged to send a white companion to effect the transaction. Equiano – always alert to finance – could not help noticing that a white man was invariably paid much more than he received.[12]

From 1763 to 1766 Equiano worked for Robert King in and around Montserrat, familiarizing himself with most aspects of King's commercial affairs. It was an arrangement which clearly suited Equiano's own varied commercial and entrepreneurial instincts and leanings. He put to good use his old ship-board training in the personal attention he paid to his owner ('I used to shave and dress my master when convenient'), he worked as a clerk, checking goods in and out, looked after the stores, worked on board King's various ships, and even took care of his master's horse. Nor did he hesitate to point out the value of these labours to his master. Characteristically, Equiano couched his efforts in financial terms: 'I was of more advantage to him than any of his clerks; though their usual wages in the West Indies are from sixty to a hundred pounds current a year.'[13]

Equiano was perhaps unusual in the *range* of skills and experiences he brought to his work. Yet he was far from unique. The more closely historians have examined the fine detail of slave history, the clearer it has become that slave efforts in the sugar islands went far beyond basic manual labour in and around the fields. While a popular image persists that the essence of slavery was brute strength and physical application, the slave colonies required and encouraged a wide range of skills and talents from their black labour force. Skilled men and women were as essential to the colonies' material well-being as the armies of field gangs toiling in the most arduous of conditions. Historians now recognize this, but in fact the slaves were acutely aware of it at the time. Equiano was at pains to tell his reading public that slaves not merely formed the backbone of the labouring gangs, but formed the basis for most of the skilled work done in the sugar colonies: 'I suppose nine tenths of the mechanics throughout the West Indies are negro slaves'.[14]

The cultivation and production of slave-grown produce in the Americas created a complex labouring and social structure among the slaves. At the bottom were the field gangs, at the top, a small elite of skilled men (and some women). The movement of slaves from one job to another, and from one level to another, was always slow, often difficult and sometimes impossible. But *all* the slave produce which was loaded into the ships bound for Europe depended on slave skill as well as slave muscle. Tradesmen of every description – masons, smiths, coopers, joiners, distillers, mechanics – men who handled the beasts, women who made the clothing, cared for the sick and the young, domestics who catered for each and every whim of local white society; these and many more were as crucial to the local slave economy as their contemporaries sweating in the sugar, rice or tobacco fields. Inevitably, slave society threw up individual slaves with the most remarkable range of talents and accomplishments: linguists and man-managers, for example, craftsmen in wood and drawing, music-makers and storytellers.[15] There were, in addition, some slaves who seemed able to turn their hand to most things. In this at least slave society came to resemble 'normal' societies in their range of human attainments and skills.

Few slaves displayed more versatility than Equiano (though we need always to bear in mind that he was anxious to persuade his British readers of his attainments). In Montserrat, and at sea for his Montserrat-based owner, he displayed, and honed, that range of skills and accomplishments which were so valuable to a slave-owner and which also allowed Equiano to profit from his own efforts. Again, Equiano was not unique, but in the range of his attainments he *was* unusual.

Looking back to the skilled slaves he had known in the West Indies – coopers and carpenters earning 2 dollars a day, masons, smiths, fishermen and others, Equiano wrote of people whose value to their owners was incalculable: 'I have known many slaves whose masters would not take a thousand pounds current for them.'[16] It was clear to Equiano that slavery was indeed a profitable system. From the sick and raw muscle power imported from Africa there had emerged a complex social and human structure which not only yielded well-being to Europe but also generated prosperity on all hands. Of course the *degree* of slave-based profitability has been a source of continuing debate among historians for decades. Equiano, however, was not concerned with the fine details of the accountancy of Atlantic slavery (how could he be?). But personal observations of West Indian slave life convinced him of the commercial worth of slaves, and hence of the economic value of slavery itself.

Equiano's own experience clinched the point. Robert King was conscious of Equiano's true value to him. Other Montserrat slave-owners were also aware of Equiano's value, trying to buy him from King for as much as 100 guineas. Equiano was delighted when such approaches were rebuffed, for he realized that Robert King was an unusually good master: 'and I used to double my diligence and care for fear of getting into the hands of those men who did not allow a valuable slave the common support of life.'[17]

The obvious point was that loyalty and hard work had its own rewards. Here Equiano was exceptionally lucky. Many (perhaps most) slaves could not hope to have such an owner, nor could they expect any reward for their efforts and application. Uncertainty and indifferent treatment was the usual lot of slaves. They were, after all, mere items in a complex local accountancy system, to be weighed in the balance alongside all other forms of investments and properties – the land, the buildings, the animals. They were subject to the caprice of ownership, the whims of their immediate drivers, the ebb and flow of local economic circumstance, and the changing tide of (white) family fortunes. Worst perhaps, it did not, ultimately, matter how hard they had worked, how loyal or persistent they had been. This had also been Equiano's experience in 1762; loyal service to his master at sea had been rewarded by resale and transportation to the far side of the Atlantic. When times were hard for their owners, when ownership of a property changed (through death, inheritance or marriage), slave life could be utterly transformed. This was most spectacularly painful when slave families were split or separated. Equiano had endured that experience *twice*; first when snatched from his family, and then when separated from his sister. Even when such catastrophic dispersals did not materialize, their threat hovered over slave communities throughout the history of Atlantic slavery. Mary Prince, the female slave who came to England in 1828, offered a similar example. Parted from her (free husband), cruelly treated both in the West Indies and in London, she was abandoned in London, sick and penniless (her case adopted by the abolitionists).[18] As long as the slave remained a thing – to be bought, sold, inherited and bequeathed much like any other form of property – then slave life would be threatened by those personal and collective insecurities which Equiano experienced and spoke about.

One of the most valued (though generally unacknowledged) of slave skills was help in the care of newly arrived African slaves. Africans stumbled ashore in the Americas in a wretched and sick condition. Some simply did not recover from their experiences in the filth and disease-ridden environment of the slave ships, and died within a short time of landing. And all, as far as we can judge, were traumatized by the succession of horrors they had experienced, from their initial enslavement in Africa, through to repurchase and relocation in the Americas (which might itself prove a protracted experience.) Newly arrived Africans could not be expected to plunge into hard work in their new habitat. Those forced to work hard on arrival soon faded away. Time and again, plantation accounts speak of new arrivals dying in their early months in the Americas, or being moved, for their own well-being and survival, to less demanding work or to a more congenial environment.

Most new Africans found it hard simply to manage. Quite apart from the new rhythms and work habits, the unfamiliar tools and alien agrarian systems, Africans could not understand the local European language (or its local patois). They needed an experienced slave to guide them. Equiano's owner, Robert King, bought and transhipped newly arrived Africans from Montserrat to other islands and even to North America, and Equiano was employed to ease their transit. On these sea journeys, the Africans were most vulnerable to assault, and sexual aggression by whites. When abolitionists began to accumulate evidence against the slave trade in the 1780s, stories of sexual licence on the Atlantic slave ships emerged as one of the more shocking themes from that litany of horror stories. It was a theme which Equiano warmed to, not simply shocked by what he had seen, but also persuaded by that potent mix of religious and abolitionist zeal which had come to influence him in the late 1780s.

Equiano felt helpless to do anything about the 'violent depredations on the chastity of female slaves' committed by whites in Montserrat and on the slave ships. It was commonplace, and only acted against when committed 'to such scandalous excess' that the white men involved had to be dismissed. The objections were largely utilitarian. Slaves, after all, were an investment; they had to yield a profit and be expected to work for their new owners. Harming them in transit undermined the economic viability of the system itself. Some may have felt moral qualms about seeing slaves fall victim to sexual aggression, but the strongest objections to such violations (as indeed to most other forms of slave maltreatment) were practical. The slave colonies (and slave ships) became infamous for acts of sexual licence, sometimes of the most grotesque kind, against female slaves. Did Equiano worry, when he thought of such horrors, about his own sister's fate? Moreover other slaves (such as Mary Prince) who told about their lives invariably mentioned the sexual threats and aggressions. Yet those same slave communities set out the most savage of penalties for sexual misdemeanours (if such they were) between black men and white women. Again, Equiano spotted the inconsistency; remarking on the dire punishment inflicted for a slave's sexual involvement with a white prostitute.[19] The issue of sexual relations between black and white was fraught with social and cultural complexities and taboos. Throughout the slave societies of the Americas, local laws were devised to render illicit relations between black men and white women (heaping savage punishment on the head of the perpetrators). Yet at the same time those same communities played host to the most persistent and horrifying sexual abuse of black women by white men.[20] Much of it went unpunished – unremarked even.

The cruelties and atrocities endemic to Atlantic slavery played a large part in the abolitionist campaign which flourished against the slave trade after 1787. Tortures, sexual violations, dismembering – each and every inhumanity doled out to the slaves was paraded before a British reading public as part of the drive to shock and to persuade. As the realities of slavery unfolded (and the most telling evidence emerged initially from eye-witness accounts of life, and death, on board the slave ships), the British reading public, which was itself emerging as a new social force, was won over to the idea that slavery was unnecessarily cruel. If such violations were needed simply to keep this economic system in place, doubts were raised about the morality and value of slavery itself. Of course this sustained

PLATE 6. 'Flagellation of a Female Samboe Slave.' Equiano never forgot his sister, or stopped worrying about her fate: 'To that heaven which protects the weak from the strong, I commit your innocence and virtues, if they have not already received their just reward, and if your youth and delicacy have not long fallen victims to the violence of the African trader, the pestilential stench of the Guinea ship, the lash and lust of a brutal and unrelenting overseer' (Equiano).

Source: John Steadman, Narrative of a Five Years Expedition to Surinam, *Vol. 1 (1796), Plate 3. By permission of the British Library.*

concentration on the cruelties of slavery, which became in effect a *leitmotif* throughout all subsequent campaigns against slavery, was only *one* of various campaigns against cruelties: against the insane, animals, children, working people. It was in effect one element (though a critical one) in the emergence of a more refined humanity. It is easy to overstate the point, but it is clearly the case that anti-slavery was part cause, part consequence, of a changing social sensibility.

We need to remember that the whole edifice of colonial slavery hinged on the chattel status of the slaves. They were, from their first contact with Europeans on the African coast, through to their dying day, things bought, bartered, exchanged, inherited and bequeathed. Yet, at the same time, the concept of the slave as chattel was fundamentally – and obviously – flawed. Whatever the slave lobby might say to the contrary, slaves were human. This simple point was reiterated time and again by abolitionists, most graphically and effectively in Wedgwood's motto, 'Am I not a Man and a Brother/Sister?' But if this was the case, how could the British tolerate such atrocities committed in their name, on the African coast, on the oceanic crossing, in the slave colonies of the Americas, and even, as we have seen, in Britain itself? These violations were not mere accidents, isolated whims, or the work of errant individuals. They were basic to the system. Indeed, many planters and their supporters felt that the slave system simply would not work without the threat of severe punishment and reprisal. More than that, the exact menu of violence to be doled out to slaves was enshrined in colonial laws (which had themselves been approved by London). The closer abolitionists looked at slavery, the more they confronted a system which depended on violence. Moreover, the violence seemed to increase, and to get worse, with the passage of time. At a time when acts of judicial cruelty in Britain were themselves in decline and under attack, violence against the slaves (by the law, by colonial whites and by maritime workers) showed no signs of abating. Not surprisingly, such cruelty prompted slave violence in response.

In the years after the Haitian revolt in 1791, when the thriving (and largely African) sugar economy of St Domingue was consumed by civil war, slave revolt and foreign invasion, fears of slave violence were at a peak. Yet the more outsiders looked at life in the West Indies (and on the slave ships), the more they perceived violence against the slaves to be the root cause of slavery's woes. Slavery seemed unable to survive without the necessary and ubiquitous use of violence. But that, in its turn, seemed merely to beget slave violence. And all this under the control of an imperial power whose domestic heartlands took increasing pride in society's progessive sophistication and humane sensibility.

Equiano's *Interesting Narrative* was a personal attack on the varied cruelties of slavery, providing readers with a highly personalized account of the sufferings of one slave. But the author frequently moved beyond his own personal experiences, lacing his book with stories of outrages he had witnessed or knew of. The stories he told were familiar examples from the lexicon of plantocratic cruelties; of slaves staked to the ground and mutilated, of slaves hanged, burned or otherwise cruelly tormented. It is clear enough that some of his examples were culled from well-known, earlier published accounts of life in the slave islands. Yet this blending of eye-witness with published account confirms rather than diminishes the strength of his case. Moreover, there is nothing in Equiano's account which contradicts what we know from other parallel evidence. Indeed the worst examples which Equiano describes fall well *short* of the most savage examples we know to have taken place, at much the same time, in the West Indies.[21]

Equiano blamed many of the worst violations not on slave-owners themselves, but on those men who managed and controlled slave properties in their name. West Indian planters were notorious for quitting the islands for Britain the moment they had secured their long-term future. In the process they established a distinctive West Indian presence in Britain, building fashionable homes across the country and strutting a particular (and particularly vulgar) style in London and their favourite watering holes, with extravagant shows of slave-based wealth. This process – 'absenteeism' – was a complex development, in part the result of success (planters who had made their fortunes and departed) but, later, a function of decline. As more and more planters fell on hard times, becoming indebted to metropolitan financial interests, they left the management of their estates in the hands of local managers.[22]

It was widely assumed that absentee planters made life harder for the slaves. Resident planters had a direct interest in their slaves' well-being. After all, they had invested heavily in those slaves and wished to see the best return on their human capital. This normally involved a degree of concern for the slaves' well-being. Managers and attorneys of absentee estates on the other hand had no such personal investment. Cases of deliberate cheating or harshness by such managers have proved elusive, but contemporaries – black and white – widely assumed that life was harder for slaves under managers than under resident planters. Equiano, for instance, was convinced that absentees, 'by not residing on their estates, are obliged to leave the management of them in the hands of these human butchers, who cut and mangle the slaves in a shocking manner on the most trifling occasions'.

The most serious and perhaps most telling of Equiano's charges against plantation managers was that they 'pay no regard to the situation of pregnant women'. Poor housing – open sheds in damp positions – exposed pregnant slaves to ailments which, Equiano claimed, 'conspires with many others to cause a decrease in the births as well as in the lives of the grown negroes'.[23] It was, needless to say, a more complex problem than Equiano alleged (though he was of course in the business of making a political argument, not an academic study).

Abolitionists quickly learned that stories of harsh treatment of female slaves provided the most persuasive criticisms of slavery. There was a widespread feeling that violence against, and neglect of, females transgressed even the bounds of contemporary slave management. Moreover, the early scrutiny of slave population figures suggested that many slave communities were in a parlous state. Without regular infusions of new Africans, some of the West Indian slave populations would simply decline.[24] This basic fact was seized on by abolitionists to illustrate the consequences of maltreatment. Their case seemed most telling when directed at the condition of pregnant slaves, and the resulting slave birth-rates.

Planters had long been aware of the difficulties of slave reproduction. Though there were great variations between the islands, it seemed generally true that slaves in the West Indies did not reproduce as they might be expected to. From the mid-eighteenth century onwards, planters became ever more concerned about this matter, especially when costs of imported Africans began to rise. They needed to pay more attention to the health, and the healthy birth-rates, of their slaves if only from a selfish economic position. From these concerns a process known as 'amelioration' emerged, a conscious effort to improve slave conditions in order to safeguard their properties' long-term future. The plantocratic hope was that better care and material conditions would facilitate a healthier slave population, hence a better birth-rate, and thus a less marked reliance on imported Africans.[25]

Equiano vigorously pointed out the shortcomings and failings of a number of planters and managers he knew, but he also singled out men who handled their slaves kindly and humanely. He frequently praised Robert King, his owner in Montserrat, and he knew of others, there and in Barbados, whose good treatment of the slaves meant that they 'need no fresh stock of negroes at any time'. Owners who allowed their slaves reasonable rest periods, who paid attention to the maternity care for pregnant slaves, and fed them decently ensured they would be 'as happy as the condition of slavery can admit'.[26] Again, he blended personal observation with evidence from the printed debates about slavery.

This demography of slavery was, inevitably, more complicated than Equiano claimed. (We now know much *more* about the overall picture than any single contemporary could have known.) But his argument provided a powerful twist to the broader abolitionist case, for here once more, was an ex-slave, whose knowledge and hatred of the slave system leapt off the page at the reader, conceding that life was *not* the same for all slaves. The particularities of the slave experience varied enormously, from place to place, crop to crop, and from one master to another. Some slaves clearly fared much better than others. More than that, slave conditions could, as Equiano showed, be greatly improved by conscious effort and goodwill on the part of slave-owners. In this Equiano was not concerned merely to improve slavery; to render it more tolerable for its victims or less troublesome for its ownership. From first to last he spoke out against Atlantic slavery and wished to see it brought to a speedy end. But there seemed little likelihood that such a major transformation would take place in his own lifetime. What was required was further amelioration; more specific efforts to improve the slaves' condition as a step towards emancipation.

Equiano's account of slave sufferings is familiar if only because the images he conveyed have become part of the folk memory about slavery itself. He recalled slaves being branded with distinguishing letters (in St Kitts). In fact, branding was common across the Caribbean. At the time Equiano was a slave in Montserrat, the Englishman Thomas Thistlewood, working in the west of Jamaica, branded newly arrived African slaves, but waited until local-born slaves were five years old before branding them. By the 1790s, branding was thought to be in decline in Jamaica, though it had already died out on other islands. Troublesome, resistant slaves, however, were commonly branded until slavery itself was finally abolished in 1834.[27]

It was, however, the periodic, regular and haphazard beatings which Equiano recalled most vividly. Slaves were physically abused for the slightest of faults; they endured floggings and whippings, family separations (that most painful of all slave sufferings), and were reduced to such misery that they took their own lives (as some had done on the slave ship). All this and more was the everyday lot of countless slaves. All flitted through Equiano's account of West Indian slavery.

Here was personal testimony to add to the growing accumulation of West Indian horror stories. And all this was in addition to the random acts of abuse, the theft of slave money and property, the brazen purloining of foodstuffs and exchangeable goods which slaves had laboured long and hard to acquire. A slave friend of Equiano in Montserrat spent his leisure moments fishing – only to have his catch regularly stolen by his master or other local whites.[28] Equiano sympathized, describing how his own possessions and money were frequently commandeered by whites. Slave possessions were always vulnerable. To make it worse, slaves who reared up in anger and reacted to this regular litany of insults and attacks with heated words, aggressive outbursts or, worst of all, with blows and physical self-defence (or assault), merely exposed themselves to still further pain and punishment.

Some slave-owners (like Robert King) clearly showed genuine concern for their slaves, but many more were motivated merely by the dictates of economic self-interest. Much of the amelioration of slave life in the late eighteenth century sprang from the dictates of commercial self-survival. Better fed, better housed, better cared-for slaves provided a better material return. But such changes did not deflect Equiano's attention from the central realities of West Indian slavery. Throughout the whole region, the critical issue was the 'small account in which the life of the negro is held'. It was a point which Equiano deftly reinforced by quoting from colonial laws. The Barbados Act of 1688, which imposed a fine of £15 for the killing of a slave, was grist to Equiano's mill. Nor was this merely a legislative hangover from the early days of colonial slavery. Only eight years before Equiano published his book, 132 slaves were murdered on board a Liverpool slave ship – and the case surfaced in an English court not, as it ought to have done, as a murder case, but as a disputed insurance claim for the loss of the murdered slaves (see pp. 152–3).

There were of course, differences between the West Indian islands, but Equiano was struck by the fact that, in the fifteen islands he had visited, 'the treatment of the slaves was nearly the same. . .' Local differences – good masters here, vile masters there – were not the core issue. It was the *system* which was at fault; a system which 'spreads like a pestilence, and taints what it touches!' Here was an economic structure, based on the slave trade from Africa, which was designed 'to debauch men's minds, and harden them to every feeling of humanity!'[29]

Equiano's account was of one ex-slave describing West Indian slavery as he had known it in the 1760s, and as he had studied it over the next twenty years. What Equiano yearned for, as he laboured for Robert King in Montserrat in the 1760s was his own freedom. His whole life, in the short term, was dedicated to that end.

Notes

1 *Interesting Narrative*, pp. 96–7.
2 See Lydia M. Pulsipher, 'Galway Plantation, Montserrat', in Herman J. Viola and Carolyn Margolis (eds), *Seeds of Change: Five Hundred Years Since Columbus* (Washington, 1991).
3 *Interesting Narrative*, p. 99.
4 James Walvin, *Quakers: Money and Morals* (London, 1997).
5 *Interesting Narrative*, p. 99.
6 *Ibid.*, p. 100.
7 *Ibid.*, p. 101.

8　B. W. Higman, *Slave Population and Economy in Jamaica, 1807–1834* (Cambridge, 1976), pp. 16; 41.

9　This is based on the calculations in B. W. Higman, *Slave Populations of the British Caribbean, 1807–1834* (Baltimore, 1984), pp. 52–3.

10　*Interesting Narrative*, pp. 101–2.

11　James Walvin, *Questioning Slavery* (London, 1996), Ch. 8.

12　*Interesting Narrative*, p. 102.

13　*Ibid.*, p. 103. In fact whites on Worthy Park Estate in Jamaica at much the same time earned a little less than Equiano claimed. See Michael Craton and James Walvin, *A Jamaican Plantation: Worthy Park Estate, 1670–1970* (London, 1970), p. 145.

14　*Interesting Narrative*, p. 103.

15　James Walvin, *Black Ivory: A History of British Slavery* (London, 1992), Ch. 8.

16　*Interesting Narrative*, p. 103.

17　*Ibid.*, p. 104.

18　Moira Ferguson, *The History of Mary Prince* (London, 1987).

19　*Interesting Narrative*, p. 104.

20　James Walvin, *Questioning Slavery*, Ch. 6.

21　*Interesting Narrative*, pp. 104–9. For the more grotesque varieties of slave tortures see the diary of Thomas Thistlewood, edited by D. Hall, *In Miserable Slavery: Thomas Thistlewood in Jamaica, 1750–1786* (London, 1989).

22　For the story of absenteeism see J. R. Ward, *British West Indian Slavery, 1750–1834* (Oxford, 1988), pp. 263–76, and Higman, *Slave Populations of the British Caribbean*, p. 112.

23　*Interesting Narrative*, p. 105.

24　The nature, cause and variations on this issue were more complex than contemporaries realized. See Higman, *Slave Populations of the British Caribbean*, pp. 72–8.

25　The details of amelioration can best be approached via Ward, *op. cit.*

26　*Interesting Narrative*, pp. 105–6.

27　Ward, *op. cit.*, pp. 204–5.

28　*Interesting Narrative*, p. 110.

29　*Ibid.*, p. 111.

6

WORKING FOR FREEDOM

Corporal punishment, or the threat of it, was universally regarded as an invaluable tool in the management of slaves. Planters were especially fond of pontificating on the indispensability of corporal punishment; remove it and slaves simply would not work. But the physical maltreatment of slaves went far beyond this. As punishment, as work-discipline, as a capricious act of cruelty, or uncontrolled expression of anger, punishment formed the bass line to slave life, its rhythm beaten out with monotonous regularity on the slave's back. Equiano's detailed account of such violence was important because it brought the voice of authenticity – a reasoned, personal memoir – to what was generally a vague and emotive debate. But even Equiano pulled back from a full and candid recitation of what he had seen and experienced: 'were I to enumerate them all, the catalogue would be tedious and disgusting'.[1]

Equiano's own life as a slave in the West Indies was not typical. Surrounded on all hands by the horrors of slavery, he managed to make the most of each and every opportunity, his natural talents and energies singling him out as an ideal worker. Towards the end of 1763, for example, he came to the attention of Thomas Farmer, an English captain employed by King in ferrying passengers from one island to another. It was a thriving business which was hindered by a chronic shortage of crew. The scarcity of suitable sailors was common throughout the West Indies and there was plenty of work to be found on the Atlantic slave ships, whose complement of crew was invariably diminished by the high levels of illness and death on such vessels.[2] This shortage of white sailors was one of the main reasons behind the employment of black sailors – free and enslaved – throughout the Americas and, indeed, throughout the Royal Navy and British merchant fleet.[3] Equiano clearly struck Farmer as an ideal candidate for his understaffed ship.

Slave sailors, however, posed problems for their owners. They might simply run away, and in the hubbub of dockside life it was clearly impossible to keep permanent watch over a potential runaway. This was, after all, the main reason why Equiano had been sold by Captain Pascal on the Thames in 1762. A year later, Equiano was reassigned to life as an enslaved sailor, but always under the sharp eye of his new captain, Farmer (who would have to compensate Equiano's owner in the event of his escape). Farmer found Equiano a good industrious worker ('better to him on board than any three white men'), an experienced sailor who was unlikely to damage his ship, and not tempted, as were so many other sailors, by drink. At first Equiano worked at sea spasmodically, spending some time under Farmer's command, then returning to work in Robert King's stores. After much pestering, however, King finally agreed to transfer Equiano to Farmer's seaborne operations. For his part, Equiano welcomed the move: 'I immediately thought I might in time stand a chance by being on board to get a little money, or possibly make my escape if I should be used ill.' He also hoped to be fed better. On shore in Montserrat he had occasionally gone hungry, despite his master's generally good treatment.

Equiano could spot a potentially good billet, and his move back to a seafaring life under Captain Farmer, after a year on land, proved a turning point in his life. He became Farmer's right-hand man, and 'did all I could to deserve his favour'. In return, Equiano received 'better treatment from him than any other I believe ever met with in the West-Indies in my situation'.[4] Equiano's clear aim was to trade and profit on his own account. Sailing between the West Indian islands would allow plenty of scope for his sharp-eyed entrepreneurial talents. Even allowing for any retrospective exaggeration – his need to convince his readers that he was an industrious and ambitious African – it is clear that Equiano came into his own after 1763. As an enslaved sailor plying his seaborne trade between the islands, and from the West Indies to the northern colonies, 'kind Providence seemed to be rather more favourable to me'.[5]

For the next four years, until 1767, Equiano sailed between various ports, always picking up information about which items were available, and what was wanted, from one place to another. From the humblest of financial beginnings (he began with a handful of pennies) he was able, by shrewd trade from one place to another, to accumulate enough cash to buy his own freedom. He began in the simplest of fashions:

> I had but a very small capital to begin with: for one single half bit, which is equal to three pence in England, made up my whole stock.[6]

Having seen the commercial opportunities available between the islands, he resolved 'to try my luck and commence merchant'.[6] Within three years he had, despite disappointments, reverses and theft, accumulated enough money to pay £70 cash for his freedom, and to spend a substantial sum on new clothes and a party (for African friends) to celebrate his release. It is a stunning story; a rags-to-riches account which could not fail to impress his readers. But it was no mere fairy tale. Nor was Equiano alone in being able to use the slave system to his own material advantage. Across the Americas, similar slave industry and initiative yielded material well-being to slaves to a degree which we scarcely imagine.

Equiano spotted various opportunities up and down the slave islands (though he claimed, in retrospect that he 'trusted to the Lord to be with me'). It proved a successful combination. On a trip to the Dutch island of St Eustatius he 'bought a glass tumbler with my half bit'. Later, he sold the glass in Montserrat for twice that amount. As his ship ferried between those two islands, he repeated the process, investing his small profits in further glassware. When he had enough cash, he invested in three pints of gin, which he again sold at a profit in Montserrat. Within the space of six weeks he had turned his half bit into a dollar and 'blessed the Lord that I was so rich'.[7]

He now had some basic capital to play with. Over the next four years, between 1763 and 1767, as he sailed between the various islands, but especially between the French islands, he 'laid this money in various things occasionally, and it used to turn out to very good account'. It was a period of permanent travel, 'and ever trading as I went'. It was a way of life which had more than its usual share of risks. Like other slaves, Equiano was exposed to the cheating and threats of local whites. He had no legal rights, he could only appeal to other people's honesty and decency, and in the world of West Indian slavery there were few non-slaves on hand to safeguard a slave's interests. He had to be permanently vigilant not to lose his money to the tricks and threats of white people he dealt with. Even when slaves were innocently enjoying themselves, they were exposed to what Equiano described as 'injuries' and 'ill-usage'. The risks were greater when slaves had money or possessions to defend.

On one trip to Santa Cruz, a slave came aboard Equiano's ship with a bag of limes and oranges; Equiano carried two bags of the same produce, and both men hoped to sell the fruit elsewhere. No sooner had they landed than two white men simply took the bags from them. The aggrieved slaves followed the men, demanding the return of their property, receiving only threats and curses for their efforts. The two slaves retreated, Equiano bemoaning his financial fate; 'in the very minute of gaining more by three times than I ever did by any venture in my life before, was I deprived of every farthing I was worth.' When they appealed to local officials, they were threatened again, and decided to return to their aggressors to plead for the goods. The thieves finally relented and returned Equiano's two bags of fruit, but kept the other man's goods: 'The poor old man, wringing his hands, cried bitterly for his loss.' Equiano gave him some of his own fruits, and the two slaves 'proceeded to the market to sell them'. Once again Equiano thought that the Lord smiled on his dealings ('Providence was more favourable to us than we could have expected') and 'we sold our fruits uncommonly well; I got mine for about thirty-seven bits'. He was amazed by his change in fortune which 'proved no small encouragement for me to trust the Lord in any situation'.

This theft was not an isolated incident. On another occasion Equiano's captain came to his defence when he had 'been plundered or used ill by these tender Christian depredators'.[8] Slaves who dealt commercially with whites were at a permanent disadvantage. In this same period, this time in Charleston, Equiano again 'disposed of some goods on my own account' but local white men, though 'buying them with smooth promises and fair words', gave Equiano 'but very indifferent payment'. He handed over a puncheon of rum to one man who simply refused to pay, despite the intervention of Equiano's captain: 'I could not obtain any thing for it; for, being a negro man, I could not oblige him to pay me.'

Equiano assembled a group of fellow blacks to seek out the man, who finally, after much badgering, reluctantly paid up – but even then partly in useless currency: 'he took advantage of my being a negro man'. When, in his turn, Equiano tried to pass on this currency in the local market he was threatened with a flogging for his pains.[9]

It was a pattern which repeated itself throughout Equiano's life whenever he tried to make money. Nor did it happen solely when he was enslaved. Much later, in 1771, when Equiano was back in the West Indies (as a free man), he again traded in goods between the islands: 'I met once more with my former kind of West-India customer.' In Grenada, a local white man took goods from him, and from other blacks, but 'without any intention of paying me'. When he pressed for payment, Equiano was threatened with violence. Though appealing to a local JP, Equiano and another black friend discovered that 'being negroes, although free, we could not get any remedy'. Only when three white sailors, who had been similarly cheated, joined with them in physically threatening the man, was he persuaded to pay up – and even then, only in part.[10]

After one successful trip to St Kitts Equiano had acquired 'eleven bits of my own' which he added to another five bits lent by his captain and 'with which I bought a Bible'. He had to search high and low to find one, however; none seemed for sale in Montserrat. This Bible replaced the one he had been parted from, along with three other books he owned, when he had been enslaved on the Thames in 1762.[11] This simple purchase is remarkable, for here was an African, with few personal possessions, able to earn and borrow money, and choosing to spend his spare cash on a Bible. Equiano's entrepreneurial talents were put to the service of his zealous attachment to his recently discovered Christian faith. Throughout his life, the two qualities went together; his ability to earn money and his attachment to piety and a Christian life.

Based in Montserrat, but sailing between the West Indian islands, Equiano became an astute observer of the daily injustices which crowded in on him and other blacks. The indignities, punishments, violations and threats doled out to blacks of all sorts and conditions formed a daily parade of unhappiness shared by untold legions of his fellow blacks. Even when blacks were freed they found it hard to escape from under the shadow of slavery. In Montserrat, a free black woman (who herself owned land and slaves on the island) wished to marry a local white man, but the clergy refused them a church wedding. The issue was resolved when the couple married at sea to avoid offending local convention. It was, claimed Equiano, hard to describe 'the irksomeness of this situation to a mind like mine' – and presumably to many others.[12] On another occasion a fellow sailor, Joseph Clipson, a 'decent free young mulatto-man', who had a free wife (and child) in Montserrat, was seized by a crew from Bermuda. Despite his certificate of freedom, despite the support of colleagues who vouched for his status as a freedman, he was hustled aboard an outward-bound vessel and shipped away, never again to see his wife or child. Equiano had seen such acts of enslavement – of free men – in Jamaica and other islands, and he had heard of similar incidents in Philadelphia. Not surprisingly, he felt deeply moved by such outrages. Was it surprising, he asked, that slaves 'when mildly treated, should prefer even the misery of slavery to such a mockery of freedom?'[13]

Slavery, then, threatened and damaged many more people than the slaves themselves. Free blacks living in the shadow of slavery were regularly in danger of re-enslavement, 'for they live in constant alarm for their liberty, which is but nominal, for they are universally insulted and plundered without the possibility of redress'. Injustice and cruelty seemed a way of life in the West Indies, and Equiano felt 'I never should be entirely free till I had left them'.[14]

By the mid-1760s and still aged only 19 or 20, Equiano had undertaken a remarkable range of jobs and visited an unusually large number of places. He had developed a special loathing for the West Indies, where slaves were treated savagely, and where his every effort to improve himself seemed to run into obstructions, threats and violations from local whites. Moreover Equiano, like other Africans (but unlike local-born slaves), had known another, very different life; an African past which, despite the passage of time, offered a memory of better times. His travels also convinced him that 'every part of the world in which I had hitherto been' seemed infinitely better, 'a paradise in comparison of the West-Indies'.[15]

The more he pondered his fate, the more he saw of life in the West Indies (dominated as it was by its brutal slave system), the more determined he became to secure his own freedom. He became preoccupied with thoughts of freedom ('if possible, by honest and honourable means'). In time, he came to believe that life was predestined; that the Lord had chosen a few select people. Not surprisingly, he eventually found George Whitfield's commitment to predestination, in the early Methodist movement, the most satisfactory religious home. He was torn, as he pondered his fate as a slave, between the sense that 'whatever fate had determined must ever come to pass' and the hope that freedom would come his way – if it were so fated. Conversely, if he were fated never to be freed 'all my endeavours for that purpose would be fruitless'. Not surprisingly, he turned to prayer and to his new Christian God for strength and succour. But throughout he remained steadfast in his efforts to free himself, using 'every honest means, and did all that was possible on my part to obtain it'.

His best hope lay in saving money: 'I became master of a few pounds, and in a fair way of making more.' In all this he was encouraged by his captain. At times Captain Farmer would 'take liberties with me'. Equiano was not a man to take lightly, however: 'whenever he treated me waspishly, I used plainly to tell him my mind.' He had witnessed too many outrages against his fellow slaves to tolerate any against himself. He told Farmer that he would rather 'die before I would be imposed upon as other negroes were'. His basic assumption was clear enough: 'life had lost its relish when liberty was gone'.[16]

Whatever frictions occurred between these two men – the English captain and the African slave – were quickly resolved, not least because Farmer appreciated Equiano's value as an industrious and enterprising workman and shipmate. It was a mutually beneficial arrangement. Farmer was rewarded by Equiano's 'great attention to his orders and his business', and Equiano was helped financially, and generally encouraged to save and prosper. It was a curious, but not uncommon, relationship. White management, dependent on enslaved effort and initiative, got the best from their human capital by granting room for economic and social manoeuvre. For their part, slaves' effort on the economic margins of their bondage enabled them to accumulate money and material well-being.[17]

Looking back, Equiano recognized that it was Farmer's liberality towards his independent economic interests which ultimately made possible his freedom. In the meantime, however, for all the economic opportunities to make small profits here and there, life at sea was, of course, dangerous and unpredictable. On a number of occasions Equiano narrowly avoided a watery grave (he could not swim) in unpleasant incidents which served merely to confirm his determination to quit the life of an enslaved seaman. Above all else he wanted to take up an earlier, perhaps casual, offer from his owner, the Quaker Robert King, of going to Philadelphia. But his main aim was his own emancipation and then perhaps heading for 'Old England'.

If his plans to buy his freedom were frustrated, Equiano planned to escape. But to escape permanently and successfully meant leaving the Americas completely. Millions of slaves doubtless harboured similar hopes, but how to effect such ambitions posed daunting problems. Equiano toyed with the idea of learning navigation, in the hope that he might somehow or other 'attempt my escape in our sloop'. He felt sure that there were plenty of others keen to join him, but he intended to embark on this wildly optimistic scheme only if he was badly treated. Just in case, he began to take navigation lessons from the ship's mate, 'for which I agreed to give him twenty four dollars' (a remarkable amount of money for a slave to possess) but the captain intervened when he heard of the scheme. Nonetheless, Equiano managed to acquire rudimentary navigation skills, and though they were not used to escape, they served him in good stead later in his sailing career.[18]

There were in fact plenty of opportunities to run away. Indeed the history of slavery in the West Indies is in part the story of slaves on the run. They ran away from hateful owners, drivers, places and work itself; they ran to loved ones, family and friends.[19] Equiano was alert to the opportunities of escape 'which frequently presented themselves'. There were plenty of ships close at hand, most of them short of crew and willing to employ men with few questions asked. In Guadaloupe some of Equiano's shipmates switched ships, joining French ships bound for France and urging Equiano to join them, but he felt a bond of loyalty to the captain who had treated him well. It seems, in retrospect, a curious decision. But Equiano already knew, from bitter experience, that Europe was not necessarily the answer to a slave's problems. He remained determined to secure his freedom formally; to have a document which would confirm in the eyes of others that he was indeed a free man. For that he needed official manumission. And for that he needed enough money to buy it.

In recognition of his application and industry, Captain Farmer gave Equiano formal instruction in navigation – though many warned the captain that 'it was a very dangerous thing to let a negro know navigation'. Indeed, a number of West Indian islands had strict laws about slave access to ships, fearing that they offered too tempting a prospect of escape, if only to a neighbouring island. Yet slave sailors were vital in the maritime trade, the coastal trades and the fishing industries throughout the West Indies and in parts of North America.[20] Equiano's own career at sea illustrates this.

In his career as a sailor, Equiano worked at any task which came to hand, as his ship loaded and off-loaded cargoes of all sorts from one island to another. But *the* most valuable of all cargoes Equiano was entrusted with was of fellow Africans. Towards the end of 1764, Robert King bought a larger vessel, the sloop *Prudence*, and Equiano joined the crew in transporting 'new slaves' (newly arrived Africans in Montserrat) to Georgia and Charleston. The new ship regularly transferred newly arrived Africans to other slave colonies. The following year, 1765, 'we took slaves on board for St. Eustatia, and from thence to Georgia'.[21] What Equiano recalled, however, was not so much the irony – of himself, a slave, working in the shipping and sale of other African slaves – but the new commercial openings which these new travels might afford him. He was pleased with the move to a new ship, and the opportunities of trading in distant and possibly more lucrative colonies. The usual difficulties surfaced (of whites trying to cheat him) but he again managed to show a profit. [22]

His hopes of freedom began to mount, especially when his owner ordered the ship to Philadelphia. As the preparations took place, Equiano 'worked with double alacrity, from the hope of getting money enough by these voyages to buy my freedom'. Robert King had long ago promised Equiano his freedom. But now, in 1765, King confessed that he feared Equiano might simply run away on arrival in Philadelphia, and planned therefore to sell him. Equiano had proved his value to King, and other men in Montserrat had noticed Equiano's worth as a worker. King felt confident that he could get 100 guineas for Equiano on the island. One local man had even earmarked Equiano as an overseer in charge of his slaves. Captain Farmer thought that Equiano would fetch 100 guineas in Carolina. Equiano had *already* been offered a post in Carolina, as enslaved captain of a local rice boat, but he distrusted the white man making the offer. Yet there is a curiosity here; an African being approached, as if he were a free agent, with the offer of a new job – but expected to remain a slave. All healthy slaves were valuable, of course, but skilled, trained and flexible slaves were especially valuable. The monetary value of skilled slaves, when they were bought and sold (normally along with the property they worked on) confirms their extra worth in local economic affairs. In Equiano's case, his industry and general usefulness were clear to all who encountered him. He was, quite simply, an attractive commercial proposition. But these same qualities also gave Equiano a degree of power of his own. He knew his own worth – even though it was a value which reduced him, like millions of others, to a crude item of trade; an artefact with its own price. Equiano recognized this – and wished to resolve the matter by his own efforts. He intended to work hard, save, and pay whatever he was worth – for his freedom.

When confronted with accusations that he planned to run away when in Philadelphia (vengeful tittle-tattle put about by a mate on board the ship who had been reported by Equiano for dishonesty), Equiano simply denied it. He pointed out that he could, had he so wished, already have escaped at a number of places: 'I thought that if it were God's will I ever should be freed . . . whilst I was used well, it should be by honest means.'

Everything hinged on the Lord: 'I could only hope and trust in the God of heaven.'[23] Captain Farmer confirmed everything Equiano said; that he had never threatened to run away and had always resisted the temptation to follow other runaways. Robert King seemed convinced, agreeing that he had always regarded Equiano as 'a sensible fellow' and had hoped, by loaning him goods and encouraging him to trade on his own behalf, that Equiano would manage to save enough money to buy his own freedom. King agreed that he would grant his freedom in return for £40 sterling.

With a loan of some rum and sugar to sell in his own name, and the gift of a silver coin from King, Equiano sailed to Philadelphia. On arrival he sold his wares 'pretty well' and was pleased to find other items 'plentiful and cheap'. Wherever he travelled, Equiano was alert to commercial openings, looking at the prices of various commodities and calculating which ones he could buy, and sell elsewhere at a profit. But the best news he received in Philadelphia was from a fortune-teller ('a *wise* woman') who told him 'I should not be long a slave'. Greatly encouraged by this news, Equiano returned to Montserrat where he sold his goods at a profit.[24] From there he travelled to Georgia (with a slave cargo) but he caught a fever and remained ill for eleven days. Worried that he might be dying, Equiano prayed for recovery, promising 'that I would be good if ever I should recover'. Helped by an eminent local doctor, Equiano recovered in time for the vessel's return to Montserrat. As his vessel slipped closer to the island, his usual business plans began to surface, but also his old unhappiness with the West Indies. Equiano thought that perhaps 'the very air of that country or climate seemed fatal to piety'. The Caribbean seemed a sump of earthly preoccupations; a region he needed to quit if he were ever to fulfil himself.

Equiano's ship had a quick turn-round, the holds no sooner empty of goods from North America before filling up with 'some of the poor oppressed natives of Africa, and other negroes' destined for Charleston. There he gathered cargo for the ship from along the local river systems, but continuing to trade in his own name.[25] Once again, he was plagued by general customer intransigence – bad debts, refusal to pay, all of which were hard to counter, even with his captain's help.[26] Things took a turn for the worse at the next port of call, Savannah, Georgia, where Equiano was badly assaulted by a drunken local doctor, Dr Perkins, and an accomplice. Equiano lost a lot of blood before being dumped in the local jail. Rescued by Captain Farmer, he was tended by local doctors (who feared he might not survive). Searching for redress, Farmer consulted lawyers, 'but they told him they could do nothing for me as I was a negro'. It was clearly a serious beating which put Equiano in bed for 16 to 18 days, and he was not able to resume work for four weeks.[27] But by the end of 1766 Equiano was back in Montserrat, where he remained for the next twelve months.[28] Equiano was not unusual in his physical sufferings. Capricious acts of violence against slaves were commonplace, and not only in the Americas.

We need, then, to think of Equiano as a man whose life was shaped not so much by what he did (or did not do), but by his status and his colour. Time and again the blows against him (the assault by the drunken Dr Perkins in Savannah; the deception and cheating whenever he traded with whites) were not simply attacks on this one man; they were symptoms and consequences of the way blacks everywhere were treated and regarded. They were, at best, the humblest of all humanity, at worse non-people for whom the normal conventions and etiquette of human exchange simply did not apply. But Equiano was quite clearly a remarkable man, able to bounce back from the latest blow, more determined than ever to press on with his aspirations – ultimately with the aim of freedom.

Thus he felt confident, in the mid-1760s, that freedom was close. After another year, working on shore in Montserrat, he was eager to return to sea, mainly to continue saving for his freedom. When in 1766 his owner bought a still larger vessel, the sloop *Nancy* ('the largest I had ever seen'), Equiano was delighted to find himself on board; the ship's extra space provided him with room to carry even more trading goods. On a trip to Charleston he bought four barrels of pork, and sold them for almost 300 per cent profit, investing the money in another consignment, but always 'trusting to God's Providence to prosper my undertaking'. When in Philadelphia, he sold his goods mainly to Quakers, with none of the troubles he traditionally encountered with other white customers:

> They always appeared to be a very honest discreet sort of people, and never attempted to impose on me; I therefore liked them, and ever after chose to deal with them in preference to any others.[29]

It was hard to avoid the Quaker presence in the city of brotherly love in the mid and late eighteenth century, and Equiano's encounters with them were to prove important in his subsequent career. Equiano was clearly a man with a great deal of social and intellectual curiosity, always willing to follow his instincts and to ask questions of people and the world around him. In Philadelphia this curiosity led him through the open doors of a local meeting house, at the time of a Quaker meeting. He was astonished to see a woman preaching. On another occasion he was amazed to see how much effort, how much sweat and energy, an evangelical preacher invested in his preaching. It was, he thought, not unlike his own sweaty efforts working in Montserrat. Gradually Equiano realized that not all Christian worship took the form he had been accustomed to. The absence of priestly effort and zest was responsible, he now realized, for 'the thin congregations they preached to'.[30] He was drawn, even while still a slave, to the evangelical mode of worship and preaching, and repelled by the staider conventions and styles of other forms of Christian worship. It may be that Equiano turned to a form of Christianity which struck a chord with the belief system, the Igbo culture, from which he had been wrenched. But it seems clear enough that these brief experiences in Philadelphia helped to confirm him in the type and style of Christian worship he found most congenial.

By the time the *Nancy* had completed this trip to Philadelphia and had returned to Montserrat (in 1766) Equiano had made enough money to buy his freedom. Before he could act, however, his owner Robert King ordered the ship to head directly to St Eustatius, discharge there and sail to Georgia. Disappointed, Equiano thought it inappropriate 'to murmur at the decrees of fate'. In St Eustatius[31] the *Nancy* was loaded with 'a live cargo, (as we call a cargo of slaves)'. But there was little for Equiano to buy in so small an island, and he was unable to secure all the goods he might have wanted for the next leg to Georgia. Though he was apprehensive about returning to Georgia – after his last dangerous and terrifying experience – Equiano took the view that each successive step of the journey brought him closer to his return to Montserrat and eventual freedom.[32] Ever alert to the prospects of earning more money, Equiano was an eager assistant to Captain Farmer in caring for a local silversmith in his final days. But the promise of financial reward failed to materialize (the silversmith, contrary to his dying promises, had no money to bequeath to the two men). In Equiano's own words, 'While we thought we were embracing a substance, we grasped an empty nothing!!'

Equiano was aware of the comedy of the situation: 'my captain and I exhibited, for some time, most ridiculous figures – pictures of chagrin and disappointment!'

They departed, leaving 'the deceased to do as well as he could for himself, as we had taken so good care of him when alive for nothing.'[33] Equiano was not above slipping into a whimsical, humorous vein, poking fun at himself and his friends. At a number of points in the text, he uses a humorous self-denigration both to lighten the text and to make a serious point.

Back in Montserrat, safe and sound, 'but much out of humour with our friend the silversmith', Equiano sold his produce, counted his assets and found that he was worth £47. Captain Farmer urged him to appear, with the cash, at Robert King's breakfast table. Understandably, Equiano approached the occasion with a great deal of apprehension. King had seemed to hesitate about the deal and had previously appeared uncertain about the wisdom of granting Equiano's freedom. When they met, King initially recoiled from the idea, quizzing Equiano about how he had managed to save so much cash: '"How did you get it"; replied he; I told him, "Very honestly."'[34] Captain Farmer intervened to confirm Equiano's story, telling how the African had worked hard and honestly, and how he was always careful with his money. King clearly regretted his earlier offer, claiming, 'he would not have made me the promise he did if he had thought I should have got money so soon'. At this point, Captain Farmer weighed in on Equiano's behalf, clapping King on the back, urging him to keep his promise, not least because Equiano had proved such a good investment:

> you have received good interest for it all this time, and here is now the principal at last. I know Gustavus has earned you more than an hundred a-year, and he will still save you money, as he will not leave you: Come, Robert, take the money.

There seemed little the Quaker merchant could do in the teeth of Farmer's prompting, and in the light of his own promise. King took Equiano's cash, and ordered him to head immediately to the Register Office for his formal manumission papers:

> These words of my master were like a voice from heaven to me; in an instant all my trepidation was turned into unutterable bliss.

Bowing with gratitude, but so overcome with emotion that he could say nothing at first, though his feelings were clear enough, he wept, and gave thanks to God. Once his initial excitement had died down, he thanked both King and Captain Farmer, and immediately left for the Register Office to secure the paper granting his freedom, with the words of the 126th Psalm ringing in his ears: 'I glorified God in my heart, in whom I trusted.'

These words, he claimed, had been in his mind from the day he had been re-enslaved in Deptford in 1762 to this, the precious moment of his freedom, granted in Montserrat in July 1766. He felt like St Peter himself, miraculously free from prison. As he strode to the office, his excitement was hard to describe. 'All within my breast was tumult, wildness, and delirium! My feet scarcely touched the ground.' He felt like Elijah as he rose to Heaven.[35] This whole episode was described as a religious experience; an emotional turmoil conveyed through biblical references and saintly images. He even alluded to freedom being like a welcome return to his mother's arms; a return to the maternal love and care he had prematurely lost in childhood.

As he hastened to the office, he told all and sundry of his new-found freedom and of his happiness. Even the island's Registrar was pleased for him and drew up the manumission document for half the normal fee (of a guinea). Clutching the document, Equiano rushed back to his master for his formal signature. By nightfall:

> I who had been a slave in the morning, trembling at the will of another, now became my own master, and compleatly free.[36]

The manumission document was dated 10 July 1766. Ten years after he had landed as an African child in Barbados, Equiano became a free man. It was, of course, a freedom *restored*. And it was a freedom won by dint of his own hard work and initiative, and in spite of periodic alarms and uncertainties.

More than twenty years later Equiano reprinted the document in its entirety. He must have kept the document, or a copy, throughout the intervening years and through all the remarkable travels he undertook in that period, for it was far too long to have been remembered word for word.

Equiano was now a free man. But black freedom was as difficult to defend as it had been to secure. In a world where the stigmata of slavery had descended on black people throughout the Atlantic world, where to be enslaved was to be black, proof of freedom was vital. In the short term, however, Equiano was keen to celebrate his newly won status. Once again, he had planned it. On his last trip to Savannah, he had bought some new clothing. Fully expecting to be freed in the near future, he 'laid out above eight pounds of my money for a suit of superfine cloathes to dance in at my freedom'. Overjoyed with his new status of free man ('to me the most desirable in the world'), Equiano organized dances to celebrate his freedom with his friends in Montserrat. Sporting his new clothes, 'my Georgia superfine blue cloathes', Equiano was pleased with the impression he made, especially with local women. Some, who 'formerly stood aloof' began, he claimed, 'to relax, and appear less coy'.[37]

From one slave society to another, slaves were famous for the care, cost and elaboration they invested in communal and private celebrations. It formed a sharp contrast to the ragged and generally miserable workaday appearance of slave life. People who shuffled off to work, reluctantly, in rags and with as much foot-dragging as could be mustered, burst into a regime of energetic, colourful and well-dressed pleasures in their spare time and at high days and holidays. As they headed for market, at Christmas, New Year, crop-over, for birthdays and funerals, for christenings – and for freedom – slaves emerged from the physical miseries of everyday life as utterly transformed people.

'Sunday best' – slave clothing of the most elaborate and costly kind – was a sure sign of slaves enjoying and distancing themselves from their owners. And this, we need to recall, was from people who (in the case of the Africans) had stumbled ashore from the slave ships virtually naked. Slave-owners were expected (and in some cases were obliged by local law) to provide their slaves with everyday working clothes; coarse but durable, osnaburg cloth, some cotton items, hats, caps and blankets. The allocation of clothing – and materials from which slaves were expected to make up their own clothes – varied, depending on the slave's age, status and health. But even among the younger, healthier, privileged slaves (craftsmen and drivers), everyday clothing was simple and basic. Not surprisingly, then, slaves set their work clothes aside to re-emerge for celebrations unrecognizably altered; butterflies from workaday grubs.

Much of the slaves' spare cash was invested in their clothes. Visitors to the colonies were generally amazed to see slaves bedecked in their elaborate clothing. At dances, 'all who can afford it appear in very gay apparel – the men in broadcloth coats, fancy waiscoats, and nankeen or jean trowsers, and the women in white or fancy muslin gowns, beaver or silk hats, and a variety of expensive jewellry...'[38] Equiano was simply joining in a well-established slave tradition when he put on the eye-catching clothes he had bought specially for his moment of freedom. And, in organizing dances for his friends, he was part of a slave tradition which was universal throughout the Americas.

Slaves danced at every social opportunity, Africans gathering together to dance throughout the night at the weekends. Energetic, loud, exaggerated, slave musical pleasures prompted Europeans to think that they were looking at Africa in the Americas. Here, they felt, were cultural signs of the slaves' African past; musical expressions of 'primitive' African cultures which whites feared, yet scarcely comprehended. It was also claimed, by planters and visitors alike, that here was proof of Africans' natural musicality. Few doubted that Africans were more attached to music than Europeans. But few stopped to consider why this might be so; why Africans, and their descendants, clung to a world of their own making, and to habits which belonged to societies from which they had been wrenched. Slaves' musical cultures changed across time. Whites were relieved when they saw local-born slaves moving ever closer to European styles; they prayed this would be part of the broader distancing of the slave community from its African past. But throughout the history of Atlantic slavery, music and dance remained a central feature of slave culture across the Americas.[39] Equiano was but one of millions when he decided to enjoy his first days as a free man through music – dressed in eye-catching and costly clothes.

Technically free to leave Montserrat, indeed to go anywhere he wished, Equiano yet felt obligated to his former owner. Though yearning to leave the Caribbean, and get back to what he called 'Old England', he agreed to stay on and to work on King's ships. But now Equiano was registered as 'an able-bodied sailor, at thirty-six shillings per month'. Even that was not enough to satisfy his acquisitive ambitions; his wages were in addition to whatever 'perquisites I could make'.[40] Planning to complete a couple of voyages, Equiano was keen (no surprise here) to make as much money as he could. He fantasized that, once back in England, he would confront his former owner Captain Pascal – for whom, despite everything, he claimed to have fond feeling – and show him 'what the Lord had done for me in so short a time'.

It is a sign of Equiano's deepening faith that he should attribute his new-found freedom, not to his own efforts, nor to his own hard work and savings, but to his

Saviour. Thus, in the summer of 1766, Equiano stepped aboard the *Nancy*, a free black sailor, day-dreaming about a future life in London, looking forward to flaunting his freedom before old friends and acquaintances, and determined to make his way in the world as a free man. He must have known – from his own bitter experience and from his sharp-eyed observation of the world of Atlantic slavery, that black freedom could be a bruising experience. Free blacks found it hard living in a world under the shadow of slavery.

Notes

1 *Interesting Narrative*, p. 113.
2 Johannes Menne Postma, *The Dutch in the Atlantic Slave Trade, 1600–1815* (Cambridge, 1990), pp. 152–7; James A. Rawley, *The Trans-Atlantic Slave Trade* (New York, 1981), pp. 285–7.
3 N. A. M. Rodger, *The Wooden World: An Anatomy of the Georgian Navy* (London, 1986), pp. 159–60; W. Jeffrey Bolster, *Black Jacks: African American Seamen in the Age of Sail* (Cambridge, MA, 1997).
4 *Interesting Narrative*, p. 116.
5 *Ibid.*, p. 114.
6 *Ibid.*, p. 116.
7 *Ibid.*
8 *Ibid.*, pp. 117–18.
9 *Ibid.*, pp. 128–9.
10 *Ibid.*, pp. 170–1.
11 *Ibid.*, pp. 118–19.
12 *Ibid.*, p. 119.
13 *Ibid.*, p. 122.
14 *Ibid.*
15 *Ibid.*, p. 119.
16 *Ibid.*, pp. 119–20.
17 James Walvin, *Questioning Slavery* (London, 1996), Ch. 8.
18 *Interesting Narrative*, pp. 121–3.
19 Walvin, *op. cit.*, pp. 125–31.
20 B. W. Higman, *Slave Populations of the British Caribbean, 1807–1834* (London, 1984), pp. 235–6.
21 *Interesting Narrative*, p. 127.
22 *Ibid.*, pp. 123–4.
23 *Ibid.*, p. 125.
24 *Ibid.*, pp. 126–7.
25 *Ibid.*, p. 130.
26 *Ibid.*, pp. 127–8.
27 *Ibid.*, pp. 129–30.
28 Equiano may have been confused about the date; see Carretta, *ibid.*, p. 276, n. 359.
29 *Ibid.*, pp. 131–2.
30 *Ibid.*, p. 132.
31 St Eustatius had emerged under the Dutch by 1720 as a market for the sale and transfer of new Africans from the Atlantic traders to merchants and traders on other islands and, in this case, even further afield (Johannes Menne Postma, *op. cit.*, pp. 270–2).
32 *Interesting Narrative*, p. 133.
33 *Ibid.*, pp. 134–5.
34 *Ibid.*, p. 135.
35 *Ibid.*, p. 136.
36 *Ibid.*, p. 137.
37 *Ibid.*, pp. 134; 138.
38 Roderick A. McDonald, *The Economy and Material Culture of Slaves* (Baton Rouge, 1993), pp. 111–28.
39 For music and dance, see Roger D. Abrahams and John F. Szed (eds), *After Africa* (New Haven, 1983).
40 *Interesting Narrative*, p. 138.

= 7 =

FREEDOM IN THE SHADOW OF SLAVERY

Africans had crossed the Atlantic from the early voyages of Columbus. The ships of all the major Atlantic explorers and settlers were dotted with black crewmen, as were the much earlier maritime fleets of the Mediterranean. On the Atlantic ships, these 'Atlantic Creoles' were part of a broader and expanding community of men who were rooted not in Africa, nor even in the Americas, but who literally floated between the two, as sailors, linguists and go-betweens.[1] With the growth of the Atlantic trade, it was inevitable that more and more black sailors would find their way onto those vessels. The slave ships were, of course, the most obvious component in this trade. Without their human cargoes the plantation-based transformation of the Americas would have been impossible. But, in their turn, the plantations, and the societies they spawned, were nurtured by the economies of metropolitan Europe. Black and white settlers (especially in the tropical Americas) were clothed, fed, housed, defended and sustained by supplies from Europe. There was, in short, a massive and expansive Atlantic trade which supported (and profited from) the slave colonies of the Americas. And as Africans spilled from the slave ships in their millions, as ever more slaves found their way into every occupational and social cranny of American life, seaborne trades naturally enough provided a livelihood for some of them.[2]

With the advance of black colonial slavery in the seventeenth century, enslaved sailors could be found on ships based in all the major seaports trading to the slave colonies. Slave-owners hired out their slaves to captains and ship-owners in return for the slaves' wages. In time, black sailors joined the ranks in the Royal Navy. Others, more desperate, fled their seaborne bondage to join the gangs of privateers and pirates in and around the Caribbean and the Bahamas. Among the eighteen men in the last crew of the infamous 'Blackbeard', five 'were men of colour'. As far as we can tell, until the early eighteenth century, most black sailors were enslaved and endured a unique mix of environments; the harsh brutalities of a seaborne life fused onto the distinctive pains and disabilities of black slavery. It was not surprising then that some of them chose the violent prospects of privateering, whereby, at least, they might enjoy the uncertain material rewards of sudden bounty.[3] If caught, a black privateer could always plead that he had been forced into piracy, and that he had little say in the matter. Piracy was effectively dead by the time Equiano first crossed the Atlantic, but black seamanship (both free and enslaved) thrived.

Colonial laws sought to restrict slave access to certain kinds of work, and to maintain a 'safe' balance between black and white. But as the sugar economy boomed the islands became ever more African in composition and style. There seemed little to be done to stem the flow of Africans into the islands. Who else could do the heavy field work – and be replaced so quickly and relatively cheaply? But as slaves spilled out into most occupations, they posed all sorts of problems. Slaves worked on the small boats ferrying people and goods to and from the Atlantic vessels lying offshore. They manned the canoes and rafts which traded up and down inland waterways, and on smaller boats which linked the economies of the smaller islands. In South Carolina, slaves in maritime work formed the third largest occupational group among local slaves. There, and elsewhere across the slave regions, seafaring slaves inevitably enjoyed a remarkable degree of mobility and freedom.[4] It was, of course, an uneven picture. On smaller islands, especially in the Leewards, there were more maritime slaves than on the larger and longer established sugar islands.

Sailing skills enabled slaves to escape, and a number of islands sought to restrict slave access to boats and ships by punishing boat owners whose unguarded vessels might put temptation in a slave's way. The critical problem, however, was the shortage of manpower. Sailors were in permanent, in some cases chronic, short supply. The Atlantic slave ships, as already mentioned, were especially vulnerable to manning problems, with the result that slaves could find work on these vessels themselves. One survey of 350 slave ships trading to Brazil in the late eighteenth and early nineteenth centuries showed that 42 per cent of them employed slaves as sailors, with an average of 14 slaves per vessel.[5] Put at its simplest, black sailors – free and enslaved – could be found throughout the Atlantic trading system.

Quite apart from their economic importance, black crewmen formed an important link between the slave communities of the Americas and heart of metropolitan Europe. London was 'the hub of the black Atlantic'.[6] It was also a clearing house for all the news, gossip and rumours that floated between all the ports of call along the triangular trade. Blacks in London learned of incidents, in the colonies and even on the high seas, even before they broke cover in the British press and public discussion. It was a position which Equiano was to experience in later years.

For the moment, in the summer of 1766, Equiano embarked on his first voyage as a free man, sailing on the *Nancy* from Montserrat, his home-base for the last three years, to St Eustatius, thence to Savannah in Georgia. Once in that thriving port, Equiano was employed on smaller boats, seeking out and securing cargoes for transhipment to the *Nancy*. But the trip was again more memorable for the dangers Equiano faced as a free black. Arguing with an aggressive slave (who belonged to a local merchant), he quickly found himself dragged into a fight. Equiano lost his temper, 'and beat him soundly'. A day later, the slave's master boarded the *Nancy* demanding that Equiano be flogged on shore, and notwithstanding his freedom, Equiano was alarmed at this turn of events and refused to step ashore, realizing that he could be exposed to arbitrary ill-treatment. He knew of others, free like himself, who had suffered imprisonment and maltreatment, and whose appeals that they were free made no impression on their aggressors.[7]

Equiano's initial fear gave way to rage at the way he had been treated, vowing to 'resist the first man that should attempt to lay violent hands on me, or basely use me without a trial'. His shipmates, however, urged caution, telling him to hide. Equiano bridled at the idea that he should hide from such an injustice, but caution prevailed and he sought the safety of a friend's house in Savannah for five days. It was a wise move, for the merchant concerned, a Mr Read, did indeed return, with local constables, to search for him. In Equiano's absence, however, work on board the ship had faltered. Both captain and mate were unwell and Equiano's help was badly missed in loading the vessel. His master therefore struck a deal with Mr Read, who promised to allow Equiano to return to work on the *Nancy* without fear of arrest or assault. To make doubly sure, the warrants for Equiano's arrest were purchased from the constables (using Equiano's money). Once again, the African's cash came in useful.

The whole miserable episode, on Equiano's first trip as a free man, was just one illustration of the dangers facing free blacks anywhere in the Atlantic world. How could a scrap of paper – an emancipation document – impress the kind of men ex-slaves might encounter, many of whom were drawn from the rougher edges of contemporary dockside life? Blacks were natural targets for abuse and even violence (albeit drunken violence – but where else was likely to be more drunken than the dockside?) In a world where arbitrary violence, personal assault and abuse were the commonplace experiences of slaves everywhere, who could distinguish between a slave and a free man or woman? Blackness denoted slavery, and the exceptions, such as Equiano, were inevitably forced to prove (and even to maintain) their freedom.

Despite such setbacks Equiano continued to pursue his commercial interests. Loading cattle from Savannah for the West Indies, he saw a chance of further profit by shipping his own beasts in this profitable trade. He squabbled over this with the captain, who claimed there was no room for extra animals. Against his better judgement, and prompted by the captain, Equiano invested instead in turkeys, doubting all the time that they would survive the voyage. In the event the journey back to Montserrat was storm-tossed and the small crew (of nine men) took turns on the pumps. The captain and the mate, already sick, got worse as the voyage progressed. The captain eventually died and control of the ship fell to Equiano, who sailed more by experience than by formal navigation.

Equiano took Captain Farmer's death badly, mourning for him and appreciating how deeply he admired him. He also realized how lucky he had been. Had Farmer died a little earlier, Equiano might never have been freed, for it had been Farmer's words and support which had in fact persuaded Robert King to emancipate Equiano in 1766.[8]

Farmer was not the only casualty on that miserable voyage. Gradually, all the cattle, loaded in Savannah, succumbed. But not so the turkeys which Equiano had bought so reluctantly. They survived and when the ship (now almost entirely under Equiano's direction) arrived in Montserrat, Equiano made a profit on them of 300 per cent. Counting his commercial blessings, Equiano again put the episode down to Providence. The fact that the vessel had weathered the storms and had been brought safely to port, despite the captain's death and the mate's illness, enhanced Equiano's reputation still further. A Montserrat merchant promptly offered him command of a sloop for trading between the islands, but Equiano refused.[9] This offer was not as unusual as it might seem. It had become more common, in parts of the enslaved Americas, for blacks to be placed in charge of vessels, as the expansion of the American-based and the Atlantic fleets pushed ever more blacks into maritime careers.[10]

The death of Captain Farmer finally removed one of the moral obligations which, Equiano felt, kept him shackled to the West Indies. He continued to feel indebted to Robert King, his Quaker employer who had formally granted his freedom. In retrospect, it seems odd that Equiano should feel any sense of duty to men involved in his slavery, or should continue to feel a debt of honour to a man who had once owned him, preferring to recall the act of emancipation rather than the years of enslavement. Once again we need to recall that Equiano was hoping to persuade his readership that they would recognize, in the author, a man of sensibility: a man for whom honour and decency brought their own rewards, and for whom moral debts, like commercial transactions, must be dutifully fulfilled.

Equiano's debt of gratitude to Robert King had, he felt, been 'pretty well discharged in bringing back his vessel safe, and delivering the cargo to King's satisfaction'. Equiano had long disliked the West Indies and began to think seriously of quitting the region, 'and of returning to England, where my heart had always been'. But he felt unable to resist King's request that he stay and make one more voyage to Georgia. With a new captain (another old acquaintance of Equiano) called William Phillips, Equiano agreed to another trip, leaving with 'several slaves on board', heading for St Eustatius and then, at the end of January 1767, for Georgia. To Equiano's surprise, Captain Phillips steered the ships more westerly than previously, a move which gave Equiano bad dreams about shipwrecks. A few days later the dreams came true.

By Equiano's account, he tried to alert the captain to the impending tragedy. For unexplained reasons, Phillips initially refused to come on deck but when he finally took charge it was too late and the current, rather than waves, drove the ship on to rocks. With the vessel cast securely on to the rocks, Equiano blamed himself for some injudicious, blasphemous curses a few days earlier. Fearing for his life, Equiano vowed that, should he be saved, he would never again curse. Taking comfort from the mercies the Lord had shown him in the past, Equiano recalled that God was forgiving, and might overlook his sinful errors. To add to everyone's worries, they had twenty slaves on board. The captain feared that, should the slaves be released, they would crowd into the small boat (capable of carrying ten at most) and everyone, enslaved and free, would drown. He therefore ordered the crew to nail down the hatches, consigning the slaves to a ghastly death on the wrecked vessel. Understandably, Equiano was alarmed by this turn of events, the more so because he was convinced that the whole episode had been brought about by his own earlier blasphemies. Berating the captain for his poor seamanship, Equiano hinted that he would tell the other crew members of his responsibility for their plight, suggesting that, in that eventuality, Phillips might be thrown into the sea for his sins. The upshot was that the hatches were *not* secured, and the slaves not doomed to inevitable death. In the meantime, however, everyone on board was in danger of drowning.

As they waited for daylight, Equiano and others began to prepare the small rowing boat (which needed some imaginative repairs). Others, faced by such terrifying circumstances, took to the bottle. Daylight brought good news. The ocean's swell had died down and they could see, about 5 to 6 miles away, a small deserted island. But even before they could put their small boat into the water they had to drag it over the reef which had trapped the bigger vessel. In the process, the men involved ripped and tore their legs on the reef. Of the small band of four who worked with Equiano on this taxing and perilous mission – rowing from the wrecked ship, over the reef, and then across 5 to 6 miles of open ocean – were 'three black men, and a Dutch Creole sailor'.[11] Here, surely, was another curious irony; a gang of (largely) black men struggling to rescue, not just themselves, but the whole of the crew and their entombed cargo of slaves. It was yet another illustration of the indispensability of black crewmen in the varied maritime business of Atlantic slavery.

Equiano was horrified by the reaction of the white crew. Not a single white member of the crew made any practical effort to help in their own rescue, preferring instead to get drunk in their moment of terror, and to lie 'about the deck like swine'. They were so drunk, that the bolder men manning the rescue boat had to drag them into the rowing boat and forcibly transfer them to the safety of the distant island. After five separate trips, thirty-two people were brought safely to the island. Not a single person was lost in this tricky operation. It proved a tiring, painful rescue, stripping the skin off Equiano's hands. But it also provided him with a morality tale to lay before his readership. Here, in time of need, salvation was secured not by whites but by blacks. It was a world turned upside-down; of inferiors caring for and securing the safety of their superiors, of slaves and ex-slaves rescuing both master and man. Who could say that virtue and Christianity were to be found only on one side of slavery's black and white divide? Where did virtue reside: among the drunken and helpless white sailors, or among the level-headed and practical black rescuers? In a world which had been persuaded that African barbarism authorized the European enslavement of Africans, examples of selfless, Christian or civic virtue flew in the teeth of the slaving ideology. Who were the godly – and who were the godless?

Equiano realized that they had been lucky. The weather was on their side and the makeshift repairs to the rowing boat held out until the rescue was completed. He clearly felt responsible (through his blasphemies) for the initial debacle but he was rewarded by the unanimous thanks and appreciation of everyone on board. He found himself treated as 'a kind of chieftain amongst them'.[12] His own reaction was to plant some limes, lemons and oranges, 'as a token to any one that might be cast away hereafter'. It was both his own thanksgiving for rescue and further proof, to his readers, of his deep-seated humanity. At a time of personal desperation, he thought of others who might find themselves in a similar position. And it did his reputation no harm to persuade his readers of his principled humanity.

This motley band, black and white, slave and free, found themselves Crusoe-like, on one of the hundreds of uninhabited keys which form the Bahama chain. It is a curiosity that this shipwrecked bunch found themselves, on this, one of the 700 islands which constitute the Bahamian archipelago, in the very year a new law tightened the legal control over local slaves.[13] All slave colonies devised their own particular legal definitions of, and control over, their own slaves. But the Bahamian law of 1767 was fierce, doling out immediate and arbitrary 'justice' to erring slaves for a wide range of offences. Legislators were especially concerned about slaves escaping, for the string of uninhabited or sparsely populated islands in the Bahamas was impossible to police. Legislators were also anxious to prevent local slaves trading and planting in their own name, and to prevent outsiders trading with them. Here was clear evidence that Bahamian slaves (like slaves across the Americas) took every opportunity to make the most of their conditions; to use local land, to capitalize on their own skills and industry, and to provide goods and services required by others. And it was, of course, in this world of independent slave industry and initiative that Equiano thrived and traded wherever he travelled. But the Bahamian island on which he now found himself cast adrift demanded more than mere industry.

They were marooned on a tiny island of about one mile circumference. The only sign of life was a group of flamingos on a neighbouring key, and the abundant fish which provided an easily caught source of food. They were also lucky to find some rainwater trapped in a cluster of rocks. Making shelter from their sails, they set about repairing their boat, and in 11 days it was ready. A small party would leave and seek help for the rest of the group. Equiano refused to be left behind by Captain Phillips (whom he clearly regarded as incompetent). Eventually the two men, along with five others, embarked equipped with firearms and three gallons of rum, hoping to head for New Providence, the capital of the Bahamas. After two days of hard, hot rowing they had run out of water, but they reached Abaco, one of the larger northern islands. Though they found temporary night-time shelter, they found no water, and pressed on for a third day, in a weakened condition, running short of food. They rowed along the Abaco coast, resting again – still without water – on the island. They travelled on (presumably southward along Abaco's eastern shore) in the direction of New Providence, hoping to catch sight of another vessel or of more hospitable land. It was a classic tale of shipwreck and rescue, written in a picaresque style which would have been familiar to his readers.

Just when hope seemed to be fading they sighted the sail of a small hoy. This vessel turned out to be already crowded with people, most of whom had also been shipwrecked – from a whaling schooner – two days earlier. The rescue ship was 'a wrecker', whose task was to scour the sea and islands looking for wrecks and survivors. This was clearly a particularly fruitful trip. Because Equiano's other shipmates had been left without adequate water supplies, the wrecker's crew was persuaded to sail directly to them. Two days later they found them, 'reduced to great extremities for want of water in our absence'. Crew from the salvage vessel stayed behind to repair the wrecked ship (and presumably to claim it as salvage) while its original crew (and slaves) settled aboard the rescue vessel for the voyage back to New Providence.

Meeting the salvage hoy had proved an amazing stroke of luck. New Providence was a long way away, and Equiano and his companions clearly stood no chance of reaching it, without drinking water, in their small rowing boat. Now, watered and fed in New Providence, they pressed on in the hoy, only to run into yet another severe storm. Captain Phillips and his mate again proved themselves to be useless (though Equiano had a habit of dismissing those in command, partly perhaps to elevate his own claims to maritime competence). Men around him, terrified of what might happen, prayed for divine help. A lull in the storm was just long enough to allow crew members to pull the hoy away from the threatening shoals and out to safer water. Equiano of course took it as a sign that God had indeed intervened to save them. When the storm had blown over, the crew repaired the hoy and headed back to New Providence.

For the past three weeks Equiano and his mates had feared they might not survive. Now, back on terra firma, each man went his own way, except for the slaves who had been part of the cargo. In Equiano's revealing phrase 'every one of my old fellow-sufferers *that were free*, parted from us, and shaped their course where their inclination led them'.[14] But not the slaves – the people who so narrowly avoided being battened below decks in the initial wreck. Having survived all the dangers and risks Equiano described, this group of wretched slaves merely swapped one agony for another. The captain set about trying to sell as many slaves as he could in New Providence. After 17 to 18 days, he hired a sloop and headed for his original destination, Georgia, carrying with him 'some of the slaves that he could not sell here.'[15]

No sooner had the vessel quit New Providence than the weather once again turned foul, forcing Equiano's vessel among dangerous rocks again. The crew worked hard to get her off the rocks, and limped her back to harbour for repairs. This string of bad maritime luck needed some explanation. Some of the crew thought that an evil spell had been cast over them in Montserrat. Others thought that 'we had witches and wizzards among the poor helpless slaves'.[16] The slaves were, of course, an easy target, notwithstanding the fact that they too would perish if the ship foundered. Such accusations about the imprisoned Africans were symptomatic of a widespread fear towards slaves in general. Africans were feared and distrusted by slave traders throughout the Atlantic system. Given half a chance, slaves – naturally enough – sought to free themselves. They needed to be shackled, kept below decks, herded in chains when on deck, kept under the eye of armed sailors, and generally suspected at every moment of a seaborne crossing. When the opportunity arose, they slipped their manacles, freed each other, attacked the crew, tried to kill them and take over the ship. Whites *assumed* that slaves wanted to harm them and that, if they could not bring about physical retribution, they cursed the whites and cast spells over them. Sixteen years earlier, John Newton, perhaps the most famous of all eighteenth-century English slave trade captains, discovered that some of his African slaves had tried to poison the ship's water supply by dropping fetishes into the water; 'which they had the credulity to suppose must inevitably kill all who drank of it. But if it please God they make no worse attempts than to charm us to death, they will not harm us.'[17]

Some of Equiano's fellow crewmen were not at all confident that African charms were quite so powerless. Equiano – a devout Christian, with his African faith far behind him – urged his shipmates to put their faith in God: 'swear not, but trust to God, and he will deliver us'. Seven days later they arrived safely in Georgia.[18]

Relief at landing safely in Savannah was quickly dispelled, yet again, by the practical and often brutal dangers facing free blacks everywhere. As soon as they docked in Savannah, Equiano headed for the home of a local friend, 'Mosa, a black man', where he expected to find lodging. In itself this may seem commonplace and unremarkable. Yet it forms another small but telling illustration of the personal links and networks which sprang up around the Atlantic rim among Africans and local-born blacks. Here was one man, recently freed from his bondage on Montserrat, visiting a black friend who lived 1500 miles away in Georgia. Of course, Equiano was a sailor who seems to have had friends in ports on both sides of the Atlantic. Yet we need to ask ourselves, how many times was this repeated; how many of those armies of black sailors and peripatetic blacks similarly found hospitality and friendship among fellow blacks wherever they put ashore? There were clearly important networks, friendships and links which connected all points along the trading routes of the Black Atlantic.

Equiano spent a pleasant evening with his friend: 'We were very happy at meeting each other; and, after supper, we had a light till between nine and ten o'clock at night.' But this simple, unexceptional event attracted attention when a passing patrol (perhaps one of the colony's slave patrols) noticed their light, and knocked on the door. Invited in to join the two blacks, the patrol 'came in and sat down, and drank some punch with us'. They also accepted some limes which Equiano had brought with him. But the mood then turned threatening, and the patrol asked Equiano to accompany them to the 'watch house', for 'all negroes, who had a light in their houses after nine o'clock were to be taken into custody, and either pay some dollars, or be flogged.' Though Equiano was a free man – and the patrol knew it – his host was a slave. The slave had the protection of his owner; Equiano was alone, and with no one to speak for him. The patrol therefore 'did not take the same liberty with him they did with me'. Complaining loudly against this treatment (the two men had caused no trouble) Equiano accompanied them, under protest, to the watch house. Locked up for the night, for no reason save being in a slave's illuminated house after the curfew, Equiano feared that he might share the flogging he saw administered to a black couple also in the watch house. Equiano argued that, since he was a free man, they had no right to treat him thus. Again he was able to use his contacts, calling for a local doctor he knew, Dr Brady ('known to be a honest and worthy man'), who secured his release.[19]

Equiano's troubles were not over. On this same trip he was waylaid by two white men 'who meant to play their usual tricks with me by way of kidnapping'. They claimed that Equiano was a runaway slave, but he warned them to leave him alone, surprising the men by the quality of his spoken English. Equiano threatened them with his stick and the men eventually left him in peace.[20] Yet how often did such incidents take place? How often were free blacks accosted like this? Equiano had already suffered the misery of re-enslavement in London; he had already encountered regular threats to his freedom and his well-being at the hands of whites who felt free to accost and assault him (and other blacks) whenever the mood took them. It seemed a permanent and inescapable problem for blacks everywhere. In a world where blacks were trussed up and handled like mere property, and where black freedom was the exception not the rule, free blacks lived under a permanent threatening cloud.

This stay in Savannah was mere time-killing for Equiano. He was anxious to return to Montserrat and finally take leave of his old master, Mr King, before heading back to England, 'and then to take a final farewell of the American quarter of the globe'. He eventually found a working passage on the sloop *Speedwell*, loaded with rice bound for Martinique, but not before he conducted the burial service, attended by both black and white, for the child of a local black woman. Yet why did the bereaved woman turn to Equiano, a visiting African sailor, to conduct the service? He openly confessed that he had no special training or qualifications for the job, but she still urged him to help.[21] We can only assume that Equiano was already known among his fellow blacks, even in a distant city where he was a mere transient, as a devout Christian. His reputation seems to have gone before him, and was to precede him for the rest of his life in various corners of the globe.

Leaving Georgia in the spring of 1767, Equiano was glad to see the back of a place that had brought little but unhappiness and grief. It was also a great relief to be on a vessel commanded by a competent captain. More striking still, on arrival at the French island of Martinique, local treatment of slaves seemed much better than on the British islands. Along with Guadaloupe, Martinique was one of the most productive and stable of colonies in the Lesser Antilles, its 83,000 slaves living alongside 10,600 whites and 5000 free coloureds.[22] Equiano landed in Martinique when it was at the height of its sugar-based prosperity,[23] and in St Pierre the island boasted a capital city which seemed to Equiano more European than Caribbean (but which was to be destroyed by the volcano in 1902). But Equiano was anxious to press on, to change ships and head for Montserrat 200 miles to the north. From there he hoped to be able to secure a position on the July sugar fleet heading for England. Any later and he would miss the ships (which tried to clear the Caribbean before the onset of the hurricane season) and would have to endure another prolonged stay on Montserrat.

Unfortunately, Equiano had made a rod for his own back. He had lent some money to his captain, who hesitated with the repayment. It was not unusual for free blacks (and slaves even) to lend money, or goods and services, to local whites, though it seems, looking back, an extraordinary state of affairs. Here were people long assumed to have nothing, able to provide money and valuables to owners or employers. In Jamaica, at much the same time, the slave lover of an Englishman, Thomas Thistlewood, showered him with valuable objects and gifts.[24] She, like Equiano, was industrious and sharp-eyed, keen to make the most of any commercial opening which came her way. But Equiano found, in this case, that his savings were threatened by his captain's reluctance to pay up. It was, of course, yet another variant on the persistent problem facing free blacks in a world of slavery. They were always, and unpredictably, exposed to the whims of local whites, who might, or might not, threaten or harm them – or might simply cheat them.

Equiano, however, was not a man to allow his financial interests to be harmed, even though he knew that the law would not come to his aid. He was forced to stay with his indebted captain as the vessel pressed on, sailing down to the Grenadines. After much pestering, he finally received repayment and promptly took ship for St Eustatius, and on to St Kitts, where he arrived on 19 July 1767. His hopes of a transfer to a Montserrat-bound vessel were again dashed, this time by the captain's refusal to accept him on board until Equiano was able to prove that he was a free man. It was an understandable position. Runaway slaves regularly sought to pass themselves off as free people, and the ships offered the obvious escape routes from the slave islands. Captains had to beware not to break local laws against providing a refuge for slaves. Equiano faced a dilemma. If, as the captain demanded, he placed a notice in the local press announcing his departure from the island (thus giving any putative slave-owner the opportunity to object), he would miss the chance to sail. It was, in any case a 'degrading necessity, which every black freeman is under, of advertising himself like a slave, when he leaves an island, and which I thought a gross imposition upon any freedom'.[25]

Fortunately, just as the vessel was about to leave, Equiano found some men from Montserrat who could vouch for him, persuading the captain that he was indeed a free man. A day later, he finally arrived in Montserrat, after an absence of six months, and after a string of narrow escapes (of all of which confirmed his sense of divine protection). Mr King was glad to meet him and to get some news of how his vessel had been lost in the Bahamas. King urged Equiano to stay in Montserrat, reassuring him that not only was he well respected on the island but that 'I might do very well, and in a short time have land and slaves of my own'. Equiano reported this remark with no comment; no suggestion that it might seem odd for an ex-slave to own slaves.

He was keen, however, to secure a letter of recommendation from King. It was a simple statement, but, like Equiano's manumission document, was repeated word for word in the book written more than two decades later:

> The bearer hereof, Gustavus Vasa, was my slave for upwards of three years, during which he has always behaved himself well, and discharged his duty with honesty and assiduity.[26]

It was, like so many aspects of Equiano's life, an unusual document; a personal testimonial from a former owner, confirming the man's stirling qualities. And, as in the earlier manumission document, Equiano was named Gustavus Vassa – not Equiano. Though he used his African name when presenting himself to the outside world in his book, he was clearly known, to large numbers of people, not by his African name but by one of the names he had been given when a slave.

Towards the end of that month, Equiano once again enjoyed 'free dances' with 'some of my friends and countrymen', just as he had when he had bought his freedom the year before. Finally, on 28 July 1767 he boarded the *Andromache*, captained by John Hamer, who paid him seven guineas for the voyage to London; 'I never had earned seven guineas so quick in all my life.' He was delighted to be leaving the West Indies for England. He was happy to see the back of all vestiges of slavery – 'adieu to oppressions'. Seven weeks later, after a swift crossing, his ship dropped anchor in the Thames, more than four years after he had last seen it. Then he had been enslaved, and crudely kidnapped from one vessel to another. Now, in September 1767, he stepped ashore a free man, and with 37 guineas in his pocket. It remains one of Equiano's remarkable features that throughout his life he remembers exactly how much money he possessed; how much he was paid, how much spent on this and that, and how much remained in his pocket or in his sea chest. He was clearly a man who kept personal accounts; a man for whom regular accounting had become a way of life. Indeed, he measured out his life – its ups and downs, its successes and failures – by tallying his financial and material possessions.

What sort of future did Equiano face that September? He was a free man, but how could that be maintained in an Atlantic economy which thrived on black slavery? He had no immediate money problems, but needed to find work. He was a man of great industry, willing to try his hand at anything to make a living. But what sort of work could England offer a recently freed African in his early 20s? He had, for some time past, yearned to return to England. In the event, life in London, the hub of the Atlantic slave empire, was to prove more difficult, more taxing, than he could have imagined. Set against his experiences on the other side of the Atlantic, however, it must have seemed, at first, a haven from the torments of slavery.

Notes

1 Ira Berlin, 'From Creole to African: Atlantic Creoles and the Origins of African-American Society in Mainland North America', *William and Mary Quarterly*, 3rd series, vol. 53, April 1996.
2 W. Jeffrey Bolster, *Black Jacks: African American Seamen in the Age of Sail* (Cambridge, MA, 1997).
3 *Ibid.*, pp. 13–14.
4 *Ibid.*, pp. 21–2.
5 Herbert S. Klein, *The Middle Passage* (Princeton, 1978), p. 59.
6 Bolster, *op. cit.*, p. 19.
7 *Interesting Narrative*, pp. 138–9.
8 *Ibid.*, p. 135.
9 *Ibid.*, pp. 143–4.
10 Bolster, *op. cit.*, pp. 24–5.
11 *Interesting Narrative*, pp. 150–1.
12 *Ibid.*, p. 151.
13 For a discussion, see Michael Craton and Gail Saunder, *Islanders in the Stream: A History of the Bahamian People* (Athens, GA, 1992), pp. 152–6.
14 *Interesting Narrative*, p. 157. Italics are mine.
15 *Ibid.*, p. 157.
16 *Ibid.*, p. 158.
17 *The Journal of a Slave Trader (John Newton) 1750–1754*, edited by Bernard Martin and Martin Spurrel (London, 1962); entry for 16 June 1751, p. 56.
18 *Interesting Narrative*, p. 158.
19 *Ibid.*, pp. 158–9.
20 *Ibid.*, p. 159.
21 *Ibid.*, pp. 159–60.
22 Robin Blackburn, *The Overthrow of Colonial Slavery, 1776–1848* (London, 1988), p. 163.
23 David Watts, *The West Indies* (Cambridge, 1987), p. 300.
24 D. Hall (ed.), *In Miserable Slavery* (London, 1989).
25 *Interesting Narrative*, p. 162.
26 *Ibid.*, p. 163.

PART THREE

AN
ENGLISH
LIFE

8

SEEKING
SALVATION

Equiano's immediate ambition had been realized. He was free and he was back in London. His first task was to seek out old friends, firstly the Guerin sisters who had been so kind and helpful to him in his earlier life in London. Tracking them down in Greenwich, he regaled them with his adventures since their last meeting; all of which had been precipitated by the treacherous actions of their cousin, Captain Pascal, in selling Equiano in 1762.

When, a few days later, Equiano confronted Pascal himself, the latter 'appeared a good deal surprised', asking how Equiano had managed to get back to England. 'I answered, "In a ship." To which he replied dryly, "I suppose you did not walk back to London on the water."' Was he being sharp, acerbic; or was he using that self-deprecating irony which he displayed elsewhere? Pascal seemed unrepentant about his actions in betraying and selling Equiano, though the latter made his own views on the matter perfectly clear: 'I told him that he had used me very ill, after I had been such a faithful servant to him for so many years.' Pascal simply turned and walked away. What could he say in the teeth of such obvious and unanswerable accusations of base behaviour?[1]

Not one to let a genuine grievance rest, Equiano raised the matter when he next met Pascal a few days later, demanding a share of the prize money to which he felt entitled for his work on Pascal's ship in the early 1760s. Pascal argued that any prize money went, not to the slave but to the slave-owner (a variant on the well-rehearsed claim that slaves could own nothing except via the slave-owner). Although he threatened to use lawyers to make his case, Equiano eventually let the matter drop for fear of offending the Guerin sisters. He was obviously a man sensitive to social niceties and feelings, even when it might interrupt the pursuit of one of his major interests: money.

Equiano had enough cash in his pocket to live reasonably well for a short while, but, always an industrious man (and just as keen to impress his readers with a sense of his worthy application to hard work), he was anxious for employment. The Guerin sisters had no opening for him as a servant. Instead, Equiano expressed an interest in learning to be a hairdresser (he had often shaved sailors and cut their hair when he was first at sea), and the Guerins helped to find him a place with a hairdresser in Coventry Court, Haymarket. Equiano worked there for six months, until February 1768. At the same time, a neighbour taught him to play the French horn. Again, Equiano seemed anxious to promote an image of himself among his readers as a man of refinement; a person of sensibility who defied the common image of the African as a mere labourer. But there was more to black music-making than that.

Black musicians were not uncommon in eighteenth-century London. Only three years earlier, in 1764, blacks in London had organized a party at a tavern in Fleet Street:

> no less than 57 of them, men and women, supped, drank, and entertained themselves with dancing and music, consisting of violins, French horns and other instruments. . . No whites were allowed to be present for all the performers were Black.[2]

There was a well-established tradition of black musicians in eighteenth-century London, and the French horn was especially popular among them. In part, the rise of black music-making was one aspect of the white belief that Africans and their descendants were especially musical. White accounts of black life, from the earliest encounters frequently referred to black musicality. Not surprisingly, the English encouraged black musicians, in stately and private homes, in military organizations. This was viewed as an arena of refinement which would blend African 'musicality' with European sensibility.

Black musicians had performed at various state and civic occasions in Britain from the late fifteenth century onwards, and certain aristocrats liked to embellish their social gatherings with black musicians. Of course, as London's black community grew in the eighteenth century, black musicians increased in number: on the streets, in taverns and at a range of social gatherings. A number of British regiments employed black musicians at this time[3] and even advertisements for slaves reflected this growing interest. A Bristol newspaper of 1757 carried a notice for a local runaway:

> A NEGRO LAD about 18 years of Age, near five Feet two inches high answers to the name Starling, and blows the French Horn very well.[4]

Black musicians were, then, familiar in eighteenth-century England. One of the most prominent young violinist in the 1790s was George Augustus Polgreen Bridgetower, whose West Indian father had been servant to a Hungarian aristocrat. At much the same time, Joseph Bologne, the Chevalier de Saint-Georges, born in Guadeloupe, was making his career as a violinist (and as a fencer). An African, Joseph Antonia Emidy, played and taught music in Falmouth, but was blocked in his career by London musicians who felt that 'his colour would be so much against him'.[5] Julius Soubise, born in Jamaica and protégé of the Duchess of Queensberry, was a keen amateur violinist (though dispatched to India in 1778 to avoid a scandal). There were black musicians on British boats, in British regiments (especially during the fad for 'Janissary' music – black musicians dressed in Turkish attire). But few of them rose to the fame of Ignatius Sancho, born on a slave ship, later a servant to the Montagu family, a Westminster shopkeeper, and letter-writer to the good and the great. His contemporary and historical fame rests on the posthumous publication of those letters in 1782. Sancho also wrote a *Theory of Music*, as well as some 62 musical pieces, in a twelve-year period (1767–79).[6]

It was precisely in these same years that Equiano learned to play the French horn. But in his case, musical skills involved more than simply joining a thriving musical tradition. It was part of Equiano's broadening cultural grounding. He was already highly literate and numerate. At every turn he sought to improve himself and to display those personal qualities of refinement and civility which marked off the man of sensibility from the common man, and certainly from the image of an African which dominated English thought. To a society which had defined the African as a beast of burden, at best forming a low link in the Chain of Being, at worst being less than human, Africans who had succeeded in shaking off slavery needed to assert their humanity. In time, with the post-1789 emergence of a universal ideology of human equality (of liberty, equality and fraternity) and, despite its obvious limitations, it was enough to argue 'Am I not a man and a Brother [Sister])'. But until the seismic impact of that revolutionary assertion, Equiano (and others) needed to persuade white outsiders that black equality could be calibrated by how closely they managed to approach those attainments most admired by fashionable society. In a word, Equiano sought, throughout his life – and specifically in his book – to portray himself as a man of sensibility.[7]

Equiano's music-making helped to fill any vacant hours that might have survived his great efforts never to be idle. He turned to another neighbour, the Rev. Gregory, for further instruction in arithmetic, before finding work with Dr Charles Irving in Pall Mall in his experiments with the conversion of sea water to fresh water. Throughout, Equiano continued to work at his hairdressing. Glad that he continued to improve himself and thanking God for his various opportunities, he nonetheless felt financially poorer than at any point in his working life. His savings (the 37 guineas he had on landing in England) had gone, his income of 12 guineas a year was substantially less than anything he had earned before, and was scarcely enough to pay for his various lessons and to keep himself. In any case, he had never really settled to life on shore, and knew that he could make more at sea:

> I thought it best, therefore, to try the sea again in quest of more money, as I had been bred to it, and had hitherto found the profession of it successful.

Leaving his employer on good terms, Equiano headed for the waterside in search of a vessel.

In July 1768 he embarked on a five-month visit to the Mediterranean on board the *Delaware* (whose cook was also black) under Captain John Jolly, 'a neat, smart, good-humoured man', who was delighted with Equiano's hairdressing skills. Equiano seemed happier with life in the Mediterranean than in any part of the world he had visited before. He loved the cities he visited – in Italy, but above all

3ᵈ Reg.ᵗ of Foot Guards.
The Band.

PLATE 7. Jean Baptiste (b. 1791), originally from Guadeloupe, was discharged from service in 1841, by which time he was deaf as a result of his military service. He retired to live in London, aged 50.

Source: Hull's Series of Costumes of the Army (1827–30), Plate 23.
Trustees of the National Museums of Scotland.

in Turkey, delighted in the foods and wines, and generally made the most of being able to satisfy 'both my taste and curiosity'. As the *Delaware* gradually became 'richly loaded with silk and other articles', Equiano, with the mate's help, also improved his navigational skills. Best of all, he was happy to find that people in the ports he visited seemed 'fond of black people' and several invited him to stay with them.[8] On his next two voyages, in 1769 to Portugal and then back to the Mediterranean, Equiano was again struck by the richness of local cultures. He recorded not only the human curiosities (galley slavery in Genoa, the large caravans from India, whose people 'are quite brown', arriving in Smyrna) but also the eye-catching beauties of different architectural styles in Oporto, Genoa, Naples and, again, Smyrna. He also regularly noted the commercial transactions (and the profits) which the ship was making as it filled its holds with local and transhipped goods. Of course, he also traded on his own behalf.[9] These travels in southern Europe and the Mediterranean in 1768–9 formed, in effect, Equiano's Grand Tour.

These were the years when Englishmen of substance turned to southern Europe, especially to Italy, for a broadening of their education and for an introduction to the more sublime of European styles, from buildings and architecture to gardens. Equiano touched on all the themes which educated readers would recognize from other contemporary accounts of southern Europe: the beauty of the country, the elegance of the buildings, the lushness of food and drink, the appearance and habits of local peoples. His was no more than a brief snapshot of the world he passed through, but it was enough to establish a claim, in the reader's mind, that he too was a man of sensibility; a man alert to the sublime in the model of the Grand Tourist.[10]

Equiano, however, gave the genre a twist, for he portrayed the non-Christian Turks as people who were more civilized and welcoming towards an African than were many Europeans. There were clearly things to be learnt from other parts of Europe, quite apart from the glories of the ancient world and the physical splendours of their cities.

Yet where had Equiano acquired this knowledge of the literary style of the Grand Tour?[11] Had he read contemporary accounts of travellers in Europe? Had he been influenced by what they wrote and how they responded to their European encounters? Though it forms only a small part of his autobiography, there is further evidence here that Equiano was alert to, or had had his attention brought to, a fashionable literary genre. We know that he was a keen reader, that he valued and owned books, especially the Bible and the major texts of English literature. But he seems also to have been influenced by a much broader range of contemporary literary fashions and styles. Whatever his point of entrée to this genre, it was reflected in the autobiographical descriptions of his own travels and how he described himself. Here again was a striking contrast for his readers to mull over: a humble African and ex-slave able to appreciate the best of European culture. It was yet another suggestion that the African had been debased not, as Europeans liked to imagine, by Africa itself, but by their violent entanglement with Europe and Europeans. Given the chance, they were as capable of refinement and sensibility as the European. Equiano stood out because he *had* been given a chance (or, more exactly, had created the chance for himself).

On his return from these journeys, Equiano spent much of 1770 in England, though he mentions nothing of his life in that period. In April of the following year he signed on as steward to Captain William Robertson on the *Grenada Planter*, 'once more to try my fortune in the West-Indies'. It was an opportunity, again, for Equiano to engage in the personal trade that had yielded his freedom. But, as before, West Indian whites were often cavalier about paying their debts to black traders. He referred to those who sought to cheat him as 'my former kind of West-India customers'. When Equiano demanded payment for his goods, shortly before his vessel sailed from Grenada, 'we found we were like to get more blows than payment'. An appeal to a local magistrate revealed the problem Equiano had faced at other places in the slave colonies; that 'being negroes, although free, we could not get any remedy'. By a stroke of luck, the same customer also owed money to three white sailors. The indebted group joined together, roughed him up, stripped him naked and took what they could find to cover some of the debts.[12] On this occasion Equiano was lucky to have the support of fellow sailors. Yet it was just the latest of a string of such incidents which underlined the helplessness of free blacks to secure their rights when they had no legal remedy. Equiano's story is one of regular and apparently inescapable deceptions and commercial treachery by men who knew they could get away with high-handed treatment towards blacks, for they realized that the law was unlikely to defend black against white.

Back in England, in December 1771, Equiano ('being still of a roving disposition, and desirous of seeing as many parts of the world as I could') signed on, again as steward, to another West India ship, the *Jamaica*, captained by David Watt and bound for Jamaica and Nevis. Jamaica was the most important of all Britain's West Indian islands, producing a range of tropical crops and with a rapidly growing slave population, in 1768, of about 167,000 slaves. Above all else, slaves were critical for the production of sugar. By the time Equiano visited Jamaica, the island's annual sugar revenue stood at £1.6 million, making it by far the most valuable possession in the Americas.[13] It had also become infamous for its widespread harsh treatment of its slaves. Equiano had seen black slavery in operation at numerous points in the Americas, but in Jamaica he thought the slaves 'exceedingly imposed upon by the white people'. He was struck by the fact that there were 'negroes whose business it is to flog slaves' and were hired, for payment, specifically for that task.

Jamaica yielded any number of slave horror stories: of violations, punishments, killings and mutilations, all of which, in time, became grist to the abolitionists' mill. And Equiano, writing in 1789, was lending his personal experience and eye-witness accounts to that broader abolitionist attack on slavery. But we also know that there was nothing exceptional – for Jamaica – in what he described. Even in the short time Equiano was on the island, he saw more than enough 'cruel punishments inflicted on the slaves', describing in detail some atrocious incidents. His accounts, however, pale in comparison with some of the more grotesque treatments devised by sadistic slave-owners and drivers.[14] Jamaica's slave system seemed to spawn violations like no other. Here, as on no other British island, violence and cruelty seemed to be the very lubricant of slavery.

Despite the grind of their daily lives, the violent threats (and realities) which hovered over them, Jamaican slaves still found time and occasion to enjoy

PLATE 8.
'A Negroes Dance
in the Island of
Dominica';
watercolour, 1810.

Source: Wilberforce House,
Kingston-upon-Hull City
Museums and Archives.

themselves. In Kingston Equiano noticed how Africans assembled together on Sunday (their one day free from work) at Spring Path: 'Here each different nation of Africa meet and dance, after the manner of their own country.'[15]

These comments form an uncanny echo of remarks made by the Englishman, Thomas Thistlewood, when he landed in Jamaica twenty-one years before, in 1750. Thistlewood wrote in his diary, that he wandered to 'the westward of the Town, to see negro Diversions – odd Music, Motions, etc. The Negroes of each Nation by themselves.'[16]

The two men – an Englishman and an African, both new to the island, both curious about slave habits and culture – were struck by precisely the same fact: that slaves gravitated to their fellow 'countrymen' for social activities. As long as Africans poured into the island, as long as the slave trade continued to disgorge cargoes of Africans bound for the sugar fields, as long as Africans dominated the slave communities, it would remain inevitable that Africans would seek out people they could understand, whose language and habits were familiar.

It was natural enough that Africans would stick to their own familiar cultures. Again, Equiano was quick to spot the pattern: 'They still retain most of their native customs: they bury their dead, and put victuals, pipes, and tobacco, and other things in the grave with the corpse, in the same manner as in Africa.'[17]

Time and again, visitors and residents on the islands were struck by the way African slaves littered their burial sites with artefacts they might need in the next world.[18] Not surprisingly, in recent years archeologists have come to appreciate the value of such evidence in recreating the world of New World slavery.[19] The cultural attachment to particular African social customs would begin to change, of course, as ever more slaves were local-born, and especially after the abolition of the Atlantic slave trade in 1807. As slaves became more Jamaican, or American, their links to Africa changed. Equiano personified the process for, though he remained, obviously, an African, he needed to adapt, and to a degree to reinvent himself, to fit into an alien society.

Jamaica brought a reprise of Equiano's old commercial problems. Here, once again, his entrepreneurial instincts came to the fore. But, once more, he found himself cheated by a local white man, a Mr Smith from Port Morant, at the easterly tip of the island, who had bought £25 worth of goods from Equiano, but who refused to pay and pretended that the African was the menacing culprit. He threatened Equiano with jail – always a potent threat in any slave society (where black could not legally testify against white). After a great deal of unsuccessful pleading, Equiano simply cut his losses.[20] He was troubled by this same problem from one slave colony to another: from the eastern Caribbean to North America, and to England. Yet it was never enough to deter his commercial instincts. Whatever losses he incurred seemed, in the long run, more than compensated by his profits. In any case, Equiano was one of nature's traders, haggling, dealing, making money – all had become as natural to him as the rhythms of the waking day.

By August 1772 Equiano's ship was safely back in London with its Jamaican cargo. Feeling the need for a break from the sea, Equiano returned to work with Dr Irving (in his continuing experiments with water) and remained there until May 1773, when he took what was the most daring of all his maritime decisions. He joined the Royal Naval expedition under the command of Constantine John Phipps (later Lord Mulgrave) to seek a passage via the North Pole to India.[21] It was a passage which, he wrote later, 'our Creator never intended'.[22] Equiano joined the Royal Navy sloop *Race Horse*, a vessel so crowded 'that there was very little room on board for any one'. Horatio Nelson, then a 15-year-old junior officer, was also on board. On 4 June, in the company of another sloop, the *Carcass*, they headed for the Pole. Prompted by the importance and unusualness of the voyage, Equiano resolved to keep a journal, but he could find nowhere to write except in the doctor's store-room, where he slept. There he was surrounded by a variety of inflammable and dangerous substances. One evening at work on his journal, a spark from his candle set fire to some material; his own clothes caught fire and he almost choked in the smoke, before fellow crewmen smothered the flames with blankets and mattresses. Severely reprimanded by his officers for his dangerous activities (i.e. writing by candlelight surrounded by combustibles), Equiano had to set aside his journal. But there was nowhere else to work and later he slipped back to the same spot to write.

By late June they had reached Greenland (their supplies *en route* aided by one of Dr Irving's distilleries for the purification of salt water). Though the sun never set, the temperature began to plummet as they sailed on, between passing icebergs, visited by curious whales and shoals of 'sea-horses' (arctic walruses). Warned by a passing Greenland ship that other vessels were already trapped in the ice, the expedition nevertheless pressed on. By mid-July they faced an impenetrable wall of ice. However they sought to skirt or outflank it, they could find no way through. The region's natural beauties impressed, and the crew spent time hunting and killing bears and sea creatures, often at great risk to themselves and their boats. But by the middle of August, the two ships had become firmly wedged in the ice and 'we were in very great apprehension of having the ships squeezed to pieces'.

The crew tried a variety of strenuous methods to escape, including sawing the ice from around the ships and painfully dragging them towards open sea. But they made little progress. Most of the men were disheartened and began to think they were doomed. It was, for Equiano, yet another occasion to ponder on the life hereafter; he was unsure, in his current state, whether he would enter the heavenly kingdom. But he found some comfort in seeing that the blasphemers in the crew 'began to call on the good God of heaven for his help'. Their prayers seem to have been answered, for, after 11 days of icy imprisonment, the weather changed, the ice broke and the crew managed to prise the vessels free. Thirty hours later, they were safely in the open water. On 19 August the expedition was effectively over and they turned their back on that 'desolate and expanded waste of ice'.[23] Though they passed through severe storms on the voyage home (throwing surplus weight overboard and shipping a dangerous amount of water) they rendezvoused with the *Carcass* off the east coast of England on 26 September 1772. By the last day of the month they were at Deptford, four months after they had departed for the Arctic.

They had ventured further north than any other expedition. But they had also proved 'the impracticability of finding a passage that way to India'. One minor aspect of this voyage was that Equiano had been the first black, as far as we can judge, to explore the Arctic. Moreover it was an exploit possibly not repeated until the American, Matthew A. Henson, made eight Arctic voyages in the company of Robert E. Peary between 1891 and 1909.[24]

Equiano once more returned to his former job in London with Dr Irving, but, shaken by his recent experiences, and acutely conscious of how close he (and his shipmates) had come to dying, he slipped into a serious crisis of faith. Always ready to ponder on the hereafter, Equiano in the wake of the Arctic experience was persuaded that he needed 'to seek the Lord with full purpose of heart ere it be too late'. Determined to set aside his previous *persona*, when his mind had been 'blinded by ignorance and sin', Equiano felt that the Lord had directed him to London so that he could work out his own salvation. He wrestled with the difficulty about how best to save his soul, regularly asking friends and acquaintances about spiritual matters. He got very little satisfaction in what was, quite clearly, a major spiritual crisis. One attempted remedy lay in regular church attendance – sometimes three times a day – at St James's in Piccadilly, and other neighbouring churches (he was again living in Coventry Court in the Haymarket). He used every means at his disposal to become 'a first-rate Christian'. But nothing seemed to help; nothing brought him that sense of religious tranquillity for which he strived. His greatest spiritual pleasure came from reading his Bible at home.[25]

Equiano sought spiritual answers from all quarters. First he went to the Quakers, whose reputation as friends of blacks had already been established on both sides of the Atlantic. Later, his dealings with London (and Philadelphia) Quakers were to prove important in the first phase of the British campaign against the slave trade. But these first sessions with Quakers were unhelpful; 'and I remained as much in the dark as ever'. Nor did he get any help from the Roman Catholics he spoke to, nor from the Jews. He asked lots of people what was the best way of getting to heaven, but there were as many answers as questions. The end result was that Equiano was thrown back on himself. He was amazed to discover no one 'more righteous than myself'. He thought he kept more of the Ten Commandments than most other people (he claimed to abide by eight) and seemed to have been especially unhappy by the regular deceptions and cheating he encountered. Although he does not specify the occasions, it seems likely that he faced continuing commercial risks and cheating. London was proving a tougher home than he had imagined, and he took comfort 'in the musical French horn, which I then practised, and also dressing of hair'. They were small compensations to set against his theological worries and his everyday practical problems.

It was unusual for Equiano to spend much time on land. He had spent most of his working life at sea, and he appears to have been troubled by the notorious difficulties experienced by sailors, after years at sea, in settling back into the mundane routines of life at home. In any case, where was 'home' in Equiano's case? But his problems went deeper than this. Whatever uncertainties he felt about his private, domestic life in London, they formed but one unsettling feature of a much deeper spirtual malaise. For the best part of two years (1772–4) Equiano was in search of a spiritual home: a church, a faith, a way of life, where he might feel at ease and feel secure in the knowledge that salvation was his.

This period of Equiano's life came immediately after the Somerset case, which had dragged on in London from January to June 1772. Lord Justice Mansfield had finally resolved that a master had no legal right to transport a slave from England back to a slave colony against that person's wishes. But whatever the fine details of that decision, slaves – and servants – took it to mean that there had been a loosening of their ties to their owners/employers. Equiano had arrived back in England three months after Mansfield's judgment. At the very time he was trying to slip back into some form of 'normal' routine in London, trying to make a precarious living from whatever jobs came to hand, wrestling with his religious troubles, he, like all other blacks in London, had to come to terms with the social and legal uncertainties of English life. These were not simply the commonplace uncertainties of the working poor, of never really knowing where the next meal was coming from, of wondering whether the accidents and haphazards of fate would knock away the precarious material props supporting their lives. They shared all these uncertainties and more. But black life in England was bedevilled by much more fundamental worries. And at every turn we can see them reflected in Equiano's troubled odyssey between 1772 and 1774.

By the spring of 1774, Equiano had had enough of London. He hated the dishonesty of people around him. He knew too well the uncertainties of black life in London and of the arbitrary, unjust treatment which might unexpectedly come his way. He clearly had no money left (important for a man so accustomed to making cash so readily) and he continued to fret about his faith. But where could he go that was better? The more he thrashed around for answers, the more disillusioned he felt, especially towards people around him, and about those 'who in general termed themselves Christians'. They seemed less good, less honest than, for example, the Turks. From conversations with friends, and from what he had seen on his voyages, he came, for a while, to believe that 'the Turks were in a safer way of salvation than my neighbours'.[26] He was on the point of rejecting completely the Christianity he had clung to so avidly for years. He had already visited Turkey in 1768, and had been impressed by local attitudes towards blacks when he visited Smyrna. No less important, he 'found the Turks very honest in their dealings'.[27] Thus early in 1774, desperate for answers to his nagging questions, and for an end to the worries of life in London, he resolved 'to set out for Turkey, and there to end my days'.[28] As he prepared to go, another deeply upsetting enslavement took place, which confirmed Equiano's decision to quit England.

In the spring of 1774 Equiano signed on as steward with Captain John Hughes of the *Anglicania*, then fitting out in the Thames but ultimately bound for Smyrna. At the same time Equiano recommended 'a very clever black man, John Annis, as a cook'. Annis had been employed for many years by William Kirkpatrick in St Kitts, but had parted on amicable terms – though Kirkpatrick had subsequently tried to inveigle him back. Kirkpatrick had asked a number of captains bound for the West Indies to kidnap Annis and ship him back to St Kitts. On Easter Monday 1774, discovering that Annis was on board the *Anglicania* in the Thames, Kirkpatrick drew alongside with two boats and six men, seized the unfortunate man and removed him.

Equiano realized that his own captain and mate had been accomplices in the kidnapping, and all this in the immediate wake of the well-publicized Somerset case, which specifically outlawed such actions.[29] Equiano's captain and mate both claimed that they wanted Annis to stay with them, but they failed to lift a finger to prevent his removal from their ship. Nor did they pay the wages already owed to Annis. Equiano proved to be his only friend on board, promptly finding out, from contacts at Gravesend, which boat Annis had been taken to. The vessel had already sailed on the first tide. Equiano promptly obtained a writ of habeas corpus against Kirkpatrick.

Two years before, the Somerset case had hinged on a writ of habeas corpus, and whether it was applicable to slaves about to be removed against their wishes from England. Indeed, for some time past, the pioneering English campaigner against enforced transportations from England, Granville Sharp (see pp. 46–50), had appreciated the critical importance of securing writs of habeas corpus to defend threatened slaves. The law, which had helped to define and secure slavery on the high seas (in English slave ships) and had fashioned slavery in the colonies, could be used to limit or control this one (admittedly small) aspect of England's involvement with slavery; the enforced movement of black people from England itself.[30] In the grand scheme of things – weighed in the balance against the massive violations against black humanity in the world of Atlantic slavery – it seems a small victory. In time, however, it was to have major repercussions, not least in sparking the initial English opposition to slavery itself. The awareness of the personal and legal violations which commonly took place against black humanity in London formed the origins of a more broadly based revulsion against slavery in its Atlantic setting.

It is scarcely surprising that the literate and politically alert Equiano would have been aware of the legal possibilities afforded by habeas corpus. With the writ in hand, and in the company of a law officer, he set out to confront Kirkpatrick at his home in St Paul's Churchyard. Kirkpatrick had anticipated such a visit and hired a look-out (a sure sign that he was aware of the significance of his wrong-doing). Even more remarkable, Equiano tried to disguise himself by whitening his face. After much manoeuvring and many feints, Kirkpatrick was eventually given the writ and brought to court to answer the charge. But since he could, truthfully, claim that he no longer controlled Annis (who by then was on the high seas), he was released on bail. Not knowing how best to respond, Equiano went straight to Granville Sharp.

On this, the first but not the last meeting between the two men, Equiano was greeted warmly and given helpful instructions on how best to proceed. Equiano felt 'the warmest sense of gratitude towards Mr Sharp for his kindness', leaving him hopeful that he would be able to secure the release of Annis. But it was not to be. His lawyer 'proved unfaithful': 'he took my money, lost me many months employ, and did not the least good in the cause'. Worse still, Annis was on his way to St Kitts, where he was vilely maltreated and flogged on arrival. Annis wrote two depressing letters to Equiano describing his wretched condition, and Equiano learned more about the case from friends in London who had seen Annis on St Kitts. There was to be no happy outcome, despite all Equiano's best efforts. Annis remained on St Kitts 'till kind death released him out of the hands of his tyrants'.[31] The case further illustrates the Atlantic networks among slaves and ex-slaves, with letters passing between the literate, and news and gossip adding to the international flow of information between black communities on both sides of the Atlantic.

This terrible story came at a bad time for Equiano. He was already unhappy, insecure about his faith, uncertain in his daily work and oppressed by life in

England. He even thought of death, though he was uncertain whether he was yet spiritually prepared to meet his Maker (uncertain even what form that Maker might take). He later wrote that his mind 'was unaccountably disturbed', and there are plenty of good explanations for his mood. He had, of course, seen many similar crimes against Africans. But this was different; he was obviously close to John Annis, and felt deep and hurtful offence at what had happened, made worse perhaps by his own failure to retrieve the situation. Equiano clearly felt helpless, and for a young man of such firm views and principles this was a serious blow. England must have seemed little better than other places he had visited; blacks were violated, transported, ill-treated and cheated at every turn. Their numbers may have been small, but in some respects that made matters worse, for Equiano *knew* the people involved. It all seemed a sharp contrast to what he remembered having seen in Turkey. It may have been a fantasy (after all he had only visited Turkey briefly as a sailor). But he determined to return there.

But what was this intention to go to Turkey all about? Did he *really* want to settle in a country he had scarcely visited? Or was it an indication of a profound unhappiness about himself – about his life in England – about the way he and other blacks were persistently treated in England? It was a frustration perhaps made all the more acute because he had invested such efforts, so much cost, and such elevated expectations, in settling in England.

He signed on as a steward with Captain Lina on the *Wester Hall* bound for Turkey, but his previous captain, John Hughes, blocked the move. In this state of limbo, obviously depressed and frustrated about the loss of John Annis and about his own failure in that case, Equiano turned to the Bible. The more he read the more convinced he became that 'what was appointed for me I must submit to'. Everything seemed predestined. Labouring under this cloud, Equiano even began to blaspheme (a trait he had always deplored in his fellow seamen). At night he was plagued by religious dreams and visions. Gradually they began to make sense for him and he came to accept that he would not be able to gain entrance to the Kingdom of Heaven unless he changed his ways. He prayed 'in the greatest agony' and 'requested the divine Creator, that he would grant me a small space of time to repent of my follies and vile iniquities, which I felt were grievous'. He awoke exhausted, vowing never again to blaspheme, promising in prayer and to himself to seek out good spiritual company and guidance, and to remove himself from the company of sinners and lesser mortals. He decided to leave his lodgings 'because God's most holy name was blasphemed in it'.[32]

Meanwhile, keen to spend his day reading the Bible, Equiano found it impossible to stay there. Rather than spend the day 'amongst the wicked ones', he took to walking during the day. By chance – or, as Equiano would have it, guided by the Lord – he ended up at the home of an old sailor who was himself deeply devout. They talked about their mutal beliefs and Equiano took great comfort from the discussion, firing questions at the old man and finding greater help in his answers than he had from any previous discussion. They were joined by a 'Dissenting Minister', who in his turn was curious about Equiano's faith. When Equiano told him about the churches where he worshipped, the minister invited him to his own chapel. Equiano left, his spirits greatly lifted by the conversation, intent on maintaining the company of the two men. But when he attended the chapel, to participate in what he understood to be 'a love feast', Equiano was bemused to discover lots of ministers, a crowded meeting filled with hymns and prayers, and guests speaking about their religious experiences. Those who spoke, however, seemed altogether more convinced about their future salvation than was Equiano himself. The service ended (after four hours) with the distribution of buns and water. 'I was entirely overcome, and wished to live and die thus.'[33]

Uncertain whether to go back to his lodgings, to the blaspheming, gambling people he lived with, or 'to hire a bed elsewhere', Equiano finally decided to go home. But the following day he went back to an old man he had spoken to the previous day, a silk weaver and his wife in Holborn. After a long, pleasant conversation with them 'about soul matters', Equiano departed clutching a book they lent him (and which he described as 'The Conversion of an Indian'), a question-and-answer book which Equiano found to be 'of great use to me, and at that time was a means of strengthening my faith'.

Delighted with his new friends, and invited to return, Equiano took the opportunity to turn his back on his old ways and from his 'former carnal acquaintances'. It proved a happy two-month period, during which he regularly went to listen to preachers, who managed to lay open 'the thoughts of my heart and actions'.

Bit by bit, Equiano was edging towards a solution to his religious crisis by coming to terms with the Methodist theology he had been drawn to. What he heard, and what was said directly to him, often confused him, if only because it clashed with everything he had previously believed or encountered. Bemused to hear of one man 'who had departed this life in full assurance of his going to glory', Equiano was told that he too could go along the same path. But he needed to experience a new birth and have his sins pardoned through the blood of Christ. The more he asked, the more theological confusion he felt. In particular, Equiano had trouble accepting that the Lord was able to forgive his sins. He did not know 'which to believe, whether salvation by works, or faith in Christ'.

He was urged to pray that the Lord might reveal the true state of his soul. What troubled Equiano was the problem of whether God had forgiven his sins – and how he could ever know that.

Greatly moved by a sermon by the Rev. Dr Peckwell in Westminster, Equiano resolved to return to Peckwell's next service, when he intended to quiz those worshippers who intended to take Communion. When the time came, Equiano faced some awkward questions about his own faith, confessing that he kept eight of the ten commandments, 'but that I sometimes swore on board of ship, and sometimes when on shore, and I broke the Sabbath'.

Peckwell would not give him Communion, urging Equiano, instead, 'to read the scriptures, and hear the word preached; not to neglect fervent prayer to God'.[34] It may have seemed bland, uninspired and obvious advice, but it was clearly of some comfort to the struggling African. He needed someone to talk to, someone who could share his concerns and talk to him sympathetically about issues which taxed his conscience. Though he was searching above all for answers, he always needed to debate his (and other peoples') religious views.

Throughout this period, in the early 1770s, Equiano had (unusually for him) been unemployed, an experience which weighed heavily on him, adding perhaps to his uncertainties. The only solution was to return to sea. He signed on as steward to Captain Richard Strange on the *Hope*, bound for Cadiz. Shipboard was not an ideal place for a man seeking religious salvation. He hated the blasphemies around him, worrying that he too might be infected by the sin of it all. He was unhappy with the thought that he could not get to heaven by his own actions. Equiano seemed as miserable as could be; he even thought of suicide and was only deterred by remembering the Scriptures, and the thought that suicide might prevent him from entering the kingdom of heaven. He was, as he later admitted, deeply depressed, thinking himself 'the unhappiest man living'. 'I fretted, mourned, and prayed, till I became a burden to others, but more so to myself.'

Life at sea, surrounded by men who seemed to have no respect for God, seemed awful and henceforth Equiano resolved 'to beg my bread on shore, rather than go again to sea'. Three times he asked his captain to release him; each time his request was refused. Other members of the crew, however, treated him well and tried to help him.[35]

Once back in London the turmoil continued, though his friends persuaded him that a life at sea was his 'lawful calling'. Equiano was particularly helped by the friendship and religious advice of George Smith, the governor of Totill-Fields 'house of correction' in Westminster, who read to him and gave him devotional books. More settled in his mind, Equiano promptly returned to his ship, sailing again for Cadiz in September 1774. On board, Equiano read and prayed whenever he could. Looking back, he knew precisely which chapters of the Scriptures he was reading on which particular days. In the evening of 6 October 1774, the religous breakthrough came:

the Lord was pleased to break in upon my soul with his bright beams of heavenly light; and in an instant, as it were, removing the veil, and letting light into a dark place.

Equiano saw Christ crucified on Calvary. He described the experience, fifteen years later, with ample biblical quotations. His whole life had flashed before him, 'from the day I was taken from my parents to that hour. . . as if it had but just then occurred'. He wept, knowing that he was saved: 'Now the Ethiopian was willing to be saved by Jesus Christ.' It was a salvation which transformed him:

the burden of sin, the gaping jaws of hell, and the fears of death, that weighed me down before, now lost their horror. . .

He thought – and prayed – for his mother and his friends, praising the Lord in loud acclamations. As he left his cabin to share his thoughts with other members of the crew, they did not believe him. He longed to get back to London and to share his experience and his thoughts with his friends and fellow believers. The Bible was now his sole companion; he saw new things in it each time he picked it up. By the end of 1774 Equiano was back in London and he hurried round immediately to his friends who 'were glad when they perceived the wonderful change that the Lord had wrought in me'. He listened to preachers, to resolve some outstanding issues, and finally was admitted as a member of New Way chapel in Westminster. Later, Equiano wrote some simple verses, reflecting on this period and appended them to his memoirs.[36]

Equiano's crisis had passed. It had lasted a little more than a year, from his return from the Arctic in September 1773 through to the end of 1774. It had clearly been a deeply troubling time, his worries prompted initially by thoughts of his close shave with death in the arctic ice, quickly followed by his frustrated fury about the fate of John Annis. A period of unemployment was followed by months of anguished religious uncertainties. For weeks on end, his sole companion seems to have been his Bible, though when he was in London he clearly drew strength and support from a small band of British friends who nursed him through his religious crisis. The solution revealed itself on 6 October 1774 – in Cadiz, a fact Equiano could recall precisely many years later. Did he keep a journal at the time? Then, and so often in his autobiography, he recalled dates and specific incidents so *exactly* as to suggest that he kept some form of written record. He clearly kept paperwork – manumission certificate, letters of recommendation – and he clearly wrote to friends regularly.[37] But the key fact of his life, at the end of 1774, was that he was now at ease with himself. He was saved. Certain of his God, of his faith, and sure of his own salvation, Equiano seemed happier than at any time in his life. His account was very much in the tradition of a spiritual autobiography which had been penned by an earlier black writer, Gronniosaw. And it was to be repeated time and again in subsequent slave narratives. Although, previous to this, he seems to have gained a great deal of satisfaction from his commercial successes – he regularly recorded his financial dealings – he had never before spoken of true happiness as he did in 1774. And it was an entirely spiritual happiness. His life had entered a new phase. Whatever satisfactions had flowed from freedom were now surpassed by knowledge of his sure salvation. His book was then, at one level, the diary of a soul. And by 1774 his African soul had found its spiritual home in a distinctively English religion.

Notes

1 *Interesting Narrative*, pp. 164–5.
2 J. J. Hecht, *Continental and Colonial Servants in Eighteenth-century England* (Northampton, MA, 1954), p. 48.
3 Peter Fryer, *Staying Power* (London, 1984), pp. 79–88.
4 *Felix Farley's Bristol Journal*, 12 March 1757.
5 Jane Girdham, 'Black Musicians in England: Ignatius Sancho and His Contemporaries', in Reyahn King et al., *Ignatius Sancho: An African Man of Letters* (London, 1997).
6 *The Letters of Ignatius Sancho*, ed. Vincent Carretta (London, 1998).
7 For the cult of sensibility, see G. J. Barker-Benfield, *The Culture of Sensibility: Sex and Society in Eighteenth-century Britain* (Chicago, 1992).
8 *Interesting Narrative*, pp. 166–7.
9 *Ibid.*, pp. 168–9.
10 On the Grand Tour, see Jeremy Black, *The British Abroad: The Grand Tour in the 18th Century* (Stroud, 1992).
11 For articles which touch on these and other issues, see Adam Potkay, 'Olaudah Equiano and the Art of Spiritual Autobiography' and Geraldine Murphy, 'Olaudah Equiano, Accidental Tourist', *Eighteenth Century Studies*, vol. 27, no. 4, 1994.
12 *Interesting Narrative*, pp. 170–1.
13 James Walvin, *Fruits of Empire: Exotic Produce and British Taste, 1660–1800* (London, 1997), p. 124.
14 *Interesting Narrative*, pp. 171–2. For more obscene outrages, see D. Hall (ed.), *In Miserable Slavery: Thomas Thistlewood in Jamaica, 1750–1786* (London, 1989).

15 *Interesting Narrative*, p. 172.

16 Thistlewood, *op. cit.*, p. 12.

17 *Interesting Narrative*, p. 172.

18 Roger D. Abrahams and John S. Szwed (eds), *After Africa* (New Haven, 1983), pp. 163–79.

19 J. S. Handler and F. W. Lange, *Plantation Slavery in Barbados* (Cambridge, MA, 1978); Roderick A. McDonald, *The Economy and Material Culture of Slaves* (Baton Rouge, 1993).

20 *Interesting Narrative*, p. 172.

21 Constantine John Phipps, *A Voyage to the North Pole Undertaken by His Majesty's Command, 1773* (London, 1774).

22 *Interesting Narrative*, p. 172.

23 *Ibid.*, pp. 172–6.

24 Matthew A. Henson, *A Black Explorer at the North Pole* (1912; reprinted Lincoln, NB, 1989).

25 *Interesting Narrative*, p. 178.

26 *Ibid.*, p. 179.

27 *Ibid.*, p. 169.

28 *Ibid.*, p. 179.

29 *Ibid.*, pp. 179–80.

30 On the law, see Chapter 4.

31 *Interesting Narrative*, pp. 179–81.

32 *Ibid.*, pp. 181–2.

33 *Ibid.*, pp. 183–4.

34 *Ibid.*, pp. 186–8.

35 *Ibid.*, pp. 188–9.

36 *Ibid.*, pp. 190–7.

37 See the reference to the correspondence with George Smith, *ibid.*, p. 193. And see surviving letter, 28 May 1792, in PRO, TS.24/24/12/2; reprinted in *Interesting Narrative*, pp. 374–8.

= 9 =

ALL AT SEA AGAIN

In his new state of mind, Equiano felt reluctant to return to sea, though he knew how hard it had been, the previous year, to find satisfactory work in London. But, encouraged by friends, he signed on again, 'in full resignation to the will of God', heading once again for Cadiz in March 1775. As his ship approached Cadiz harbour it was damaged in a collision and was in danger of sinking. While others cried to God for help, Equiano tells how he remained calm, not worried that he might be about to meet his maker. He was, he felt, in a state of grace. With the help of some passing Spanish ships, Equiano's vessel was saved; quickly emptied of goods, then run aground and repaired. Once seaworthy, the vessel sailed on to Gibraltar and then Malaga. Though Equiano was impressed by the local cathedral he was shocked, in that same city, by 'the custom of bull-baiting, and other diversions which prevailed here on Sunday evenings, to the great scandal of Christianity and morals.' Here again Equiano was trailing his coat as man of sensibility; a man offended by examples of barbarous customs which belonged to past times.

It is a remarkable coincidence – which Equiano is very unlikely to have realized – that only a year before he published his *Narrative*, one of England's most prominent and traditional bull-running customs, in Stamford, had first come under serious social and political attack. This was part of a much broader propertied onslaught on violent and bloody popular entertainments and games; an element in the drive to change the cultural habits of the common people, to wean them away from the gory turbulence which so characterized many of their traditional pleasures.[1] But it was also an aspect of the effort to refine the manners of the people at large; to render them more civilized, more biddable and less tinged by the crudeness of past ages.[2] It was to prove an uphill struggle, in which many propertied campaigners made exceptions for their own interest in field sports and the necessity of allowing public executions, if only *pour encourager les autres*.

Yet it seems odd that Equiano should raise *Spanish* bull-running as an affront to Christianity. It was, again, part of his intention of persuading readers that he was strongly opposed to violence, to unchristian behaviour, to outbursts of popular blood-letting. That an African should feel this way was doubly ironic for the British had, over the past century, been nurtured on a printed diet which cast Africa and its inhabitants as primitive and violent; beyond the pale and the ken of European sensitivities and refinements, a continent of primitive barbarisms from which slaves were taken with no offence to local morality or utility. This was, in broad measure, the slave lobby's justification for the Atlantic slave trade and American slavery. If Africa and Africans were beyond the pale of civilization (as Europe understood it), the act of enslavement, of transportation and American bondage were morally neutral. Indeed, in removing Africans, and bringing them into contact with the 'higher' cultures of Europe and the Americas, the Atlantic slave system could even be seen as a force for good. In reality, this argument, which rumbled on for two centuries but which reached a crescendo in the late eighteenth century in conflict with abolitionists, was mere posturing; a smokescreen to disguise economic self-interest. Yet it is within this context that we need to place Equiano's insistence, time and again, on Christian morality. He portrayed himself as a man of refined Christian morality; an enlightened African of civilized feelings. If *he* could reach such attainments, how many countless others might not do the same – if only Europeans could be persuaded to treat Africa and Africans differently?

Characteristically, Equiano protested about the bull-running to a Spanish Catholic priest, with whom he had struck up a theological discussion. This simple event was itself surely significant. How many other sailors – and how many African sailors – passing through a major European port, engaged clerics in theological discussion? In this case, the Spanish priest tried to convert Equiano to Catholicism, and Equiano in return tried to convert the priest, producing his Bible to make a point. (This in itself was surely unusual; an African wandering round a Spanish city, Bible in hand.) The Spanish priest disliked what he had seen of religion in England, especially the widespread popular access to the Bible 'which was very wrong'. Equiano countered by arguing that Christ wanted his followers to search the Bible for themselves. It was, at heart, a clash between a Protestant from a society where popular literacy was on the rise, and a Spanish Catholic who wished to see biblical exegesis remain solely in the hands of a privileged priesthood. Urged to attend a Spanish university, Equiano was assured that he could even become a priest. Such a future held no attractions for him, not least because he could 'not in conscience conform to the opinions of his [the Spaniard's] church'.[3] Once more, it did Equiano's image no harm to tell his readers that he had been encouraged to think of attending university and entering the priesthood. Along with the book from which these cultured images emerged, it was another example of Equiano's determination to speak to African potential. He wrote not merely for himself, but for Africans at large. How many other Africans might flourish if the shackles of slavery were permanently removed?

Equiano's ship, already loaded with fruits, wines and money, moved on to Cadiz, where it took on 'about two tons more of money', before returning to England in June 1775. On this, as on other voyages, Equiano actively promoted his religious ideas among his fellow sailors. When, in the teeth of contrary winds, the captain blasphemed, Equiano joined in a young passenger's criticisms of such talk, urging blasphemers to give thanks for their blessings. Within the day, Equiano's ship had picked up a small boat of 11 shipwrecked men, all half-drowned and on the point of starvation. They were Portuguese, from a ship which had suddenly capsized when its load of corn shifted, and they would surely have died had they not been rescued. They promptly 'bowed themselves on their knees, and, with hands and voices lifted to heaven, thanked God for their deliverance'. The captain seemed especially thankful that the Lord had spared him, and Equiano took the opportunity 'of talking to him on the providence of God'.[4] It seems, again, an unusual encounter: an African and ex-slave discussing theology with a distressed shipwrecked Portuguese mariner on the high seas. Though it may seem unusual today, in that swirling mixture of humanity and cultures which was the Atlantic slave system, such encounters were commonplace on both sides of the Atlantic. Most such encounters took place on land, of course, but many were at sea.[5] What, after all, was the Atlantic slave trade, but a massive, prolonged (and violent) encounter between utterly different cultures? This single incident was perhaps more symptomatic than it might seem.

From mid-summer to November 1775 Equiano was in London, happy to be 'once more amongst my friends and brethren'. (Were these 'brethren' his fellow worshippers – or fellow blacks?) He was clearly on friendly terms with Dr Irving, for whom he had previously worked on the water experiments, and was now persuaded by friends to join Irving in a new adventure: to work as a planter in Jamaica and on the 'Musquito Shore'. Interestingly, Equiano sounded out and heeded the advice of friends on this and other matters. Clearly, he placed great value on his biblical readings (he seemed to have read the Bible on most days) but he also had a circle of close friends in London whose advice he valued and followed. Irving's venture was quite unlike anything Equiano had experienced before. Moreover it would depend on slave labour.

Equiano had already been in charge of slaves at sea. Both as an enslaved and a free sailor he had supervised the loading and unloading of African slaves at various points in the Americas. Although he regularly denounced slavery and was, eventually, to commit the latter part of his life to campaigning against it, he was inevitably dragged into an involvement with slavery in ways he must have found distressing. Hitherto he had had no say in the matter, but had been forced to obey orders, and to ignore or relegate his own feelings. Now, in 1775, he had to make a conscious choice. And he chose to work with an old associate on plans to develop a new slave settlement.

Dr Irving wanted Equiano to be in charge of an estate he was planning to establish: he 'said he would trust me with his estate in preference to any one'.[6] Throughout the slave colonies it was common to place reliable (or strong) blacks, themselves normally slaves, in charge of slave gangs. But it was very unusual not to have white man in charge of the overall estate. What Dr Irving proposed was the creation of an entirely new settlement, a proposal more akin to the pioneering settlements in English colonies in the previous century. By the last quarter of the eighteenth century, the plantations of the English-speaking Caribbean had reached maturity, and the hierarchies of race and status had taken on a classic and familiar form.[7] This venture – expedition, really – was a return to an older pattern, where black, white (and Indian), free and unfree, would work side by side to impose order and control on the wilderness, and bring it to profitable cultivation.

Equiano had his own ideas about what this venture might achieve. He saw it as an opportunity to spread the gospel, and 'of bringing some poor sinner to my well-beloved master, Jesus Christ'. It was in effect an opportunity to become a missionary. Equiano began with four Mosquito Indians (one of whom was a prince), who had already been in London for 12 months, could speak English, and were about to return home. Horrified to discover that no one had bothered to take them to church, Equiano took the matter in hand. But time was short, and a few days later, in November 1775, his ship, the *Morning Star,* a sloop of 150 tons captained by David Miller, sailed for Jamaica.[8] Equiano spent much of the voyage instructing the Mosquito Indian prince, concentrating on Christianity (which 'he received with gladness') and the basics of literacy. By the end of the journey, the Indian had begun to spell, and seemed happy enough browsing through Equiano's copy of Fox's *Book of Martyrs.* Equiano was delighted with the progress the man had made, especially his insistence that they pray together regularly, late at night and before meals. It was a remarkable example of cultural transformation. An African, who had himself been taught and converted at sea by British sailors, helping to convert an Indian *en route* to the Americas.

It proved too much, however, for some other people on board ('Satan's messengers' in Equiano's words) who, towards the end of the voyage, began to mock the Indian, undermining his commitment and deterring him completely from further biblical study. Though he would not drink or enjoy himself with his tormentors, nor would he return to the Bible or to Equiano's instruction. Confused by the tension between the two sides – Equiano's expositions on sin and the hereafter, and the mockery of other men – the Indian drifted into depressed isolation. By the New Year 1776, the *Morning Star* had made landfall, skirting Martinique, then Montserrat and Antigua, before arriving in Jamaica on 14 January 1776.[9]

Once in Kingston, Equiano was keen to press home his progress with the Mosquito Indian, taking him to a local church, but the man was more impressed by the colourful and teeming market which stretched from the church door right down to the Kingston dockside. Visitors to the West Indian islands were often amazed by their first sight of local Sunday markets, with their rich mix of peoples, produce, animals and goods. Slaves walked for miles to their nearest market, to sell the foodstuffs they had grown, the animals they had reared, the goods and items they had crafted (clothing, bedding, rope, baskets, pottery, matting). They sold and bartered from slave to slave, African and local-born, to free blacks and to whites.[10] It was a scene which testified to the extraordinary industry and enterprise to be found within slave society. Slave-owners complained at every turn of the slaves' basic laziness, yet these same people shaped key areas of the local economies, in the process improving themselves by application and industry. It was a world from which Equiano himself had emerged so successfully.

On this trip, Jamaica was only a stopping-off point *en route* to the Mosquito Coast of Central America, a region, even then, scarcely settled by Europeans, and notoriously dangerous, unhealthy and resistant to outside conquest. Whatever else Dr Irving's adventures required (and they needed good luck in abundance), they required slave labour. Thus, just before they quit Kingston, Equiano and Dr Irving went 'on board a Guinea-man, to purchase some slaves to carry with us, and cultivate a plantation; and I chose them all of my own countrymen, some of whom came from Lybia'.[11]

Equiano recorded this transaction with no comment. Yet we need to consider what lay behind this transaction. Here was a freed African stepping aboard an Atlantic slave ship to select Africans for a new plantation. His own experiences on the slave ship, twenty years before, had – obviously – been among his formative and most traumatic experiences. Now here he was, twenty years on, a free man, plucking newly arrived Africans from the bowels of a slave ship, to steer them to a lifetime's bondage on a plantation.

Equiano selected Africans, 'my own countrymen', with whom he had some contact; this almost certainly meant fellow Igbo people. The Igbo were a 'distinct ethno-historical group' from the Nigerian hinterland of the Calabar coast who formed upwards of one and a half million captives in the Atlantic slave trade. Almost one-half of that total crossed the Atlantic in the years between 1750 and 1807 (the years spanning much of Equiano's life) and the bulk of them were carried in British ships and taken to British possessions.[12] Equiano was a natural agent to deal with newly arrived Igbo, his fellow countrymen, as indeed he had been earlier when dealing with the transhipment of slaves at St Eustatius. With the unhappy Africans on board, Dr Irving's vessel left Kingston for the Mosquito Coast, arriving six days later. Again, his dating was precise (leaving on 12 February 1776, arriving the 18th) a clear indication that Equiano kept a regular account of events.

The Mosquito Indians made their fond farewells, taking with them a few cases of liquor (along with Equiano's admonishments). The *Morning Star* then cruised south along the coast to Cape Gracias a Dios where they found plentiful fish and tortoise, and made contact with friendly Indians. Using the Indians as guides Irving and Equiano began the search for a suitable settlement site. They opted for an area of rich soil near a river bank, quickly clearing the bush and planting foodstuffs. They had settled in what seems to have been present-day Nicaragua. Their vessel then sailed north to trade at Black River – but was promptly impounded by Spanish coastguards. Indian peoples from the interior soon began to arrive at the crude settlement, attracted by what the Europeans and Africans could offer them, and the resulting trade seemed mutually beneficial. The Indians brought 'a good deal of silver in exchange for our goods'. They also provided 'turtle oil, and shells, little silk grass, and some provisions'. The most prized service they received in return was the medical attention of Dr Irving, whose treatment and assistance made him a popular figure among the Indians.

Like Europeans everywhere in their early settlements in the Americas, this new band of pioneers was unable to persuade the Indians to work for them. Indeed, one of the most powerful reasons behind the decision to turn to Africa for labour, especially after the development of sugar plantations in the seventeenth century, had been the unsatisfactory nature of Indian labour. Indians either died out, refused to work, or simply melted away into the inaccessible interior, rather than bend their backs to the unrelenting work demanded on new plantations. This pattern was repeated in this small settlement on the Mosquito Coast. Equiano remarked that the Indians 'would not work at any thing for us, except fishing; and a few times they assisted to cut some trees down, in order to build us houses'. He was also struck by the fact that the Indians worked much like the Africans, 'by the joint labour of men, women, and children'.[13]

Wherever he travelled in the world, Equiano had a sharp eye for local and human detail. Living among the Indians, he was struck by their distinctive social customs, especially by relationships between men and women. While the women cultivated the land, the menfolk fished and made canoes. They all travelled together to Irving's plantation; they seemed monogamous, the women always taking up positions behind their husbands, but they ate their food separately. Men and women were both fond of decorating themselves, but their homes were simplicity itself. More pleasing still to Equiano was his belief that they had no real swear words; he claimed that the most severe oath they uttered was 'you rascal' – and even that had been acquired from English. But he was unhappy to realize that they appeared to have no religion. On the other hand, neither did many of the white people at the new settlement. In the sheer grind of securing the settlement, days simply blurred into each other and after a while it was hard to know which day was which. It proved impossible to keep the Sabbath holy when they did not know which day of the week it was.[14]

The Europeans were glad to note that the Indians were fundamentally honest. The settlers were able to sleep under open lean-to huts, and never had to secure their material or personal possessions against theft: 'we slept in safety, and never lost any thing, or were disturbed'.[15]

They found some Indian habits unattractive, however. The Indians formed a bellicose group, fond of claiming that they had never been defeated by the Spaniards. They loved strong liquor, distilling a form of rum from pineapples, and inevitably drink caused unrest and friction. When a major Indian figure (described as a governor, travelling to see his various outposts) visited the settlement, drink quickly became a cause of serious trouble. Having plundered other Indians *en route*, he arrived to a fanfare of drunken revelry, and obviously expecting to be provided with the best the settlement could provide. Equiano and friends fed the visitors all day, and by the evening, the Indian governor was quite drunk. He struck a local (friendly) Indian chief and stole his gold-laced hat and in the ensuing commotion, Dr Irving fled to the forest, leaving Equiano to restore peace. Equiano confessed he would have liked to flog the man responsible. Since that was not possible, he took the next best step and invoked the Almighty.

Recalling a story of how Columbus had been able to quell Indian troubles by pointing to the heavens (at the time of an eclipse), Equiano tried a similar ploy. Pointing to the sky, Equiano told the Indians that God lived there, and unless they behaved he would read the Bible, and would '*tell* God to make them dead'. This had the desired effect. The clamour subsided and, clutching their gifts of rum, the visiting Indians dispersed.[16] Relations between Indian peoples, Europeans and Africans throughout the Americas were bedevilled by the effects of alcohol. Though many Indian societies had their own forms of alcohol, Europeans introduced new brands of potent drinks as a gift, as a means of lubricating trade and of securing friendship or agreement – or simply to induce drunken powerlessness and incapacity among the Indians. Thanks to the labour of African slaves in the Caribbean, there was always plenty of cheap rum available to dope and seduce Indian peoples into that drunken haze which was as advantageous to the European aggressors as it was corrosive of Indian life.[17] It was a miserable story which was repeated, with local differences, clean across the Americas. Here, in 1776 on the Mosquito Coast, Equiano was only the latest of outsiders to feel unhappy about what he saw unfolding in front of his eyes.

Drink was also basic to Indian ceremonies. Local Indians, keen to fête Dr Irving, prepared one of their traditional festivals – a celebration which seemed characterized, again, by vast drinking of potent alcohol (made from pineapple and cassava, and brewed in and served up from an open canoe). It helped to wash down roast turtle and alligator meat. At the appointed time, the settlers arrived to be greeted by a large friendly crowd of Indians, already making-merry and dancing. Dr Irving tried to dance with the women, but since men and women danced separately he had to move over to the men's group. Equiano was struck by how similar the musical instruments were to those 'of any other sable people. . . [but]. . . much less melodious than any other nation I ever knew'.[18] It proved a colourful and lively evening, as the food and drink passed from hand to hand by calabash, some Indians dressed and decorated in skins, feathers and headpieces (one wore what looked like a grenadier's hat). The whole evening passed off peacefully, 'without the least discord in any person in the company, although it was made up of different nations and complexions'.[19]

Despite such occasional pleasures, Equiano was unhappy with life on the plantation settlement. Like frontier life everywhere, life was rough and crude; Equiano had experienced nothing like it before. More than that, it was an irreligious community. God, the Bible, the calendar of the Christian week, the refined sociability of Christian life – all were absent. Equiano was in the midst of apparently godless Europeans and Africans and cheek by jowl with Indians who knew nothing of Christianity. Over the past twenty years Equiano had changed fundamentally. He was now a devout Christian, more at home in the company of fellow worshippers than in the company of his fellow Igbo on a Central American plantation (though in fact he scarcely mentioned the Africans throughout this period). The sheer grimness of daily toil, of working each and every day, of not realizing which day was the Sabbath, took its toll on this devout man. Equiano found it impossible to observe that regime of devotion and worship which had become so important to him.

The summer of 1776, with its heavy rains from May to August, forced Equiano's hand. Rivers overflowed, crops were washed away and Equiano – typically – put it down to God's wrath; 'a judgement upon us for working on Sundays'. He wrote that 'living in this heathenish form was very irksome to me'.[20] His Bible was his only refuge, though what he read sometimes brought little comfort: 'What does it avail a man if he gain the whole world, and lose his soul?'

Plucking up courage, he asked Dr Irving for his release in June 1776. Reluctantly, Irving agreed, handing over a testimonial of good behaviour to his African employee. Like other paperwork from his earlier life, Equiano was able, years later, to reprint the document word for word. It was, again, a document made out not in the name of Equiano, but Gustavus Vassa:

The bearer, Gustavus Vassa, has served me several years with strict honesty, sobriety, and fidelity. I can, therefore, with justice recommend him for these qualifications; and indeed in every respect I consider him as an excellent servant. I do hereby certify that he always behaved well, and that he is perfectly trust-worthy.

CHARLES IRVING.

Musquito shore, June 15, 1776

Dr Irving was not the only person saddened by Equiano's impending departure. The slaves he had selected from the Atlantic slave ship in Kingston were all similarly unhappy:

All my fellow countrymen, the slaves, when they heard of my leaving them, were very sorry, as I had always treated them with care and affection, and did every thing I could to comfort the poor creatures, and render their condition easy.

That is all he said. Not unlike the story of his choosing these Africans in the first instance, Equiano's comment about a group of African slaves – possibly Igbo like himself – is stark, but revealing. It is a passing reference, as much to do with himself, his treatment of and his feelings for them, as it is about the Africans. Of course there was little practical he *could* do. Whenever he had a hand in the business of slaving, he was in no position to prevent the sale of slaves. He was but a tiny cog in a massive Atlantic machine. Any form of protest, objection or gesture would surely have been counterproductive and might merely have made a rod for his own back. So, it seems, he simply resolved to do all he could 'to comfort the poor creatures, and render their condition easy'.[21] But their good fortune – if such it was – was not to last. Equiano's departure was to prove a disaster for this group of Africans, for the man who replaced him turned out to be a violent, cruel driver. They tried to escape from their driver's oppressive control by canoe, but all were drowned in the attempt.[22]

Equiano took his leave of all his friends and fellow settlers on 18 June 1776, heading south in a hired canoe manned by Indians and accompanied by Dr Irving. When they met a sloop bound for Jamaica, Irving took a tearful farewell of Equiano. No sooner was Irving out of sight than the ship's owner, keen to transfer Equiano as a sailor to another of his ships, began to menace him, to challenge his freedom, threatening – once again – to enslave him. In very different parts of the world, he never seemed able to escape the threat of slavery, and white men regularly threatened him with bondage, despite his loud protestations of freedom, and despite their having seen him living and working as a free man. It was yet another illustration of a much broader phenomenon; the difficulty facing free blacks in an Atlantic community dominated by black slavery. When blacks were assumed, by their very blackness, to be slaves, individual black freedom was tenuous and sometimes elusive.[23]

Understandably, a furious row erupted between the ship's owner, a man named Hughes, and Equiano, who told him he had 'been twice amongst the Turks, yet had never seen any such usage with them'. Hughes seemed especially angered by Equiano's evocation of Christianity: 'much less could I have expected any thing of this kind among the Christians'. Hughes hurled blasphemy and abuse at Equiano, telling him he would only get off the ship if he could walk across the water.[24]

Equiano was trapped. Hughes ordered him to be tied up, and the crew secured him with ropes round his ankles and wrists, another round his body, and he was hoisted off the deck:

> Thus I hung, without any crime committed, and without any judge or jury, merely because I was a freeman, and could not by the law get any redress from a white person in those parts of the world.[25]

As he knew all too well from his own enslavement in London in 1762 and from the case of John Annis in 1774, such arbitrary and cavalier actions were not peculiar to the Americas.

Dangling, in great pain, just above the deck, Equiano begged for help. This merely prompted Hughes to threaten to shoot him. Not a single white man on the ship offered to help, as Equiano dangled there from ten or eleven o'clock at night till about one o'clock in the morning, when other slaves on board slackened the ropes, despite the obvious risk to themselves. Slightly relieved, Equiano continued to dangle there until daylight, but praying all the while. Hughes was unrepentant the next day, as the ship sailed, but Equiano was finally released. Fortunately he seems to have known the carpenter, a Mr Cox (who also knew Dr Irving) who petitioned the captain on Equiano's behalf, confirming that he was indeed Irving's steward and ought not to be treated in so vile a fashion. The captain relented and allowed Equiano to head for the shore in a canoe. But all this took place unknown to Hughes who, when he discovered what had happened, threatened to shoot the departing Equiano. As Hughes and the captain argued, the ship was slipping away, and Equiano decided simply to make a break for it, quickly paddling the canoe towards the shore and out of range of Hughes's musket. It had been a close-run thing. Equiano might easily have been re-enslaved – yet again. He could have been killed in one of those random acts of viciousness which so often erupted in the world of slavery; he might simply have disappeared from sight, and from the record, like legions of Africans before and afterwards. But luck, on this occasion, was on his side.

Once ashore, Equiano made his way to the joint owner of the vessel from which he had just escaped, complaining of his treatment at the hands of Hughes. Here he was treated kindly, refreshed and fed. As he set off once more, alone in a canoe, he felt exhausted and had abdominal pains from being trussed up for so long. Finally arriving at an Indian community, he was taken in, fed and rested in a hammock. The Indians 'acted towards me more like Christians than those whites I was amongst the last night, though they had been baptized'.[26]

This was a refrain which now ran throughout Equiano's ideas and writing. How could people who were nominally Christian, behave so badly? And what was to be made of non-Christians (Turks, or, in this case, Indians) behaving better than Christians? Equiano expected Christians to be guided by their faith in everything they did. It was not a faith for the Sabbath alone but should, instead, inform and shape each waking moment. Yet other unanswered issues lurked behind his bald statements. How were Christians to regard other, non-Christian peoples: peoples who often displayed many of the social and humane qualities to which Christians themselves aspired? In the balance sheet of good and evil, it was apparent that the line did not neatly separate Christians from others.

The ABOLITION of the SLAVE TRADE.
Or the Inhumanity of Dealers in human flesh exemplifyd in Captn Kimbers treatment of a young Negroe Girl of 15 for her Virgin Modesty.

My Eyes Jack our Girles at Wapping are never flogd for their Modesty

Dam me if I likeit I have a good mind to let go a good 'un

By G—d that's too bad if he had taken her to bed to himd it would not be so bad through Shett me I'm almost sick of this Black business

PLATE 9.
'The Abolition of the Slave Trade'; cartoon, 1792. Equiano experienced this form of torture.

Source: Wilberforce House, Kingston-upon-Hull City Museums and Archives.

Equiano had been raised in an utterly different culture, in a world as yet untouched by Christianity. What memories did he bring to bear, from his distant childhood, of personal and collective qualities and virtues; of the interplay between good and evil in a non-Christian setting? Of course, the whole biography was an exercise, at one level, of reconciliation; of delving into the distant past and trying to make sense of that past in relation to the present. What was the *Narrative* but an effort to reconstruct a past crudely fissured by a series of emotional upheavals and separations?

In any event, Equiano had seen enough of the non-Christian world – in Turkey and the Americas – to appreciate that humane behaviour and society came in many different forms. But he had committed himself to the Christian life, the one and true path to salvation. Not surprisingly, unchristian behaviour hurt him in many ways. It affected him directly: the physical agonies of being trussed up like an animal (and that at the hands of Christians); the confusion of knowing that nominal Christians could behave like 'savages'; and the glaring fact that 'savages' could behave like Christians. Making sense of the world was no easy matter for an African, who, by turns, had been enslaved, freed, frequently threatened with slavery, converted to Christianity and finally secured to Methodism. Equiano had not simply been buffeted around the world – cast here and there on the changing tides of the slave system – but had undergone a series of emotional, intellectual and devotional transformations. In common with millions of others, his had been a life of innumerable upheavals and confusions. And the world he had adopted, or had been adopted by (the Christian England of the late eighteenth century) was no easy place for a free, African Christian.

When Equiano had rested and recovered, a group of Indians ferried him by large canoe to a port 50 miles distant. It proved a difficult trip, at times dragging the canoe across spits of land, and spending two nights in swampy, mosquito-infested campsites. But on the third day they made contact with a sloop, apparently ready to sail for Jamaica. Equiano signed on as a working sailor, but again disappointment intervened. Instead of heading for Jamaica, the vessel headed south along the coast, the crew – Equiano included – employed in the strenuous work of logging mahogany (the region's key export, and the basis for so much fashionable eighteenth-century furniture in Britain).[27] Equiano felt deceived once more. Having been assured by the captain that the vessel was ready to sail for Jamaica, Equiano found himself, instead, working as a labourer at strenuous work on shore. 'This fretted me much; but, as I did not know how to help myself among these deceivers, I thought patience was the only remedy I had left, and even that was forced.'[28]

For sixteen days the vessel cruised the coastline collecting timber (again, Equiano's precision about the timing suggests a journal), their meagre food supplies augmented by what they could catch from the sea. They encountered a small sloop, the *Indian Queen*, under the command of an Englishman, John Baker, who claimed he was looking for sailors so that he could sail for Jamaica. Equiano offered to raise crew for the journey and was offered 45 shillings a month for the voyage. But Jenning, Equiano's captain on the original vessel, would not release him, instead making ready to sail, with Equiano on board (against his will). Not to be trapped yet again, Equiano (with the help of a sailor he had known earlier on the North Pole expedition) managed to get on board the *Indian Queen* on 10 July 1776. Even that narrow escape brought its own disadvantages, for his new boat headed, not easterly to Jamaica, but south to Cartagena, trading along the coast. Provisions were scarce, the crew having to make do with what they could find along the shoreline, from islands they passed and from the sea. When good luck came – when food unexpectedly materialized, Equiano thought it was, of course, God's will. But life on the *Indian Queen* was hellish, thanks to Captain Baker, 'a very cruel and bloody-minded man, and a horrid blasphemer'. Violent towards everyone, he seemed to have a particular hatred for his mate, a man named Stoker, and towards 'some negroes he had on board'. He beat them, cast Stoker ashore on a desolate key, and continued his mistreatment when the man returned. Stoker's miseries ended when he drowned a short time later.[29]

Equiano also attracted the captain's wrath, in what Equiano described as a 'wild, wicked, and mad career', and suffered various beatings by whatever came to hand. It culminated when Baker, alone on the vessel with Equiano (the rest of the crew were on shore trading) threatened to blow up the ship.[30] Equiano prepared to kill him with an axe, praying throughout but convinced that he was about to do the right thing. With nightfall, the man's volcanic anger subsided. Through all these upheavals, up and down the coast of Central America, on a number of different vessels plying their varied trades in the region, Equiano had stumbled from one problem to another. He had been lied to at every turn. He had been threatened with enslavement. Rival captains had struggled over his services. He had been tortured, beaten and threatened with death. All this – and more – from Europeans; from civilized, Christian people. He had no complaint against local Indians (save their love of drink). Yet all he sought was a berth back to Jamaica, thence to England.

This cycle of confusion and uncertainty – would he ever be able to quit the Mosquito Coast and get back to England? – was soon broken. Equiano hoped to make a quick escape when he discovered Dr Irving on another English ship (*en route* to Jamaica to buy replacement slaves) but Irving was powerless to effect Equiano's transfer to his own ship. Eventually, however, the *Indian Queen* docked in Kingston on 14 October 1776. Equiano had calculated precisely how much he was owed for his labours: £8. 5s (shillings), but Captain Baker refused to pay anything 'although it was the hardest earned money I ever worked for in my life'. Dr Irving helped Equiano scour Kingston for redress. They visited the town's nine magistrates, but none could help. It was an old and familiar problem. They all told Equiano that 'my oath could not be admitted against a white man'. To make matters worse, Baker threatened to beat Equiano if he saw him, and Equiano was understandably concerned not to give him the opportunity. He managed to avoid this problem when Irving placed him under the protection of a Royal Naval officer, Captain Douglas of the *Squirrel*.[31]

Equiano was not alone in his complaints, and he was depressed to see how similar incidents (of whites cheating blacks and threatening them with violence when challenged) seemed all too common in Jamaica: 'Such oppressions as these made me seek for a vessel to get off the island as fast as I could.'

Within the month, he had signed on a ship heading in convoy to England, having turned down Irving's invitation to join him in his latest venture (sugar refining in Jamaica). It proved a rough but uneventful passage, enlivened only when the *Squirrel*, also part of the convoy, captured an American privateer. (Britain was now at war with the breakaway American colonies.) On 7 January 1777 Equiano's ship arrived at Plymouth, after a little more than a year's adventure and dangers in the Americas: 'I was happy once more to tread upon English ground...' Interestingly, Equiano knew people in Plymouth, and in Exeter, and spent some time with them. They were he wrote, 'pious friends, whom I was happy to see'. How did he know people in the remote far west of the country, when he had spent most of his time in England in London? (He had of course visited the West Country on first landfall on earlier voyages.) Were these friends members of his own church – friends acquired by common worship in the same church? Or had he made friends on his earlier visits? Whatever the explanation, he was soon on his way back to London 'with a heart replete with thanks to God for all his past mercies'.[32]

This might strike modern readers as an odd remark on a period which had been characterized by a succession of near-disasters and acute worries. But Equiano's faith enabled him to find solace, and the Lord's bounty, in most events. After all, he had indeed been spared the worst of sufferings. He had avoided being re-enslaved, he had skirted death, and even his physical punishments had left him with no permanent damage. Yet from first to last, this period of his life had been precarious in the extreme (as indeed it was for most people living on the raw edges of pioneering settlements). The violence and precariousness of life at sea, on pioneering settlements and on the volatile slave colony of Jamaica, were simple facts of life. Of course Equiano was also anxious to *emphasize* such incidents for his readers (a ghastly fate narrowly avoided, death averted) by way of underlining his own divine protection, and the rewards which came to those who led a blameless life. Though the incidents at the heart of Equiano's account were appalling – persistent cruelty and double-dealing, casual violence, capricious inhumanity – they were not out of keeping with what we know of life for armies of slaves and free blacks in the region. But more than that, they also served to tell the story of triumph against all the odds.

It was in essence the account of an African, redeemed by his discovery of true religion, who overcame every threat and danger which man could throw at him. Between 1775 and 1777 Equiano had avoided death, disease and maltreatment, and had, against the odds, returned to England reassured in his faith. He was happy to be back in England. It was a tale of Christian – and English – triumph. The hero, however, was not an Englishman but an African. And what sort of a home did England actually afford him?

Notes

1 Robert W. Malcolmson, *Popular Recreations in English Society, 1700–1850* (Cambridge, 1973); Richard Holt, *Sport and the British* (Oxford, 1989).

2 J. M. Golbey and A. W. Purdue, *The Civilization of the Crowd: Popular Culture in England, 1750–1900* (London, 1984).

3 *Interesting Narrative*, p. 200.

4 *Ibid.*, pp. 201–2.

5 W. Jeffrey Bolster, *Black Jacks: African American Seamen in the Age of Sail* (London, 1997).

6 *Interesting Narrative*, p. 202.

7 The details of plantation life and population in the last generation of British slavery can be approached in B. W. Higman, *Slave Populations of the British Caribbean, 1807–1834* (Baltimore, 1984).

8 *Interesting Narrative*, p. 203.

9 Equiano is so specific about these dates that it seems very likely that he kept a journal of his movements.

10 James Walvin, *Questioning Slavery* (London, 1996), pp. 146–7.

11 *Interesting Narrative*, p. 205.

12 Douglas B. Chambers, '"My own nation": Igbo Exiles in the Diaspora', *Slavery and Abolition*, vol. 18 no. 1 (1997).

13 *Interesting Narrative*, p. 206.

14 *Ibid.*, pp. 206–7.

15 *Ibid.*, p. 207.

16 *Ibid.*, p. 208.

17 James Axtell, *The European and the Indian: Essays in the Ethnohistory of Colonial North America* (New York, 1982), pp. 257–8.

18 *Interesting Narrative*, p. 209.

19 *Ibid.*, p. 210.

20 *Ibid.*

21 *Ibid.*, p. 211.

22 *Ibid.*, pp. 217–18.

23 Walvin, *op. cit.*, Ch. 5.

24 *Interesting Narrative*, p. 211.

25 *Ibid.*, p. 212.

26 *Ibid.*, pp. 213–14.

27 Narda Dobson, *A History of Belize* (London, 1973), p. 62; Higman, *op. cit.*, pp. 177–8.

28 *Interesting Narrative*, p. 214.

29 *Ibid.*, pp. 215–16.

30 *Ibid.*, p. 216.

31 *Ibid.*, p. 218. See also p. 294, n. 606.

32 *Ibid.*, p. 219.

10

LIFE IN ENGLAND

Equiano returned to England in the New Year of 1777 in the first full year of the war against the rebellious North American colonies. Though it was a distant conflict, it was to have profound consequences for the black community in England, and ultimately for Equiano himself. In the wake of that war, Equiano was to gain a public prominence, indeed notoriety, which he could never have predicted.

Looking back, from 1789, he remarked that, 'Since that period, my life has been more uniform.' The upheavals and alarm, the threatening incidents which had so characterized his life hitherto, faded into memory and he settled into a more tranquil way of life, based mainly in London. During his earlier stays in London (which were never very long) he had often found regular work hard to find, flitting from job to job before returning, time and again, to sea. But now, in 1777, the sea had lost its charms. He confessed that 'I became heartily disgusted with the seafaring life, and was determined not to return to it, at least for some time.' Equiano's main objection to maritime life, however, was not the danger, not the threats he periodically faced, but the economic troubles: 'I had suffered so many impositions in my commercial transactions in different parts of the world.'[1]

Equiano's 'commercial transactions' were, of course, that string of small-scale deals, the bartering and haggling, the buying cheap and selling dearer, which had been so prominent a feature of his life from the early days of his story. Equiano the freedman and trader found himself frustrated by the inherent problems of being black, trading in a world dominated by whites who often sought to gain unfair advantage and to cheat. Equiano had been regularly cheated in England, the West Indies and North America, on the high seas, and in Central America. Wherever he sought to profit, others sought to take advantage of him. Nor was this merely a matter of the normal give-and-take of trading life; the profit and loss of anyone in trade. Time and again, Equiano was cheated because he was black and because his opponents knew they could take advantage of a black person. The law, especially in the slave colonies, simply could not be rallied to the side of blacks (slave or free). No court was about to accept the word of an aggrieved black man against a white man. To do so would create the solvent of slavery itself.[2] Even when the law seemed sympathetic to a black cause – as English law had clearly become post-Somerset (see pp. 49–50) – practical problems often proved insuperable. A writ of habeas corpus had not sufficed to prevent poor John Annis being shipped back to St Kitts.

If a white person refused to pay, or refused to pay the agreed amount, the black person had little hope of satisfaction. They could, like Equiano, appeal to their opponent's better nature, invoking a host of issues: honesty, Christianity, decency. But on the whole, whites did not appreciate having their vices highlighted in this way, and few cared to have blacks tell them that their behaviour had fallen below acceptable levels. Of course, an aggrieved black could threaten physical retaliation, and might be able to rally enough friends and sympathizers to shake the money out of a reluctant customer. But physical threats were, in general, not a good idea. They were counter-productive and might easily bring still more trouble on the head of the black complainant, especially in the slave colonies where plantocratic violence was an unquestioned way of life. No sensible black would casually threaten whites in a slave society, or even at sea, in the teeth of the fearsome and often arbitrary violence they knew would inevitably follow.

By 1777 Equiano had had enough. After twenty years of trading and higgling, in whichever corners of British trade and settlement his travels had taken him, he had little to show for his efforts, save of course his personal freedom, and even that had been narrowly secured. Set against the enormous risks he had faced (and overcome), he must sometimes have felt that it had hardly been worth the effort.

From 1777 to 1784 Equiano worked in England as a servant. He had already been employed at that trade in his earlier sojourns in London, and even at sea much of his time had been spent as a steward. Domestic work, by then a well-established position for blacks in England, was reflected in a host of contemporary pictures, accounts and commentaries. Black domestics caught the eye. Often dressed in fashionable and eye-catching regalia, black servants provided social cachet for their employer, drawing attention to the latter's wealth and standing, forming a stark contrast to prevailing concepts of beauty and, in general, enhancing the employer's status. By the late eighteenth century, however, black servants were no longer the unusual object of attention they had once been. In part this was because they had become more commonplace and their employment was no longer a novelty. Some are well remembered: Francis Barber, servant to Dr Johnson; Dido Elizabeth Bell, servant (and distant family member) in the home of Lord Mansfield, the judge at the centre of the 1772 Somerset case; and of course Ignatius Sancho, man of letters and Westminster grocer. All three, like Equiano himself, were captured in portraiture, itself a sure indication of their standing within contemporary fashionable society. Why paint a portrait of an eighteenth-century domestic servant?[3]

The use of black servants in England was, of course, a social fad. There was no real practical or pressing reason to employ black servants, recruited (initially at least) from abroad. After all, there was no shortage of white servants. Indeed, Britain was awash with cheap labour, fresh from the countryside and willing to be trained up

PLATE 10. Bill Richmond, boxer. He and Tom Molineaux were the most important of a number of black boxers of the period.

Source: Hulton Deutsch Collection Limited.

in the varied tasks demanded of servants. Black servants, however, were more than a reflection of their employer's status. They were also a reflection of Britain's Atlantic empire and maritime power; people who had been cast ashore in Europe, like the human flotsam and jetsam of British military and commercial power in the Atlantic.

Like all fads, this one began to change. By the late eighteenth century, aristocratic tastes were changing. Some prominent families adopted Chinese servants; part of the emergent interest in *chinoiserie*. But the key to the persistence (or decline) of black domestic labour was the nature of British involvement with its slave colonies. As long as the ebb and flow of people continued between Europe, Africa and the enslaved Americas, there would be a movement, albeit a trickle, of Africans and their descendants back to Britain. Should the relationship between Britain and that Atlantic slave system change, so too would the migrations of black people to Britain.

When Equiano returned to England in 1777, he became part of a small, largely anonymous, community of blacks living in London, working, like so many others, as a domestic servant. Wherever he settled he took with him his fierce religiosity, and a determination to win others to his religion, and to his habits of worship and daily life. It was no easy matter. When working for Matthias Macnamara (formerly Governor of James Island and later Senegambia), Equiano asked other servants in the house to join him at family prayers, 'but this only excited their mockery'.[4] Was this simply a result of his intrusive religiosity – or was it a racial issue? Were they amused by the presumptions of a black Christian, urging them to observe the white man's faith, or was it mere social or religious indifference?

Though his fellow servants seemed indifferent, Equiano's employer noticed 'that I was of a religious turn'. Equiano told Macnamara that he was 'a protestant of the church of England, agreeable to the thirty-nine articles of that church'. Equiano confessed that he was happy to listen to whoever preached that doctrine. After further discussions, Macnamara put the idea into Equiano's head that he might even think of becoming a missionary in Africa. Initially, Equiano baulked at the idea. He had had enough hostile treatment when, on his last voyage, he had tried to convert the Mosquito Indian prince. He was worried, understandably, about returning to Africa, though his employer (who had been there more recently than Equiano) tried to reassure him. Macnamara, however, had not been enslaved and Equiano was alert to the problems. It was precarious enough, living as a free black in London or Kingston, without tempting fate by returning to West Africa, where Europeans were actively trawling for ever more slaves to ship into the Americas. Macnamara won Equiano over to the idea by flattering him with offers of ordination by the Bishop of London.

Thus, in March 1779, the two men wrote to Robert Lowth, the Bishop of London, hoping for ordination. Proclaiming that he had been a Christian since 1759, Equiano expressed a hope 'of returning to Africa as a missionary, if encouraged by your Lordship, in hopes of being able to prevail upon his countrymen to become Christians'.

He pointed to Portuguese and the Dutch successes in converting Africans by using educated blacks, the latter being 'more proper than European clergymen, unacquainted with the language and customs of the country'. Equiano claimed that his only reason for wanting the task was to reform his countrymen and to persuade them 'to embrace the Christian religion'. Macnamara gave the idea his full backing, testifying that he thought Equiano (though he used the name Gustavus Vassa) to be 'a moral good man'.[5] To strengthen his case, Equiano also enclosed a testimonial from Dr Wallace, who had also spent time on the Senegambian coast of West Africa.

The Bishop of London received Equiano personally, and treated him politely, but felt unable to ordain him, 'from some certain scruples of delicacy'. In addition, he added that 'the Bishops were not of opinion in sending a new missionary to Africa'.

In fact they had already dispatched one African, Philip Quaque, as a missionary to West Africa thirteen years earlier. Quaque, the son of a Cape Coast ruler, had been the first African ordained into the Anglican priesthood in 1765 and had set to work at Cape Coast Castle in 1766. Amazingly, he was to remain there for half a century, but throughout he faced a wall of local hostility, as well as indifference to his work from London, and could show only meagre results for a lifetime's toils.[6] The Anglican church was in no hurry to double their team of African missionaries by adding Equiano to the list. There was a host of good reasons not to convert West Africa, not least (and despite Quaque's remarkable durability) the high mortality rates on the African coast. Moreover, the Anglican church had not decided to embark on the conversion of slaves in the American colonies.[7]

Equiano's life as a domestic servant did not involve those routine excitements and alarms, the moments of danger and interest so commonplace in his earlier life. His mundane work passed unobserved. Even when he switched employers, from working with Macnamara to serving with an officer in the Dorset militia, life in military camp proved too uninteresting to discuss. Whereas Equiano had spelled out his earlier exotic experiences in small detail, sometimes describing events by the day, now, living in England, years slipped by with scarcely a mention. Understandably, an English readership was unlikely to find stories of life below stairs as interesting as life on board an ocean-going ship, or in the slave colonies. The curiosities Equiano described were less interesting the closer they came to home. It is also possible that Equiano was running out of narrative energy. There is a limit to how much detail a single author can include in his story. And who, in 1789, wanted to read about everyday life in England, especially when prefaced by the history of such dramatic events over the previous twenty years?

There was, to be sure, the occasional highlight: a tour of eight Welsh counties in 1783, which he visited 'from motives of curiosity', and his adventure down a Shropshire coal mine, which involved a narrow escape from serious injury, or worse, in a rock fall.[8] Quite clearly, Equiano was a man with resources and with contacts (which he was to put to good use when he wrote and promoted his autobiography). More than that, he was a man with a sharp intellectual curiosity. It was unusual – perhaps impossible – for most working men to head off to distant parts of the country, in the late eighteenth century, simply from 'motives of curiosity'. This curiosity was present in abundance throughout Equiano's account of his earlier travels, and his writing bubbles with detail and curiosities – eye-catching facts to titillate and entertain the reader, but which also speak to the author's enquiring spirit.

The Welsh and the Shropshire incidents, however, were exceptional events in a narrative which casually skips seven years of Equiano's life in England after his return from sea in 1777. We know very little about his life in the years between his return to London in 1777 and his decision, in the spring of 1784, to go back to sea. He was now about forty years old, had experienced the full range of life's perils at sea, and had survived more than enough by way of threats and dangers. So why return to that most perilous of professions? We can only speculate on what drove him back; boredom with life as a domestic, lack of money (the factor which had driven him back to sea before), a search for further adventures?

Whatever the reason, in the spring of 1784 'I thought of visiting old ocean again'. He signed on as steward on the *London*, captained by Martin Hopkins and bound for New York. Impressed by that buoyant and thriving city, Equiano stayed on with Hopkins, 'an agreeable man', for the next voyage, this time from London to Philadelphia. Equiano had visited Philadelphia before, describing it as 'this favourite old town', but what pleased him this time was his encounter with local Quakers. Philadelphia Quakers were active, 'freeing and easing the burthens of many of my oppressed African brethren'. Equiano's experience with Philadelphia's black community was to prove a turning point in his career.

Philadelphia was a thriving port, epicentre of the revolution which had driven the former colonies down the road to full independence, and was home to a growing black community, large numbers of whom were free. Of those, a substantial proportion found careers at sea. Perhaps a quarter of all sailors based in Philadelphia at this time were black.[9] More than that, Philadelphia was a magnet for blacks from across the eastern seaboard, and even further afield. A local abolition law had seen the gradual erosion of slavery in that city, and blacks naturally gravitated to the attractions of living in a free black community. By the time of Equiano's visit in 1785, only about 13 per cent of Philadelphia's black population were slaves. To add to its attractions, Philadelphia had developed distinct communities in the southern sections of the city where black churches and black schools had become 'vital centres of black community life', thus encouraging further black migration and settlement.[10]

Philadelphia's black churches were critical, for they formed the heart of social life, forging a direct link 'between the distant African past, the more proximate slave past, and the present and future as free persons'. Founded in the late eighteenth century Philadelphia's black churches have long been recognized as a landmark in the history of black America. More than that, they took the name 'African' – a term applied to a plethora of local black organizations (schools, mutual aid organizations and others) – in order to give themselves a particular identity and to distinguish themselves from white society.[11] In 1787, for example, two ex-slaves, Richard Allen and Absalom Jones, founded the 'Free African Society' in Philadelphia.[12] When, two years later, Equiano published his memoirs, he adopted the same tactic. He used an African name – despite the fact that he signed all his paperwork hitherto with the name Gustavus Vassa – and publicly referred to himself as 'the African'.

What Equiano witnessed in Philadelphia was the early flowering of a distinct and autonomous free black society, based around a strong family system, rooted in local black communities and sustained by a range of independent economic and labouring activities. This society was partly a function of the upheavals in American life which had been spawned by the successful break from Britain (1776–83),

PLATE II. Billy Waters, dancing fiddler. He was a well-known and popular entertainer
who busked outside the Adelphi Theatre in the Strand, London. Waters and his companion,
African Sal, were immortalized in Staffordshire pottery figures.

Source: Mansell/Time Inc/Katz.

partly a result of harsh rejection by local white society. It stood in sharp contrast to anything Equiano had seen elsewhere on his travels. Rapidly changing, it was utterly different from any of the slave societies Equiano had experienced in the Americas, and it was quite unlike that small black community which Equiano had been a part of in London for the past few years.[13] Black Philadelphia in the 1780s seems to have been an enlightening experience for Equiano, a man with a sharp social eye, sensitive to black injustice, and anxious to promote black interests.

In 1785 Equiano made contact with Philadelphia Quakers (the Society of Friends), themselves of course central to that city's history – and to the struggle against slavery. As early as 1750, the Quaker Anthony Benezet had estabished a night school for blacks in Philadelphia. Quakers had long formed a small (though generally ignored) opposition to black slavery in the Atlantic. Benezet was the best-known Quaker publicist against the slave trade, prompting Friends on both sides of the Atlantic to agitate against what he described (in 1773) as 'the grievous iniquity and great danger attendant on a further prosecution of the Slave Trade'. The end of the American war in 1783 enabled Quakers to renew their activities and focus attention on the need to end the slave trade.[14] At this precise moment, in a climate of mounting Quaker agitation in both Philadelphia and London against the Atlantic trade, Equiano made contact with American Quakers. What they showed him in Philadelphia was exciting:

> It rejoiced my heart when one of these friendly people took me to see a free-school they had erected for every denomination of black people, whose minds are cultivated here, and forwarded to virtue: and thus they are made useful members of the community.

Equiano took this as an example to the planters, using a biblical reference to make the point: 'Go ye, and do likewise'.[15]

Black education would elevate slaves and ex-slaves from the misery into which the slave system had pitched them. Equiano for his part needed no persuading of the benefits of learning. He had, after all, learned the hard way, taught by fellow sailors at sea, acquiring first a rudimentary, later a more sophisticated literacy and numeracy thanks to friends and employers. Throughout his life Equiano had struggled to improve himself through reading and learning. Though much of his recent personal effort had been directed towards biblical study, Equiano's book learning was clearly considerable (his autobiography is peppered with literary and scholarly references). He knew that his own status and well-being had been secured, in large part, by the benefits of education and of learning. Though he could have made his way in the world as a simple higgler and trader, making money from this or that economic activity, his life had been transformed by his command of English, and by his education. Indeed, his autobiography was itself testimony to this central fact. If he could improve himself in this way, how many more slaves might be similarly helped – if only they were given access to learning?

The Quaker connection was to prove vital. Equiano was clearly close to Quaker circles. Once invited to a Quaker wedding, he was struck – like many before and since – by the simplicity of the ceremony: 'This mode I highly recommend.'[16] On his return to London late in 1785, Equiano led a deputation of Africans to Quakers in London, thanking them for their anti-slavery efforts. It was early days, but already the Quakers had struck out against the slave trade. Indeed the initial, pioneering steps towards formal abolition had been taken by Quakers, and the early years of English abolition were dominated by Quakers. They were to remain a powerful influence throughout its progress until the final ending of British colonial slavery in 1834.[17] It was, then, no surprise that as early as 1785 Equiano and other Africans in London appreciated the importance of the Quakers.

It is also revealing that when Equiano approached the Quakers at their main London Meeting House in Gracechurch Street, he was not on his own, but in the company of other Africans. There had clearly been a meeting, or meetings, of Africans to draft a petition of thanks to the Quakers. How did the Africans keep in touch with each other, and what prompted them to choose Equiano as their leader and spokesman? Who organized the petition and why; why then, and why Equiano?

On 21 October 1785 a letter was handed over to the Quaker gathering 'by Gustavus Vassa and Seven others'.[18] It was prompted, claimed the Africans, 'By reading your book, entitled *A Caution to Great Britain and her Colonies, concerning the Calamitous State of the Enslaved Negroes.*' This, a tract written by Anthony Benezet, had been first published in Philadelphia and then, in 1784–5, by the London Quaker printer, James Philips, who had, since the American war, published a number of American tracts.[19] American Quakers had a stock of anti-slavery material, and British Quakers found it easiest to launch their own initial campaign on the back of North American abolitionist publications. Thus the first organized attack on slavery in London came courtesy of Quakers in Philadelphia.

The Africans' letter was a hymn of praise for Quakers' efforts on their behalf. We do not know who drafted it, but it has all the signs of Equiano's style and tone. Speaking as 'part of the poor, oppressed, needy, and much degraded negroes', they thanked the Quakers 'with our inmost love and warmest acknowledgments' in their efforts 'towards breaking the yoke of slavery'. This devout tone and the pious phrases smack of Equiano. God (the word was used three times in a short sentence) gazed down 'upon all his creatures, and always rewards every true act of virtue, and rewards the prayers of the oppressed'.

The Lord would, the Africans thought, reward the Quakers with 'blessings which it is not in our power to express or conceive'. This letter was clearly drafted by a devout Christian, in a style which parallels Equiano's own, with its regular and periodic insistence on God's blessings.

Not surprisingly, the Quakers received the Africans warmly 'and with a promise to exert themselves on behalf of the oppressed Africans'. Few at that meeting could have expected, within twenty years, that the movement which the Quakers effectively launched would bring an end to the Atlantic slave trade.

Throughout the mid-1780s, Equiano continued his working trips to North America. In March 1786 he was employed as steward on the American ship *Harmony*, captained by John Willett. It proved another difficult experience, for Willett 'began to play me the like tricks as others too often practise on free negroes in the West Indies'. We can only assume that Equiano was once more being cheated of his just rewards. But on this occasion he was helped by friends, 'who in some measure prevented him'. When Equiano returned to London from the USA in August 1786 he became involved in a scheme which utterly changed his life, transforming him into a public figure. He was pleased to discover that a government-sponsored plan was under discussion, 'to send the Africans from hence to their native quarter, and that some vessels were then engaged to carry them to Sierra Leona'.[20]

It was a complex, difficult – ultimately disastrous – scheme which had its roots in the recent story of London's black population. It seems inevitable that Equiano would, at some stage, become involved in the scheme. He was an African who had now become a familiar figure in London, he was known to influential Quakers, had met senior Anglican clerics and was a regular worshipper at prominent London churches.

The scheme to repatriate Africans, the Sierra Leone scheme, emerged as a solution to the growing problem of the black poor in London. There had been a noticeable increase in the number of poor blacks in England, but especially in London, in recent years. It was, in part, a continuation of the trickle of Africans and of New World blacks to England from the various corners of the Atlantic slave system. It was a movement of people which aroused conflicting passions (as indeed it did in France at much the same time).[21] Planters were especially vociferous, and often vicious, in their denunciation of black settlement in England (even though many had brought slaves with them). They viewed the removal of slaves from the Americas as a loss to the slave-owning regions, and they disliked what they saw of black life in London.

It is tempting to quote the unpleasant words of exiled planters, writing in England, about the risks and dangers of allowing a black society to thrive in England. They and their supporters fulminated against what they saw as an emergent black community. Prompted by particular incidents – by a law case for example – they speculated on the numbers of blacks in England (invariably alarming readers by exaggerations) and called on their readers to help bring an end to black migration and settlement.[22] It would be wrong to doubt the strength of their views if only because they formed the bedrock of a prototypical plantocratic racism which was widely diffused in English life in the late eighteenth century. If we need confirmation of the hostility which lay in wait for blacks in England, on a regular basis, we need only look back over the troubles Equiano faced throughout his life in London. Yet this hostility also needs to be weighed in the balance with a very different force; of daily friendship and succour, of social and humane equality, and of white support in times of trouble. Again, using the example of Equiano, he had as many friends and helpers, encountered as much goodwill and assistance, as he faced dangers and hostility.

The slave lobby, a federation of planters, shippers, financiers and others whose material well-being was intimately linked to the survival of the Atlantic slave system, disliked the development of a black society in England. It helped to spread the truth, the horror stories, throughout British society of what happened in the plantation colonies and on the slave ships. Blacks in London formed one branch in the Atlantic network for information, gossip and news from Africa, the slave ships and the slave colonies. They also served as a reminder of all that was wrong with the skewed world of colonial slavery. Black life in England offered an antidote to everything the planters held dear; it encouraged black freedom where they required slavery, it prompted black initiative, where they expected obedience and humility, it fostered familiarity (especially sexual) between black and white, where the planters demanded isolation and separation. Yet as much as the slave lobby might not approve of black society in England, it was bound to thrive and grow as long as the African diaspora itself continued. As long as large numbers of Africans continued to be ferried across the Atlantic to serve the economic and material interests of white settlers and metropolitan interests, some – if only a trickle – would inevitably arrive in London, the hub of the whole Atlantic system.

In the wake of the 1772 Mansfield judgment, the numbers of free blacks had seemed to increase. This was not so much a consequence of that legal decision, but rather a social custom. Enslaved blacks simply quit their posts, running away to secure a marginal but free existence on the streets of London. Their precise numbers remain uncertain, and even the most painstaking archival research leaves a wide margin of statistical error. There were probably between 5,000 and 10,000 blacks in London at the end of the eighteenth century, and that from an overall population of about 1,117,000 (in 1800–01).[23] It was, by any calculation, a small fraction of the overall total.

Yet this relatively small minority inspired some of the late eighteenth century's fiercest debates, prompted a bitter polemical warfare between West Indians and abolitionists (and other supporters of the blacks), and led to the costly government Sierra Leone scheme. The events leading to that scheme in 1786–7 cannot be explained solely – or even largely – in terms of the numbers of black people involved. It was, in effect, evidence of a much deeper set of conditions, and bore witness to a complexity of attitudes, of cultural values about black and white humanity which, though shaped in and around the core of Atlantic slavery, had taken on a domestic English vernacular. Atlantic slavery had, in effect, come home to roost.

Black slavery, and the free black communities which it inevitably spawned, were not designed for England. Yet they had clearly taken root there. As long as blacks remained few in number, and lived under the care of employers (as slaves or as free workers), they prompted no serious concern. Black domestics, in prosperous homes, had long adorned English life, forming a social curiosity which prompted only favourable remarks. Black independence, however, was an entirely different matter. And it was an independence which seemed to increase in the late years of the century. Equiano was of course a personification of this very process, and it was fitting that he should be recruited to discuss the problems of black life in London, especially the problems of the black poor, when he returned from sea in 1786.

London's black population had increased sharply in the early 1780s with the return of refugee loyalists, and the flight to England of black servants, soldiers and sailors following the British defeat in North America in 1783. The British had offered freedom to slaves who fought for them against the Americans. In any case, how many blacks, after the British defeat, would want to return to their former American homes when that would necessarily involve a return to slavery? Not surprisingly, then, London's black poor were augmented by people who had fled from North America. After 1783, contemporaries *assumed* that 'the black poor' were refugees from the American conflict; 'Loyalists from America', 'loyal Blacks' were among the phrases used to describe them.

Thus it was, by the mid-1780s, that the black community had come to be seen as a 'problem'. Indeed the phrase 'the black poor' began to recur in discussions about the nature of London life. Poverty had, of course, been a persistent theme in the history of London since time out of mind. But this particular brand of poverty in the 1780s seemed new. It was black, and was therefore alien. And because it was alien it could be dealt with – solved – by methods inapplicable to the traditional poor. There had been a long tradition of returning the poor to their home parish (a legacy of the Elizabethan Poor Law). But the 'black poor' posed problems of an entirely different order. Where could they be returned to? To Virginia or South Carolina (i.e. back to slavery, when they had been promised freedom), or to Africa (still cursed by the marauding bands of coastal slave traders and their interior suppliers)? It was clear, from the initial discussions about how to handle the black poor, that all the alternatives under serious discussion involved some form of repatriation. Equiano thought that the decision to encourage this repatriation, 'redounded to the honour of all concerned in its promotion, and filled me with prayers and much rejoicing'.[24]

Whichever scheme was to be adopted, it would clearly need the help and co-operation of a black leader who had the respect of fellow blacks in London. Who better than Equiano?

Notes

1 *Interesting Narrative*, p. 220.
2 For a broader discussion of the relationship between slavery and law, see Orlando Patterson, *Slavery and Social Death* (Cambridge, MA, 1982), pp. 192–3.
3 Gretchen Gerzina, *Black England: Life before Emancipation* (London, 1995), Ch. 2.
4 *Interesting Narrative*, p. 220.
5 *Ibid.*, pp. 221–2.
6 Paul Edwards and David Dabydeen (eds), *Black Writers in Britain, 1760–1890* (Edinburgh, 1991), pp. 101–16; Peter Fryer, *Staying Power* (London, 1984), pp. 426–7.
7 See Mary Turner, *Slaves and Missionaries* (Urbana, 1982).
8 *Interesting Narrative*, p. 223.
9 Gary B. Nash, 'Forging Freedom. The Emancipation Experience in the Northern Seaport Cities, 1775–1820', in I. Berlin and R. Hoffman (eds), *Freedom in the Age of the American Revolution* (Charlottesville, NC, 1983), p. 6, n. 4.
10 *Ibid.*, pp. 40–3.
11 *Ibid.*, p. 45.
12 Peter Kolchin, *American Slavery* (London, 1995), p. 84.
13 For the latest estimates of the size of London's black population, see Norma Myers, *Reconstructing the Black Past: Blacks in Britain, 1780–1830* (London, 1996).
14 Judith Jennings, *The Business of Abolishing the British Slave Trade, 1783–1807* (London, 1997), Chs 1–2.
15 *Interesting Narrative*, p. 224.
16 *Ibid.*, pp. 225–6.
17 I have greatly benefited from discussions with Mark Jones on the issue of anti-slavery and the Quakers.
18 John Kemp, *Commonplace Book, 1786*, MX Box X3/2, fols 152–4. Friends' Meeting House, Euston Road, London. Full letter reprinted in *Interesting Narrative*, p. 225.
19 Jennings, *op. cit.*, pp. 8–9.
20 *Interesting Narrative*, p. 226.
21 Sue Peabody, *'There Are No Slaves in France': The Political Culture of Race and Slavery in the Ancien Régime* (Oxford, 1996).
22 Peter Fryer, *Staying Power* (London, 1984), Ch. 7.
23 Norma Myers, *Reconstructing the Black Past* (London, 1996), pp. 34–5; B. R. Mitchell, *European Historical Statistics, 1750–1970* (London, 1978), p. 13.
24 *Interesting Narrative*, p. 226.

PART FOUR

PUBLIC
FIGURE

= 11 =

BACK TO AFRICA

The effort to help London's black poor in 1787–8 owed its inspiration to the Quakers. Though few in number (their total numbers never rose above about 60,000), the Quakers had come to exercise an influence in British life out of all proportion to their numbers. Moreover, their power rested on some remarkable family fortunes, as Quaker business and family dynasties had thrived on the application, self-help, networks and prudent housekeeping, which had been their hallmark since their seventeenth-century origins.[1] In the process, Quakers had also developed a refined social conscience and a commitment to doing good works, which was inspired, in the first instance, by their own sufferings and persecutions in the previous century. They had been among the first to denounce the slave trade despite the economic conflict for certain Quaker businesses.

Few were more keenly anti-slavery than Dr John Fothergill, doctor and scientist, friend of Benjamin Franklin, keen botanist and horticulturist (who ran the best experimental garden in England). Fothergill had come to the conclusion that one sure way of undermining the slave trade was to establish a free colony somewhere in West Africa. There the fruits of free labour would, in time, undermine slave labour by producing tropical staples more cheaply. It was, in essence, an early and simple form of the free trade argument more memorably proposed in 1776 by Adam Smith and, much later, by a host of *laissez-faire* abolitionists in Britain. Along with other contemporary men of science, including Sir Joseph Banks, Fothergill had supported the experimental adventures of the maverick Henry Smeathman to West Africa. Smeathman spent four years in and around Sierra Leone, returning with enthusiastic (and exaggerated) claims for the long-term benefits and potential of the region, for both trade and colonial settlement.

Smeathman returned to Europe (via the West Indies), full of elaborate schemes for scientific experiments and for agricultural settlements. He proposed the creation of commercial settlements in West Africa – the kind which might offer free black labour a chance to challenge the dominance of the slave trade. The Quakers, to whom he proposed these ideas (though he also talked about them to anyone who would listen) were sceptical about some of the practicalities, nor did they like the necessary reliance on arms to secure the settlements. His keenest audience was Granville Sharp, evangelical, member of the Clapham Sect, saviour of many distressed blacks in London, and long-time opponent of the slave trade. Sharp, the first effective campaigner to help poor blacks in London, was naturally interested in any such schemes. He was also, as we have seen, an acquaintance of Equiano.

By the mid-1780s few doubted that large numbers of London's recently arrived blacks were destitute. They were poor because they had no work, and their prospects of finding work were slim. It was also impossible to give them traditional charity (returning them to their home parish). They had, in the words of Thomas Clarkson, later to be the most influential campaigner against the slave trade, 'no parish which they could call their own'.[2] They were not alone in the 1780s, of course. Poverty among 'Lascar' sailors and among the Spitalfield weavers was also appalling. But most observers agreed that the black poor formed a special and a pressing case. Thus early in 1786 a 'Committee for the Relief of the Black Poor' was formed, its original eighteen members drawn from the city's more prosperous businessmen and financiers, and most of them linked by their opposition to the slave trade. The committee was led by Jonas Hanway, an Anglican philanthropist whose efforts for the dispossessed ranged far and wide

The committee's public appeal for financial help received a steady flow of money, prompted in part by the awareness that many of the black poor had opted for the British side in the American war. In the words of a correspondent to *The Public Advertiser*, 'the greater part of them, have served Britain, have fought under her colours'.[3] Needless to say, Quakers were among the more prominent (and generous) contributors.[4] The committee also opened a 'sickhouse' in Warren Street, and dispensed money, clothing and food from public houses in Mile End and Marylebone. As word of the scheme spread, more and more black supplicants turned up for assistance. Requests for help quickly outstripped resources. Many wanted work, asking to be sent to sea or to be shipped abroad if work could be guaranteed. Gradually the idea evolved both among the black poor themselves and within the committee, that settlement abroad might offer a suitable solution. The task of relieving the black poor had become overwhelming. By April 1786 some 460 people had been given relief, funds were drying up, and plans for migration were so daunting they could only be effectively handled by government.

But *where* could the black poor be resettled? Plans were discussed to relocate in Nova Scotia and in the Bahamas. We need to remember that this issue was just one of a number of social problems which generated ideas of transportation. There was a wider debate about transportation (and penal colonies), culminating in the best-known example of all: the First Fleet to Botany Bay in 1787.[5] At this point, Henry Smeathman's proposal for a black settlement in Sierra Leone resurfaced, with Smeathman dangling before the committee and the subsequent government officers a seductive image of fertile land, benign climate and economic potential for all involved. There was no mention of ill-health – or of the critical fact (critical at least in the eyes of the blacks they sought to attract) that Sierra Leone was the

PLATE 12.
'Foot Pad's – or much ado about nothing'; cartoon, 1795. Anxiety about London's poor black community motivated the Sierra Leone scheme.

Source: Courtesy of the Print Collection, Lewis Walpole Library, Yale University.

centre of a thriving slave trade. Smeathman won over both philanthropists and government ministers. By early summer 1786, the government began to organize an official, state-funded settlement of volunteers from among the black poor, 'back to Africa'. They were to be transported in Royal Naval ships, clothed, housed, equipped and provided with all the necessary means for settlement, all at British government expense. The black settlers were expected to be self-sufficient after three months.

The scheme, however, needed more than money and practical assistance. It needed, initially, the confidence and the support of the potential settlers. Men were chosen – black 'corporals' – who would be in charge of small groups of settlers. Of the eight men chosen to be corporals, four had been born in North America, two in Africa, one in Barbados and one in Bengal. Each rallied a group of 24 other potential black settlers. By July 1786 the corporals claimed that they spoke for about 400 people.[6] But the turning point in the scheme was the decision that relief to the black poor would henceforth be paid *only* to those blacks who signed a contract agreeing to settle in Sierra Leone. Only 130 took the decision to sign, a sure indication of the widespread doubts about the scheme among London's blacks.

Among the men who formed the committee to relieve the black poor, the most powerful influence was a Christian determination to see the establishment of a Christian beachhead on the African coast. Henry Smeathman on the other hand was convinced that the Sierra Leone scheme was commercially viable. By the summer of 1786 the blacks themselves were clear that they would settle *only* in Sierra Leone. All the other potential destinations discussed – the Bahamas, various points in Canada – were unpopular and unattractive. Smeathman had his way (though by now he was dead) when in July 1787 the committee and the government opted to send the black settlers to Sierra Leone.

The first decision was to find a replacement for Smeathman as leader of the venture. In the event, the decision to appoint Joseph Irwin, who had been closely associated with Smeathman, was to prove critical and was to have repercussions on Equiano's future career. In August 1787 the Treasury and the Navy began preparations in earnest, hoping to dispatch the settlers within four months. The *Atlantic* and the *Belisarius* were positioned at Gravesend to await their passengers. Later, a third ship was added. Vital supplies and skilled personnel were recruited for the settlement's practical needs. Inevitably, delays occurred; the first black settlers did not board until late November (a month behind schedule).[7] There were far fewer volunteers than expected (certainly fewer than the numbers already receiving relief from the Committee). To persuade more to join, city authorities ordered pressure to be put on blacks begging on the streets (to the approval of some in the press).[8] But why did so many of the black poor show such reluctance to enlist for the scheme?

Only a small number had been attracted to the plan in the first place. Sierra Leone was not 'home' in any sense of the word. The Africans had already had more than their fair share of horrifying oceanic travels, especially on the slave ships. And it was widely known that slavery still thrived on the West African coast. Could anyone really guarantee their future safety there? Many may also have suspected *any* maritime travel organized by whites; their previous encounters with similar voyages had been miserable beyond words. In any case, and despite its practical miseries, London provided security of a kind: a home, a black community and access to philanthropy (if not always to work). Discussions were openly in train about other possible destinations for the black poor who, in their turn, made it clear that 'no place whatsoever would be so agreeable to them as Sierra Leona'.[9]

Rumour also began to spread that they were to be sent, not to Sierra Leone, but to Botany Bay. The links between the two schemes were closer than we might imagine. The government organized them in harness. Clothes from one expedition were passed to the other. There were black transportees – black convicts – on the ships heading for Australia. And it was intended that the two convoys would rendezvous with their naval escorts side by side at Spithead. The fact that two major overseas expeditions were being equipped and dispatched at precisely the same time inevitably created confusion, not least in the minds of many of the black poor.

The press also played its role in unsettling London's blacks. Newspapers discussed the similarities between the two expeditions. Reports about one of the expeditions were invariably tagged onto comments about the other. Readers would naturally assume some connection, however remote. And black readers would certainly have made the connection. We do not know how many blacks were literate, but among those who were, the news in the newspapers was not encouraging. From the first therefore the scheme had its black critics. Most of them were evident in the refusal to volunteer. Others, more prominent, complained in print. Ottobah Cugoano (John Stewart), an African associate of Equiano's, and like him a literate ex-slave, published his own criticisms in 1787. The scheme had, he claimed, 'neither altogether met with the credulous approbation of the Africans here, nor yet been sought after with any prudent and right plan by the promoters of it'. It was not planned or thought through carefully. No efforts were made to discuss the scheme with people in the region to be settled. And the whole matter was far too rushed. But the critical factor was that many of London's blacks were Africans, enslaved by Europeans, by 'barbarous robbers and pirates, and like sheep to the market, have been sold into captivity and slavery'. They were, quite simply, fearful of returning to Africa and 'afraid of being ensnared again'. They knew that European traders 'have a prejudice against Black People, [and] that they use them more like asses than men, so that a Black man is scarcely ever safe among them'.[10]

There was talk in the press of banning all forms of black organization and political expression and even following the French example, of trying to ban the entry to Britain of all black people.[11] For those already on the boats, waiting week after week, conditions began to deteriorate. They were short of supplies, were inadequately clothed as the autumn turned to winter, and generally short of essentials. It was at this point that Equiano entered the scheme.

Equiano had been in Philadelphia and at sea when the Sierra Leone scheme had been in the making. When he returned, in August 1786, he was pleased to learn of the initial schemes to help the black poor. It was he said a scheme which 'filled me with prayers and much rejoicing'. Equiano was known by a number of the men serving on the Committee for the Black Poor 'and as soon as they heard of my arrival, they sent for me to the committee'.[12] This was a revealing turn of events. Some of the best-placed men in the city – prosperous businessmen, devout

Quakers, even men from the West Indian interests[13] – assumed that Equiano could help them. He was of course *the* obvious African to turn to. He had moved on the edges of polite – and certainly devout – London society, was familiar with a number of prominent contemporaries, and was well known for his devout style and intentions. He had, after all, only recently been recommended to the Bishop of London for ordination as a missionary to West Africa.

When Equiano presented himself to the Committee they 'seemed to think me qualified to superintend part of the undertaking, [and] they asked me to go with the black poor to Africa'. Like Cugoano, Equiano pointed out the obvious problems (it is impossible to imagine that the two Africans did not discuss the scheme at some point). There were, said Equiano, several objections to joining the expedition: 'and particularly I expressed some difficulties on account of the slave-dealers, as I would certainly oppose their traffic in the human species by every means in my power.'

These were fundamental and major issues. Yet Equiano records that the Committee overruled his objections and 'prevailed on me to consent to go'. They recommended him to the Royal Navy Commissioners 'as a proper person to act as commissary for government in the intended expedition'. Appointed officially in November 1786, Equiano received his formal written instructions from the Navy Office on 16 January 1787, taking the title, 'Commissary of Provisions and Stores for the Black Poor to Sierra Leone'.[14]

Even more telling, Equiano was to be charged with offering the local ruler in Sierra Leone the 'present' (a gift) in return for the land to be used by the settlers. It was an extraordinary role and rank for an African to be offered in 1786. The position was offered by the Navy Board, whose head, Sir Charles Middleton, was a prominent evangelical.[15] Equiano was clearly a beneficiary of the early abolitionist sentiment present in high circles in London. Equiano was known to be devout, was keen to proselytize in Africa, wished to see an end to slavery and had good contacts both with other blacks in London and with prominent men in and around the capital. He was to be the only African involved in an official capacity in the scheme. His appointment was very soon regretted.

The scheme clearly needed a black leader or spokesman, one who could command trust and respect from the body of poor emigrants. In fact Equiano's terms of employment were quite specific. He was put in charge of the provisions for the black poor on the voyage and, after they had landed in Sierra Leone, the clothing, tools 'and all other articles provided at government's expense'. He was given a list of people for whom the supplies were intended, and was ordered not to allow any white people to join in the venture. However, since those supplies were ordered for more settlers than had, in the event, volunteered to travel, there ought in theory to have been a great deal of material left over. Equiano was therefore expected to dispose of this surplus 'to the best advantage you can for the benefit of the government, keeping and rendering to us a faithful account of what you do therein'.[16]

Government officials clearly knew that Equiano was a capable and practical man. They entrusted him with large amounts of stock (much as Robert King had done when Equiano had worked as a slave in Montserrat). They knew he was an efficient stock-keeper, able to write and to do basic arithmetical accounting. Unlike

PLATE 13. Joseph Johnson, sailor-beggar; etching, 1815. Johnson was a merchant seaman whose injuries and resulting poverty meant that he became a 'Regular Chaunter' singing and begging for a living on the streets of London.

Source: Guildhall Library, Corporation of London.

those critics who subsequently came to doubt Equiano's literate and numerate abilities, government officials – ever alert to the interests of the public purse – had no qualms about granting him considerable power over men and material in 1786–7. Their confidence, however, rested on more than Equiano's commercial or business skills. He was a man whose probity they never doubted. But if government officers thought that they had acquired in Equiano a compliant agent, they were quickly disabused. They had, in effect, chosen a man who saw his task as not merely to defend government interests, but also to safeguard the well-being and interests of the black settlers. He set out to defend the interests of what he called his 'countrymen'. Looking back, this seems scarcely surprising. But it was to be a volatile force in the crowded and increasingly squalid, poverty-stricken decks of the vessels preparing to ship the black poor back to Africa.

Life on board the emigrant vessels had quickly descended into destitution. There was a shortage of berths, clothing and other supplies were scarce, and even the water began to run out. Whatever discipline existed among the settlers began to disintegrate. There were worries about 'the disposition of the Blacks and their want of discipline' and two of the vessels were moved to Blackwall to ease the problems.[17] Worries began to surface about the physical control over the emigrants, though the ships' captains reassured the Navy Office that the ships' arms 'are perfectly safe and secure'. To make matters worse, sickness had broken out in the last weeks of the year. Orders were issued that new clothes were to be distributed, 'to each of the Blacks and that their old ones to be thrown overboard to prevent infection'.[18] Ships' officers complained that the blacks on board were indisciplined, in particular highlighting 'their irregular behaviour in burning Fires and Candles all night and wasting the Water'. The naval commanders wanted to depart immediately.[19]

From December 1786 to 24 March 1787 Equiano was at the centre of the unfolding misery on board the emigrant ships. Gradually his role shifted; from government agent, to black spokesman and, in the eyes of white officials, black agitator. To the black poor he was their defender, to outsiders he was a troublemaker. In the words of Captain Thompson (of HMS *Nautilus*), Equiano was 'turbulent, and discontented, taking every means to actuate the minds of the Blacks to discord'.[20]

Equiano may have facilitated and expressed black complaints. He certainly did not cause them.

One major cause of friction and complaint was the corruption of Joseph Irwin, appointed as Smeathman's replacement to lead the expedition, a man with no experience of West Africa and none of leadership. From their first encounter, Equiano began to suspect Irwin's management of the expedition. Theirs proved to be a stormy, unhappy relationship which disintegrated week by week, and culminated in Equiano's dismissal amidst accusations of trouble-making in March 1787. From the very first, Equiano suspected Irwin of misappropriation and of not passing on supplies to the settlers. He told the captain of the *Nautilus* about these fears, and they were passed on to the Navy Office and thence to the Treasury:

from the beginning [Equiano] expressed his Suspicions of Mr Irwin's intentions in supplying Tea Sugar and other Necessaries allowed for the use of the women and children. . .[21]

Later, when he wrote his version of this unhappy episode, Equiano spoke of 'the flagrant abuses committed by the agent'. Though he tried to have them remedied, it was all to no avail. Equiano cited chapter and verse of his complaints; clothing ordered and paid for by the government, but nothing to show for the expenditure; bedding and other essentials, again paid for, but nowhere to be found. The people who paid the price for these problems were of course the black poor. Equiano appealed, in writing, to Captain Thompson of the *Nautilus* for proof of his assertions, quite unaware that Thompson had written a damning report on him to the Navy Board.

Thompson was clearly in some despair about the state of affairs between Equiano and Irwin, as the vessels waited in the Thames and then, in the New Year, headed out on the first leg to Plymouth. He was convinced that there was no sign from Irwin 'which might indicate that he had the welfare of the people at heart'. Whatever the cause of the dispute between the two men, Thompson felt that Equiano needed to be curbed: 'unless some means are taken to quell his spirit of sedition, it will be fatal to the peace of the settlement'.

This 'spirit of sedition' seems to have been a loud and persistent complaint about the way blacks were treated. To campaign on shore was one thing, but to agitate on board a Royal Naval ship, in the late eighteenth century, was an altogether different matter.[22] But this was no ordinary naval expedition, and the passengers no ordinary complement. Moreover, in Equiano the expedition had the only African aboard in a position of authority. He was clearly a critical conduit for the flow of ideas and information, back and forth, between the wretched passengers, the ship's officers and the expedition's backers, thence to and from the Admiralty.

Moreover this was no normal convoy. It was not like the Botany Bay expedition, which consisted of convicted criminals, travelling under a severe disciplinary regime. The Sierra Leone emigrants were not so easily cowed. After all, they were people who, having once been enslaved, were conscious of their status as free people, however poor they might be. Indeed, throughout this whole episode the emigrants were at pains to insist on their rights as free people. They were not about to be moved around the globe against their will, or treated in ways which infringed their best interests. They were free people destined for what they had been assured would be the 'Province of Freedom'. Yet for months they found themselves idling in the Thames, in physical circumstances at least as miserable as they had endured on the streets of London. Those conditions worsened when, on 23 February 1787, they slipped their moorings in the Thames.

Severe storms battered the fleet as soon as it reached open sea. One ship lost its foremast, the *Nautilus* was damaged and stores were swept overboard; two of the ships were ordered to put in at Plymouth while the *Nautilus* made for Torbay, 'the ship labouring very hard, and waist full of water'. The fleet was not repaired and ready for departure from Plymouth until mid-March.[23] By then, Captain Thompson – and others – had had more than enough of Equiano. Complaints from prominent blacks about conditions on the ships (and about Irwin) had already surfaced in the London press. It was clear enough that the simmering trouble between Equiano and Irwin had already affected relations between other people on the ships.

From Plymouth, Equiano took the extraordinary step of writing to his African friend, Ottobah Cugoano, attacking Irwin (and others) and publishing his case in *The Public Advertiser*. It was a bitter, withering attack, quite unlike anything we find in any other piece written by Equiano. He claimed that the leading white men in the expedition, led by Irwin, 'mean to serve (or use) the blacks the same as they do in the West Indies'. Equiano denied the accusations which he knew were already circulating in official circles that 'I use the white people with arrogance and the blacks with civility, and stir them up to mutiny'. This was, he argued, 'not true, for I am the greatest peace-maker that goes out'. What outraged Equiano was that numbers of the poor blacks had *already* died because of the shortages brought about, he claimed, by the corruption on board.[24] It was true that fifty people had died even before the main voyage had started. The fact that the vessels were largely resupplied while in Plymouth suggests there was more to Equiano's case than the organizers were prepared to admit.[25]

Captain Thompson was in an unenviable position. He had ranks of discontented and miserable black passengers. Equiano was in open and public hostility to Irwin (who was technically in charge of the settlers) and Irwin himself was threatening to quit and return to London. Following discussion between four government departments, Equiano was dismissed on 24 March. The evidence, it has to be said, is confusing. The Navy Board, for example, felt that in all his dealings with them, Equiano 'has acted with great propriety and been very regular in his information'.[26] Perhaps Equiano had been given an impossible task; an African official, with a great deal of responsibility, in a scheme which would inevitably generate friction and discord between poor black emigrants (who were already uncertain and insecure about their fate) and the white organizers and naval officials in charge. Who was Equiano expected to side with?

Equiano was deeply angered by the events unfolding around him. He was charged with the material well-being of large numbers of blacks, in conditions which, as time passed, rapidly deteriorated. Living on board ships for months at a time, in an English autumn and winter, would have been grim enough. But without many of life's basic necessities, conditions became intolerable. It must have been all too familiar to any African who had endured the even starker privations of their first Atlantic crossing. The ingredients seemed much the same. Ships filled with Africans, manned by Europeans, heading for a destination the blacks knew nothing about. But more than that, Equiano had learned by bitter experience the trickery and deception which whites played on black victims. He had spent much of his adult life avoiding the traps whites set for him; cheating him of money, of goods, threatening him with slavery, physically assaulting him. Life was a constant struggle; a permanent vigil against white threats and violations.

Now, in the first months of 1787, Equiano found himself with responsibility, but with little power, obliged to watch unnecessary sufferings of blacks around him. It seemed to him a reprise, on a major scale, of the troubles which had plagued his own life as a free man. Now, however, people were dying on a regular basis. How many succumbed because of normal circumstances, and how many had their end hastened by material deprivations, we cannot tell. Whatever the cause, Equiano was in no doubt that the expedition was riddled with wrong-doing and corruption. His dismissal was perhaps inevitable. He had become a thorn in the organizers' side; a permanent, nagging reminder that something was wrong and that someone was responsible for those shortcomings.

This constant criticism from the only African in authority raised, in a particular form, the awkward problem of internal discipline and control. Who precisely was in charge? And what sort of discipline could be exercised over a collection of voluntary emigrants? Captain Thompson looked anxiously ahead and wondered what course events would take once the ships arrived at Sierra Leone. As the convoy pitched its troubled course along the south coast of England it was, clearly, a worrying time for everyone, but for none so much as for the black poor themselves. Most of them had been uprooted before; Africans first from their homelands, then from the Americas, and American-born from their birthplace, after the recent war. They had found a temporary and precarious home in London. That, too, was abandoned as they headed, in miserable conditions, for an uncertain fate in Africa. Moreover, at each critical juncture in their lives, the key players deciding their fate had been white. Sold into and out of slavery by whites, organized for emigration by whites, they were, once again corralled and organized on the emigrant ships by whites. The one single exception was in the person of Olaudah Equiano.

He was one of them. An African, conscious of their sufferings and the dangers they faced, alert to insults and threats alike, a man hardened by a lifetime's miseries but sensitive to their interests. How could he remain silent and idle in the teeth of what unfolded around him, irrespective of who was responsible? Equiano had never hesitated to speak out before, in his everyday life. Now, in the early months of 1787, he had a great deal to complain about. But his complaints, however real, however justified, were corrosive of the precarious stability and discipline on the emigrant ships. It was inevitable that Equiano would speak out about the problems facing the black emigrants; and it was no less inevitable that he would be dismissed from his post. Looking back, he felt the problem had been personal. But there was, throughout, an undercurrent of racial tension which ultimately served to undermine Equiano's position. It was a racial dimension which surfaced in the press in the immediate aftermath of Equiano's dismissal.

As the ships lingered for repairs in Plymouth, local magistrates became concerned about blacks wandering around that city's streets, fearing that some would be left behind. The naval commander was therefore ordered to detain them on board. Finally, on 9 April 1787 the convoy left for Africa, with 350 black passengers and 59 white wives. A month later, they landed in Sierra Leone (by which time a further 35 people had died). Whatever troubles the settlers had faced so far – in the Americas, in London, on board ship – paled into insignificance compared to the traumas of life as settlers in Africa. After four years, only 60 of the initial 374 settlers remained alive. It was a disaster made worse by the fact that it had been predicted by its black critics from its inception. In the words of Cugoano, the blacks had been 'hurried away at all events, come of them after what would'.[27]

Their fate did not surprise Equiano. He, more than anyone left behind in England, knew precisely the condition of the settlers:

Thus provided, they proceeded on their voyage: and at last, worn out by treatment, perhaps, not the most mild, and wasted by sickness, brought on by want of

medicine, clothes, bedding, &c. they reached Sierra Leona just at the commence-
ment of the rains.

Equiano was bitter about his dismissal. He felt it unjustified, and took the terrible
fate of the settlers as proof of everything he had claimed about the scheme's
organization. The cost, however, had been born by the hapless settlers; poor,
innocent people, already bounced from one corner of the British Atlantic empire
to another, and now, back in Africa, consigned to a miserable fate. Both Equiano
and Cugoano went out of their way to say 'told-you-so' in print, though both
continued to show an interest in the Sierra Leone settlement (which was revitalized,
after 1792, by the relocation of more than 1, 100 black settlers from Nova Scotia).
Equiano thought that, however troubled its progress and outcome, the Sierra
Leone scheme 'was humane and politic in its design'.[28]

Debate about Equiano's dismissal flitted in and out of the press from March
to July 1787. *The Public Advertiser* in particular gave plenty of space to criticisms
of him. Such coverage clearly stung him. Keenly aware of his status as an upright
man born into high African status and of unimpeachable integrity, he felt that
public criticism, much of it unjust, inflicted damage on his reputation. One
correspondent urged readers to ignore Equiano's side of the story ('the improbable
tales propagated concerning the Blacks'), not least because 'the cloven hoof of the
author of those reports is perfectly manifest'.[29]

What was this devout African to make of such a gross reference to his devilish,
satanic work? Clearly meant to wound, this remark struck home, not only because
Equiano felt that its substance was wrong, but because it was couched in such
offensive and racially motivated terms. There were powerful cultural associations
between contemporary images of the devil and blackness. To accuse a man of
having cloven hooves was to speak of his devilishness. And few readers would be
unaware that the devil was black.[30]

The same newspaper continued to be hurl insults at Equiano. A few days later
the paper accused him of lying about events on the ships, showing 'him to be
capable of advancing falsehoods as deeply black as his jetty face'. The whole tone
of this attack was racial:

> Let us hear no more of those *black* reports which have been so industriously
> propagated: for if they are continued, it is rather more than probable that most of the
> *dark* transactions of a *Black* will be brought to *light*.[31]

It was, obviously, a deeply offensive racial attack, playing on the accepted English
cultural implications of lightness and blackness, with their deeper meanings of
truth and untruth, of beauty and ugliness, of good and evil. It could only have
been hurtful to Equiano, as it was intended to be. He never sought to play down
his blackness. Indeed, he flaunted his African origins with pride. But he also
boasted those personal qualities – of refinement, piety, industry and sensibility –
which he felt he had acquired as a Christian. And he was, from first to last, an
honest man of integrity. To be accused of lying, to be libelled in the press as a
devilish deceiver and mischief-maker, clearly depressed him. He was unhappy
that a number of prominent men seemed to be behind the campaign against him

in the press and could not understand why they should 'descend to a petty contest with an obscure African'.[32] By then, however, Equiano was anything but obscure.

Equiano was at a loss to understand why he had been dismissed. He took a narrow view of his role, judging himself simply on the conduct of the tasks given to him by the Navy Board. When he petitioned the Treasury about his dismissal he claimed that he had 'acted with the most perfect fidelity and the greatest assiduity in discharging the trust reposed in him'. He assumed that his 'conduct has been grossly mispresented to your Lordships'. In addition to the loss of public face, which Equiano felt acutely, he complained that he was badly out of pocket, having 'sunk a considerable part of his little property in fitting himself out, and in other expences arising out of his situation'. He typically – but perfectly properly – attached a claim for expenses of £32. 4s, plus his loss of wages. A few months later, he was paid £50. Equiano concluded his account of this unhappy episode with a typical financial flourish. 'Certainly the sum is more than a free negro would have had in the western colonies!!!'[33]

By the early summer of 1787 Equiano's involvement with the Sierra Leone scheme was finally over. He may have been given fair recompense. But, more important perhaps, the past twelve months had seen him raised from 'an obscure African' to a man in the public eye. He was better known than ever in governing circles and among men of influence in London (some of whom were sympathetic to abolition). Equiano remained on friendly terms with some of the men who had been behind the Sierra Leone scheme. And a number of those same men had begun to stir themselves in the early campaign against the Atlantic slave trade. Equiano was an accepted example of what the ending of slavery could achieve. One abolitionist even suggested that Equiano should be positioned, with a publication against the slave trade, to greet every MP arriving at Parliament.[34] For all the disappointments, set-backs – and racial insults – of the past year, Equiano was now in a position of some influence, better placed than ever before to denounce the Atlantic slave system. Who better to speak of the horrors of enslavement, of the Atlantic crossing and New World slavery? And who better to tell the story of what could be achieved when freedom was bestowed? Equiano was *the* obvious African to speak for abolition.

Notes

1 James Walvin, *Quakers: Money and Morals* (London, 1997).
2 Quoted in Stephen J. Braidwood, *Black Poor and White Philanthropists* (Liverpool, 1994), p. 32.
3 *Ibid.*, p. 68.
4 The Committee papers, the subscriptions, and the moneys dispensed – and to whom – can be found in the Public Record Office. T 1/630–647.
5 Alan Frost, *Botany Bay Mirages: Illusions of Australia's Convict Beginnings* (Melbourne, 1994).
6 Braidwood, *op. cit.*, pp. 91–2.
7 *Ibid.*, pp. 105–7.
8 Peter Fryer, *Staying Power* (London, 1984), p. 199.
9 Minutes, 15 July 1786, in T.I. 633/1815.
10 Ottobah Cugoano, *Thoughts and Sentiments on the Evil and Wicked Traffic of the Slavery and Commerce of the Human Species* (London, 1787). Reprinted in Paul Edwards and David Dabydeen, *Black Writers in Britain, 1760–1890* (Edinburgh, 1991), pp. 49–52. For a description of Cugoano, see Keith A. Sandiford, *Measuring the Moment* (London, 1988).
11 Fryer, *op. cit.*, p. 200.
12 *Interesting Narrative*, p. 226.

13 For the composition of the Committee, see Braidwood, *op. cit.*, pp. 64–7.

14 *Interesting Narrative*, pp. 226–7.

15 Braidwood, *op. cit.*, pp. 153–4.

16 Orders to Equiano, 16 January 1787, in *Interesting Narrative*, p. 227. Here again, Equiano was addressed by the name Gustavus Vassa.

17 Minutes, 24 October 1786, T.I. 638.

18 Minutes, 1 December 1786, T.I. 638.

19 1 January 1787, T.I. 641.

20 Letter, 21 March 1787, T.I. 643.

21 23 March 1787, T.I. 643.

22 N. A. M. Rodger, *The Wooden World: The Anatomy of the Georgian Navy* (London, 1986), Chapter 6, 'Discipline'.

23 Braidwood, *op. cit.*, p. 149.

24 Letter, 4 April 1787, reprinted in *Interesting Narrative*, pp. 325–6.

25 Fryer, *op. cit.*, p. 201.

26 23 March 1787, T.1.643.

27 Cugoano, *op. cit.*, p. 50.

28 *Interesting Narrative*, pp. 228–9.

29 *The Public Advertiser*, 11 April 1787, reprinted in *ibid.*, p. 301, n. 653.

30 This is discussed in Winthrop Jordan, *White over Black: American Attitudes toward the Negro, 1550–1812* (New York, 1968).

31 *The Public Advertiser*, 14 April 1787, reprinted in *Interesting Narrative*, p. 301, n. 653.

32 *Interesting Narrative*, p. 229.

33 *Ibid.*, pp. 229–31.

34 Braidwood, *op. cit.*, p. 157–8.

12

THE CAMPAIGN AGAINST THE SLAVE TRADE

Few could have imagined, in the mid-1780s, that the Atlantic slave trade could be destroyed within the space of a mere two decades. It was a colossal economic and human system, which ensnared three continents and whose economic benefits (in European eyes) far outweighed its terrible human costs. The dead and the sick in the ill-fated Sierra Leone scheme were only a tiny number from among the millions whose sufferings formed the story of Atlantic slavery. And Equiano was but one person from the army of uprooted Africans, but he came to play a significant part in the initial British drive against the slave trade. Like so many other African features of the history of Atlantic slavery, his role has been minimized. But to understand that role, and to grasp the significance of his major contribution (i.e. his autobiography) we need to know more about the emergence of the campaign against the Atlantic slave trade.

Though the British campaign to abolish the slave trade began in earnest in 1787, like all political campaigns it had deep-seated roots. In fact the Atlantic slave system had had its critics from the earliest days of European settlement in the Americas. From the first, some men of conscience, scruples, or men with religious or humane worries, found it hard to accept that Africans should be brutalized on so vast a scale. Such objections, beginning with the sixteenth-century Dominican friar, Las Casas,[1] were simply swept aside; overwhelmed by the rising tide of material benefits which enslaved labour yielded to settlers and Europeans alike. Moral scruples seemed a luxury in the face of the wealth and material well-being disgorged by ships returning from the West Indies or the Chesapeake.

This was especially true in eighteenth-century Britain, for the rise of British power in the Atlantic seemed inextricably linked to the slave system. The money which flowed to the Treasury, the strategic power which accrued to the Royal Navy, the social habits which developed from the widespread British consumption of slave-grown produce, all and more served to integrate slavery into the fabric of British life. It was a system which flourished in the Americas, and the grotesque sufferings of the slaves were hidden from direct British view (though they were observed at close hand by generations of sailors and others involved in colonial trade and settlement). Yet the material and social benefits of slavery were so obvious, so tangible (and could be bought across the counter in a myriad corner shops)[2] that few wished even to raise the question of how these benefits were provided – and how much suffering was necessarily involved.

It would be wrong, however, to suggest that the slave system was ever morally neutral. Even though slavery's core activities were far away – on the far side of the Atlantic, in Africa or on the high seas – Britain was inevitably dragged into a debate about the ramifications of the slave system. There were periodic reminders of the moral, but above all the legal, problems spawned by the slave empires. True, they often took local, specific and sometimes confusing form. Throughout the eighteenth century, as we have seen, a number of legal cases had raised the question of slavery in England (and Scotland). In most of those cases the issue emerged indirectly, nonetheless forcing contemporaries to confront the question of slavery in Britain itself. Equiano had been both victim and activist in two such cases and in the process had made himself known to Granville Sharp, the driving force behind the campaign to use English law to defend black interests (and secure black freedom) in England (see pp. 46–50).

Sharp could boast of a number of small triumphs on behalf of blacks in London, of violated and maltreated blacks who were cared for and restored. But his major triumph was really the Somerset/Mansfield decision in 1772. Though that case did not achieve its primary objective of having slavery outlawed, it secured a legal judgment that people could not be removed from England against their wishes. Thereafter there was a steady erosion of slavery in England. Set against this, however, was Sharp's major failure, the *Zong* case of 1783. Even by the standards of the day, the stark details of this affair were horrifying. Captain Luke Collingwood of the Liverpool slave ship, the *Zong, en route* from Africa to Jamaica in November to December 1781, found his ship running short of water. To safeguard the lives of the healthier slaves, the captain ordered batches of sick slaves to be thrown overboard. Altogether 131 were murdered in this way. When the case surfaced in an English court it did so as an insurance case, as a claim on property deliberately destroyed by the captain.

The legal hearing about the claim was reported in a London newspaper, and Equiano immediately went to see Granville Sharp, on 19 March 1783:

Gustavus Vassa Negro called on me with an account of 130 Negroes being thrown live into the sea, from on Board an English Slave Ship.[3]

Sharp promptly alerted friends and contacts, initiating a legal case against the alleged murderers. He sought to persuade the Admiralty to bring charges against the men accused of this crime, claiming that he had 'been earnestly solicited and called upon by a poor Negro for my assistance, to avenge the blood of his murdered countrymen'.[4] Curiously though, Equiano makes no mention whatsoever of this, the most chilling of all maritime slave outrages in his lifetime, in his autobiography written only six years later.[5] It was an event which provided some of the most graphic and damning evidence about the Atlantic slave trade, yet Equiano chose not to use it in a book which was specifically designed as a contribution to the abolition debate.

Sharp's efforts for justice got nowhere. The *Zong* affair, though providing powerful ammunition in subsequent abolitionist campaigns, simply faded away, its perpetrators unpunished, its victims unmourned. It prompted the melancholy remark by Ottobah Cugoano, 'our lives are accounted of no value, we are hunted as the prey in the desert, and doomed to destruction as the beasts that perish'.[6]

The legal debate about compensation for slaves lost on board English ships simmered on, however. Both sides, abolitionists and the slave lobby, were keen to secure their own positions. Inevitably, Parliament intervened to regulate the question of slave insurance, and it is worth repeating the clause in the Act passed by Parliament in 1790 which determined that:

> no loss or damage shall be recoverable on account of the mortality of slaves by natural death, or ill treatment, or against loss by throwing overboard of slaves on any account whatsoever.[7]

Moreover this Act was passed *after* the campaign against the slave trade had begun to make a major impact.

Shortly after the debate about the *Zong* case, the loyalist blacks who were to form the bulk of the 'black poor' began to arrive in London. The resulting debate about the establishment of a new, black settlement in West Africa prompted a growing interest in West Africa itself. And that, in its turn, led to an emergent awareness, among small but critical groups, that Africa might offer much more than a hunting ground for slaves destined for the American plantations. The initial case for Sierra Leone had been advanced by Henry Smeathman, though much of what he said and wrote seems, in retrospect, pure fantasy:

> Pleasant scenes of vernal beauty, a tropical luxuriance, where fruit and flowers lavish fragrance together on the same bough! There nature animates every embryo of life: and reigning in vegetable maturity.

For all the romantic gloss of this argument, Smeathman made a critical intervention, by suggesting that Africa could yield a range of goods and commercial possibilities which might, in time, overtake the slave trade as the main attraction for the Europeans. 'It is not improbable, that most of the riches of the East, may be found, at one fourth of the distance.' He thought that various points on the African coast might yield rice, cotton and tobacco, sugar and gums. The establishment of 'modern' (i.e. European) agricultural systems would form a beach-head for the modernization of West Africa.[8]

Smeathman's case appealed to a small group of English Quakers (Quakers had first sponsored Smeathman's work in West Africa). But the Quaker interest in West Africa – and in the slave trade which so blighted the region – also had other, non-utilitarian roots. Quakers were ever alert to new commercial opportunities (and a non-slave West African trade looked economically tempting), but Quakers also had an honourable record of dissent against the Atlantic slave trade. Indeed the Friends had been among the first to speak out against slavery. When George Fox visited Barbados in 1671 he had urged that local slaves (at the time the key force in developing the island's sugar-based prosperity) should be converted 'in the fear of God', much to the alarm of local slave-owners. Inevitably, some Quakers, especially those living in slave colonies, became entangled in slavery. How could shippers and merchants distinguish between slave and non-slave produce in the varied confusion of import/export trade? Robert King, Equiano's owner in Montserrat, was a Quaker. Nonetheless, English Quakers were cautioned against slave-owning with increasing regularity in the eighteenth century. A warning of 1727 was repeated by the London Yearly Meeting in 1758, urging Friends not to participate in a trade which was so 'evidently destructive of the natural rights of mankind'.

One Quaker who took this to heart was Dr John Lettsom, who, though born into a slave-owning family on Tortola in 1744, freed all his slaves on his return from his British education in 1767.[9] In later life, Lettsom opted for gradual, rather than immediate freedom for the slaves. Lettsom was a friend of Smeathman and backed his plans to form pioneering settlements in West Africa.

The most aggressive denunciations of slavery, however, came, not from London, but from North America. As early as 1758 the Philadelphia Yearly Meeting resolved to exclude those Friends who continued to buy and sell slaves, urging Friends, instead, to free any slaves they might own. By 1776 they had resolved to exclude anyone from the Society of Friends who persisted in keeping slaves. Three years later they urged that compensation should be paid to freed slaves.[10] This was far in advance of anything formally proposed by Quakers in London, though American Quakers lived cheek by jowl with slavery and saw its grim reality in ways which English Quakers could only imagine. Nonetheless British Friends were, bit by bit, nudged towards abolition by the words of their American cousins.

Quakers criss-crossed the Atlantic, often in search of commercial openings and trade, but always keen to share their ideas with fellow Quakers. In the 1760s and 1770s two American Quakers in particular, Anthony Benezet and John Woolman, pressed British Friends to speak out against the slave trade. During the American war of 1776–83, the Quakers were inevitably preoccupied with commercial survival and with the ethical problems they faced in wartime. Yet Philadelphia kept up the abolitionist pressure on Friends in London and finally, in 1782, English Quakers formed a committee to investigate the slave trade. By June 1783 the London Yearly Meeting was ready to discuss the issue.

Some of London's prominent Quakers wanted to move the matter forward more quickly than the cumbersome organization of the Society of Friends might allow, and among a group of six prosperous businessmen, some of whom had seen slavery at first-hand on their travels in North America, convened in 1783 with that in mind. Their main aim was that 'the public mind should be enlightened'. To that end they initiated a series of abolitionist pieces in newspapers across the country. And among the arguments they sought to promote was the case (recently advanced by Adam Smith in *The Wealth of Nations*) that slavery was uneconomic. Quakers assumed that slavery was morally and theologically flawed; some of them now saw it as economically unjustifiable. Yet economics was the main justification of the entire Atlantic system. By the end of 1783, ten batches of articles had been distributed to twelve newspapers in London and the provinces.[11] The formal Quaker committee weighed in, at the end of 1783, with a powerful tract, *The Case of Our Fellow Creatures, the Oppressed Africans*. Backed by Quaker wealth, published by Quaker printers and distributed through the Society of Friends' extraordinary national network, tens of thousands of copies of the tract fluttered down on the reading public in 1784. Other abolitionist pamphlets came spitting from the Quaker presses, employing each and every argument – moral, religious, economic – to denounce the slave trade. British consumers were called on to express their private revulsion by not consuming slave-grown produce.[12]

By 1785 abolition had begun to move out of its Quaker compound, winning over Anglicans, notably William Wilberforce and Thomas Clarkson. The latter wrote his Cambridge prize-winning essay in that year, *An Essay on the Slavery and Commerce of the Human Species, Particularly the Africans*, which was published (1786) in both England and America.[13] The gratifying sympathetic response persuaded Clarkson to devote his life to the abolition cause. His first aim was to extend the reach of the abolition message, to move it outside its largely Quaker confines to reach as wide an audience as possible, though he remained at home within the inner circle of influential Quakers, whose advice, money and networks he used to promote the cause. Clarkson in effect sought to popularize abolition. He also began to accumulate evidence on the slave trade by visiting as many slave ships as possible. What struck him was not merely the enormity of the Atlantic system but the economic potential of Africa itself. Clarkson began to collect as many goods and products from Africa as possible, filling a small trunk and displaying them wherever he spoke. Africa could yield more than the slaves required in the Americas.

At much the same time, William Wilberforce was persuaded that the abolition of the Atlantic slave trade would be his own crusade inside Parliament. Thus the abolition cause had acquired a parliamentary spokesman (Wilberforce) and a brilliant public spokesman and lobbyist (Clarkson). Quaker networks and Quaker money gave abolition a ready-made framework to become a nationwide campaign, quickly and with a minimum of effort.

In May 1787 the London Abolition Committee was formed to agitate and publish information 'as may tend to the Abolition of the Slave Trade'. It was a trade which they denounced as 'both impolitick and unjust'.[14] Their aim was to end the Atlantic slave trade, not to emancipate slaves in the West Indies (though many members privately wanted to see full black freedom). Appropriately, the Committee was chaired by Granville Sharp. In their first correspondence, the largest group of potential sympathizers across the country (Clarkson claimed a majority) were Quakers.[15]

The Committee launched a war of words against the slave trade, publishing tracts and articles across the country, and showering the reading public with printed arguments against the slave trade from all angles. The first attack came from a friend of Equiano, the Rev. James Ramsay, in his *Essay on the Treatment and Conversion of African Slaves in the Sugar Colonies*, first published in 1784.

Ramsay knew what he was talking about. He had been a cleric in the West Indies for 19 years, and his words had a major effect on winning over his readers to oppose the slave trade.[16] He had also been involved earlier in helping distressed blacks in London. But all this was just the start of an abolitionist onslaught which surprised even the staunchest of supporters by the reaction it provoked.

The response was remarkable. Abolitionist groups sprouted across the nation and emblems were devised which quickly came to symbolize the movement. Wedgwood's medallion with its motif, 'Am I not a man and a brother?', and the plan of the slave ship the *Brookes* were to remain a fixture in the popular memory as symbols of the drive against the slave trade. Money poured in and dozens of tracts and pamphlets flew off abolitionist presses. Abolition had clearly struck a rich vein in distant parts of the nation; it was not to be simply a metropolitan force.

Nowhere was this more striking than in Manchester. When, in the winter of 1787–8 abolitionist petitions were launched, the petition in Manchester led the way, with 10,000 names expressing the local demand for abolition. More than 100 petitions calling for an end to the slave trade were dispatched to Parliament from around the country in 1788. It was the beginnng of the mobilization of popular feeling which surprised the abolitionist fathers by its extent, and which concerned the proponents of the slave system. It seemed, by 1788, that abolition had become a genuinely popular phenomenon.[17] There was a veritable blizzard of abolitionist publications issuing from the London presses and being distributed across the face of urban Britain. The country had expressed a collective choice for abolition, and it seemed but a matter of time before Parliament would agree.[18]

Among the shoal of petitions drawn up against the slave trade in 1788, perhaps the most striking was the one presented by Equiano, 'on behalf of my African brethren'. Unlike most others, which were directed to Parliament, this African petition was addressed, on 21 March 1788, to Queen Charlotte, wife of George III. It was a highly personal petition, written in the first person, and signed (with the name Gustavus Vassa) 'The oppressed Ethiopian'.[19] Equiano's petition was not to 'solicit your royal pity for my own distress. . .' With his own troubles now forgotten, Equiano's purpose was to 'supplicate your Majesty's compassion for millions of my African countrymen, who groan under the lash of tyranny in the West Indies'.

Equiano's petition was intended to parallel the campaign against the slave trade recently debated in Parliament, and to reinforce the abolitionist petitions. Though he described the document as a petition, it was as much a personal letter, designed 'to implore your interposition with your royal consort, in favour of the wretched Africans'.

Equiano hoped that the time had come to put an end to the slaves' misery:

> that they may be raised from the condition of brutes, to which they are at present degraded, to the rights and situation of men, and be admitted to partake of the blessings of your Majesty's happy government . . .[20]

This letter demanded much more than the ending of the slave trade. It spoke the language of equality, or at least the aspiration of equality, for the slaves, at a time when the Abolition Society wanted simply to end the Atlantic slave trade.

ANTI-SACCHARRITES, – or – JOHN BULL and his Family leaving off the use of SUGAR.

To the Masters & Mistresses of Families in Great Britain, this Noble Example of OECONOMY, is respectfully submitted.

PLATE 14.
'Anti-Saccharrites,
– or – John Bull
and his Family
leaving off the use
of Sugar'; cartoon,
1792. James
Gillray's cartoon
of George III and
his family is a
caricature of the
campaign to
boycott slave-
grown sugar in
the 1790s.

Source: © The
British Museum.

Even abolitionists who wished to see an end to slavery felt constrained not to press for full freedom. The debate about the timing of black freedom, and how to pursue it, was to continue for a further forty years.

No doubt Equiano was keen to alert the monarch's wife to the general problem, and to the fact that Parliament and the country had, finally, begun to debate the slave question. It is, however, curious that he should do so on a much broader front than the abolitionist movement itself. He specifically mentioned the West Indies and made use of the imagery of the lash, that potent (but, for the slaves, real) emblem of daily violation. Along with his fellow petitioners to Parliament, Equiano felt that slavery is 'as impolitic as it is unjust and what is inhuman must ever be unwise'.[21]

It is a remarkable document. Whatever its influence, and whatever its aim, it was a crisp and stylish letter from an African at a time when Africans were deemed to be slaves to their white masters. The letter in itself was a demonstration of the case for black freedom. Literacy, loyalty and sensibility; all were here, in the words of an African writing to his monarch. Equiano had already been involved in a publicized debate about black issues. Letters from Africans had already been published in the London press, mainly about the ill-fated Sierra Leone scheme. Equiano's letter to his friend Ottobah Cugoano had been published, and both Africans had signed other published letters about abolition. The two men were in touch personally and by letter with Granville Sharp. In 1787 Cugoano published his own abolitionist tract *Thoughts and Sentiments on the Evil and Wicked Traffic of the Slavery and Commerce of the Human Species.*[22]

All this formed a small beginning. But it was important. The simple fact that Africans had entered the literary/political debate on their own behalf was bound to impress readers, accustomed to an altogether different view of Africans. Other activists in those early months of the abolitionist campaign were seized with the idea of presenting Africa, and things African, in a positive light. If the non-slave side of Africa could be made public, British people might begin to distance themselves from the view of Africa and Africans which was determined largely by slavery. Goods and produce manufactured and cultivated by free African labour, materials more easily acquired in Africa than in other parts of the world, Africans capable of more than heavy, labouring work; all were part of a piece – an attempt to reinvent Africa in the eyes of the British public. Though abolitionists might be able to woo and persuade, by speeches and publications which appealed to a range of contemporary moral, economic or theological themes, they could never hope to carry the conviction and the punch which Africans themselves might deliver. And who better to do this than the man who had already proved his remarkable qualities: Equiano?

The key issue facing Equiano in the aftermath of the Sierra Leone scheme in 1787 was how best to make a personal contribution to the rising tide of abolition? He clearly saw himself as a leader of other blacks in London. So too did white sympathizers. Indeed, the government had appointed him as commissary to the 1787 expedition, in part, for that very reason. He was the most prominent African in London. How could that prominence be best applied to the campaign for abolition? It was no accident that Equiano was to opt for a form of activity which, at once, would promote the abolitionist case and have the additional prospects of making money. Equiano decided to write a book.

Notes

1 David Brion Davis, *The Problem of Slavery in Western Culture* (Ithaca, NY, 1966), Ch. 6.

2 James Walvin, *Fruits of Empire: Exotic Produce and English Taste, 1660–1800* (London, 1997).

3 19 March 1783, Extracts from Diary, 1783–1798. I consulted these papers when they were in Hardwicke Court. They are now lodged in the Gloucester Record Office.

4 Sharp's account of this miserable story can be found in Prince Hoare, *Memoirs of Granville Sharp* (London, 1820), Ch. VIII.

5 His friend Cugoano, however, did mention it.

6 Ottobah Cugoano, *Thoughts and Sentiments on the Evil of Slavery. . .* (London, 1787), pp. 111–12.

7 F. O. Shyllon, *Black Slaves in Britain* (Oxford, 1974), p. 206. This book provides the best analysis of the legal debate around the *Zong* affair.

8 Henry Smeathman, *Plan of a Settlement to be made near Sierra Leone on the Grain Coast of Africa* (London, 1786), p. 8.

9 James Walvin, *Quakers: Money and Morals* (London, 1997), pp. 126–7.

10 Roger Anstey, *The Atlantic Slave Trade and British Abolition, 1760–1810* (London, 1975), Ch. 9.

11 Judith Jennings, *The Business of Abolishing the British Slave Trade, 1783–1807* (London, 1997), pp. 22–5.

12 *Ibid.*, pp. 26–8. See also J. R. Oldfield, *Popular Politics and British Anti-Slavery* (Manchester, 1995), and Clare Midgley, *Women against Slavery* (London, 1992).

13 Ellen Gibson Wilson, *Thomas Clarkson: A Biography* (London, 1989), Ch. 2.

14 British Library, MSS, *Minute Book of the London Abolition Society*, Vol. 1, MS 21, 254, 22 May 1787.

15 Jennings, *op. cit.*, p. 39. For a complete list of members of the society see, 'Published list of Members of the Society instituted in 1787 for the Purpose of effecting the Abolition of the Slave Trade', 1787, Quaker Manuscript Collection, Tracts, Box H. Friends' Meeting House, Euston Road, London.

16 Anstey, *op. cit.*, pp. 248–9.

17 Seymour Drescher, *Capitalism and Antislavery* (London, 1986), Ch. 4.

18 Jennings, *op. cit.*, p. 48.

19 *Interesting Narrative*, pp. 231–2.

20 *Ibid.*, p. 232.

21 *Ibid.*, p. 231.

22 See Paul Edwards, 'Introduction' to Ottobah Cugoano, *Thoughts and Sentiments. . .* (1787; reprinted London, 1969).

= 13 =

THE BOOK

In 1789 Olaudah Equiano published his autobiography in London. The first edition ran to 530 pages in two volumes – much like many other memoirs and also contemporary novels – and was entitled *The Interesting Narrative of the Life of Olaudah Equiano, or Gustavus Vassa the African*. Equiano chose to highlight his African name, relegating the name he used on all his manuscript writings and which he had used in his earlier dealings with government officials, the name by which all his friends and acquaintances had known him. He had, in effect, chosen to present his African persona to the public.

The book is Equiano's best-remembered legacy. The very great bulk of what we know about him is derived from this text, and from what we can cross-check against it. It was not, however, the first of his publications. In the months between his dismissal from the Sierra Leone scheme, and the publication of the book, Equiano had gone out of his way to place his name before the reading public. He had crossed literary swords with supporters of slavery in the press and had attracted criticism for his much-publicized role in the Sierra Leone scheme. He had inevitably drawn the racist fire of those who disliked seeing an African agitator so effectively promoting abolition.

'Civis', a supporter of slavery, told the readers of one London paper:

If I were even to allow some share of merit to Gustavus Vasa [*sic*], Ignatius Sancho, &c., it would not prove equality more, than a pig having been taught to fetch a card, letters, &c., would shew it not to be a pig, but some other animal.[1]

Equiano was clearly known for his public activities (why else challenge him in so public and so dismissive a fashion?) In this author's mind Equiano was linked with the work of an earlier prominent African in London, Ignatius Sancho, whose own posthumously published letters in 1782 had established his reputation as an accomplished African of letters and attainment.[2] Both men, of course, were not *typical* of other blacks in London; both were well known, had caught the imagination, and both were literate. It seems to have been their level of sophistication which irked 'Civis' so much, and it was their literate accomplishments which 'Civis' sought to diminish by racist slurs and insults.

Such attacks raised Equiano's public profile still further. It was, in many respects, an ideal prelude to the publication of his book, preparing the reading public, itself already primed by abolitionist agitation, for what he had to say. It was a very unusual situation: an African writer addressing an English reading public. It is true that a few years earlier the *Letters of Ignatius Sancho* had developed a fashionable following, but times had changed dramatically in the course of the 1780s. Equiano prepared to publish his book in a very different climate, one changed by the abolition campaign. Abolition had generated a more receptive mood, and the reading public was well disposed to each new twist of the abolitionist argument. Equiano provided a new recipe.

There was no problem about financing abolitionist literature, either from the Abolitionist Society, or from the Quakers. But perhaps the most remarkable feature of Equiano's book was that he published it himself, using the well-tried method of subscribers, who by paying for the book in advance provided the necessary capital for publication. Why did Equiano go down this route? He was obviously not a rich man, and clearly did not have his own capital. But he had a knack for spotting commercial openings and here, once again, was a commercial venture in the making; a prospect of profit-making which would, at one and the same time, advance abolition and reward the author. The publication of Equiano's autobiography was, in effect, the latest in a long string of commercial deals assiduously promoted by this remarkable African.

The book was sold at a dozen of London's best booksellers. The bookshops were carefully chosen for their positions in strategic spots in that teeming city.[3] Later, thanks to Equiano's own promotional efforts, it was available from major outlets across Britain. It sold for 7 shillings (perhaps 6 shillings to subscribers). It quickly sold out, and by the end of 1789 Equiano had issued a second edition. A third followed in 1790, a fourth was published in Dublin in 1791, a fifth in Edinburgh in 1792, two more in London in 1793. The eighth was issued in Norwich in 1794 and the ninth in London that same year. It was also published in North America in 1791, and was translated into Dutch, German and Russian in the same period. The book was reviewed in many of the major outlets in London, sometimes warmly, sometimes (for example by Mary Wollstonecraft) rather frostily. But whatever the critics felt, Equiano's autobiography was a bestseller. It was perhaps 'one of the best-selling new books of that half decade'.[4]

When Equiano died in March 1797 he left an estate worth almost £1000.[5] This was a considerable amount and much of it seems to have derived from the book. Anyone familiar with Equiano's commercial activities in his earlier life would not find this surprising, and it is fitting that he should be remembered by the last of his many entrepreneurial activities: the publication and promotion of his own autobiography. He had bought his own freedom by his sharp-eyed commercial efforts. And he bequeathed a substantial estate by similar activities. At the same time, he made a major contribution to the abolitionist cause. It was quintessential Equiano; to the very end of his life, self-improvement went hand in hand with agitation for the black cause.

Equiano's book has, in recent years, developed an iconic status. It has become the 'prototype of a uniquely African-American literary genre, the slave narrative'.[6]

It has been reissued, anthologized and cited more often, perhaps, than any other comparable work.[7] In fact, in recent years Equiano's book has been grafted on to an American tradition, when in reality it belongs more properly elsewhere. There is a *British* slave narrative tradition where Equiano is more properly located and which includes Gronniosaw, Cugoano and Sancho. Positioning of Equiano in the American tradition has served to remove him from his immediate, defining context. His was an African testimony, aimed at the English-reading public, and designed to woo readers to the side of abolition. It was also of course designed to persuade the reader – and the wider world beyond – that an African could aspire to all that was good and worthwhile, all that was refined and sensitive. Equiano presented himself to his readership as a man of sensibility. Yet he was, as the title page proclaimed, 'The African'.

There are inevitably many levels at which we can read and interpret the book. Much of the recent study of Equiano's book has been literary, and has tended to abstract the book and the man from the world of British abolitionist activities in the late 1780s. It is important to recognize that this book, whatever its resonance at other levels, was a contribution to the continuing debate about the abolition of the slave trade. Its genesis, tone, substance – even its very existence – makes little sense unless we remember that fact. It was a tract for the abolitionist times.

The book was 'Printed for and sold by the Author', with help from subscribers. The subscription system of publication had a long and honourable tradition and was, in essence, a variant of the old aristocratic patronage of writing and publication. By the late eighteenth century, subscription had become an accepted way for unknown writers to break into print. The list of subscribers was printed in the book, at once flattering them and revealing the author's connections with distinguished patrons. Equiano's list is as revealing as it was vital. Among the 311 names, prominent abolitionists stood out, but so too did a number of contemporary theologians, intellectuals and politicians. Members of the Royal family, various peers, clerics and a host of well-placed men (and women) also subscribed. That an African could muster such a collection of prominent people is in itself testimony to Equiano's unique appeal and standing in contemporary society.

Calculations about the numbers of books printed are inevitably uncertain, but it is likely Equiano made about £100 profit on the first edition. The success of that edition, in 1789, enabled Equiano to move on to a second edition. Normally, authors chose to sell the copyright to a publisher for subsequent editions, but Equiano with his sharp eye for profitable business did not do this. His book had proved too lucrative to hand over to others. Furthermore, his commercial dealings with white people had traditionally been plagued by problems; he had been cheated, short-changed and threatened. From his slave days to his most recent involvement with the Sierra Leone scheme, Equiano was happiest and at his best when operating in his own economic interests. From the first (1789) to the last English edition (1794) Equiano therefore published his own book. The profits were his alone.

We do not know *where* Equiano wrote the book, though we know he stayed with friends when revising a subsequent edition. In March 1792 Thomas Hardy, the Scottish shoemaker and founder of the radical, plebeian London Corresponding Society (which Equiano joined) told a friend in Sheffield that 'my friend Gustavus Vassa, the African, (who) is now writing the memoirs of his life in my house'.[8]

The exact composition of the book remains a mystery; where and how it was written, which papers Equiano had access to, which people he consulted in the process. There is no serious doubt, however, that it is his own work. When it was completed, on 24 March 1789, Equiano registered his book by depositing nine copies at Stationers' Hall, to protect his copyright. (In October 1790, when he published the third, one-volume edition, he repeated the exercise.[9]) The book was then put on sale at twelve London booksellers, with the added claim that it 'may be had of all Booksellers in Town and Country'.[10]

The story of what happened to Equiano's book is quite remarkable. But commentators have not fully recognized that the story of the book forms an extraordinary testimony to the determination, industry and persistence of Equiano himself. Though the *Narrative* emerged from, and clearly belonged to, the earlier genre of abolitionist literature (the list of subscribers in London and the provinces reads like a *Who's Who* of abolitionist sentiment), the book quickly took on a life of its own. This was entirely due to the author's promotional efforts. For the next six years he criss-crossed Britain promoting and selling the book.

He began (1789) on the crest of the abolitionist wave, but the political climate changed, and was not always sympathetic to his efforts. By 1792 his efforts overlapped with the broader politics of reform, driven forward by the Corresponding Societies, which also spawned a massive upsurge in cheap and popular publications, most notably Tom Paine's *Rights of Man*. By 1793, however, all that was in rapid and worried retreat, in the face of wartime reaction, fuelled by Pitt's government and its supporters. Faced by successful revolutionary armies abroad, and by thriving radical societies at home, Pitt and his friends harried, repressed and ultimately marginalized reform – of all kinds. The confident demands for an end to the slave trade in 1789, like the widely supported pleas for parliamentary reform in 1792, were effectively silenced or driven underground, not to reappear until the immediate wartime dangers had passed (along with Pitt himself). Yet through all this, Equiano soldiered on, promoting his book, issuing new editions and selling substantial numbers. When he died in March 1797, he was a man of substance.

The success of the first and second editions in 1789 established a formula which Equiano stuck to in subsequent editions: drumming up subscribers and publishing the book himself. His first list of subscribers was a remarkable testimony to his ability to raise support among the good and the great. Provincial editions might have been expected to pose problems. How could an African, who had lived all of his English life in London, tap into circles of supporters in provincial and distant localities? In fact, even his *first* list of subscribers had contained a scattering of people (11 per cent of them women) who lived in the provinces. Moreover, the abolition cause had already made its own impact in provincial life. Indeed, the real impetus behind abolition, in its first, petitioning phase, came from the provinces. This was particularly the case, as mentioned, in the emergent cotton town of Manchester.[11] There were, in effect, pockets of people scattered across Britain who had been alerted to the question of the slave trade, who had strong views about abolition, and who were willing and able to put up cash for the cause.[12]

There could have been few more obviously worthy causes than an educated and persuasive African author, already in the public eye, and keen to promote abolition on the back of his own autobiography. Equiano and his book made for a unique mix. They combined the appeal of abolition, by now well rehearsed in print, in public and in Parliament, with the lure of a narrative which was replete with exciting and remarkable stories. It was also a tale of self-improvement, of an African raising himself from the most wretched of circumstances to become an educated man of refinement. Here, then, was a book which appealed to a host of contemporary fashions and feelings. Not surprisingly, Equiano seems to have had little trouble (though he invested lots of effort) in recruiting subscribers for his various editions.

Each new edition saw some names dropped from the list of earlier subscribers. But Equiano was successful in keeping the famous, the well-known and the aristocratic on board. New editions secured a roster of local names for a local edition; 211 names in Hull, 81 in Bristol and 248 in Norwich. The Edinburgh edition attracted 159 subscribers, including a range of lawyers and most of the University's professors.[13] Equiano travelled widely to promote the book, speaking for abolition wherever he went. He became so successful in selling his book that some abolitionists saw him as a threat. When Equiano visited Shrewsbury, a local abolitionist feared it would only tend 'to increase the difficulty of getting subscriptions, when wanted, for carrying on the business of abolition. . .'[14]

Even Equiano's plans for his wedding – to Miss Cullen of Soham in Cambridgeshire in 1792 – seem to have been arranged around his publishing plans. He wrote to a friend in Nottingham that 'when I have given her about 8 or 10 Days Comfort, I mean Directly to go to Scotland – and sell my 5th Editions'.

Equiano hoped that his book would help the wider cause of abolition, and was assured by a prominent abolitionist that 'I am more use to the Cause than half the people in the Country I wish to God, I could be so.' Wherever he went, whoever he contacted, he urged them to think about, and to discuss the plight of Africans. He beseeched a clerical friend in Nottingham, 'Pray mind the Africans from the Pulpits.'[15]

By the early 1790s Equiano's fame went before him. He was consulted (by Lord Stanhope) about the slave legislation currently passing through Parliament. He spoke publicly against the slave trade, and in May 1792 he addressed the General Assembly of the Church of Scotland, thanking them (while he was in Edinburgh to promote his book) for their unanimous support for abolition. He wrote as 'one of the oppressed natives of Africa', thanking them and giving 'testimony against that iniquitous branch of commerce the slave trade'. But he also spoke on behalf of 'my much oppressed countrymen'. Yet it is surely revealing that in this correspondence, Equiano combined his political and social message with an advertisement for his book. He addressed a letter to an Edinburgh newspaper from: 'At Mr M'Laren's, turner, second stair above Chalmer's Close, High Street – where my Narrative is to be had.'[16]

In all the fragmentary manuscript material we have in Equiano's hand in the years after the publication of his book, he refers to his *Narrative*. Even when writing to friends, he took the opportunity of reminding them of the book, its progress and its impact.

By 1792, with five editions published, Equiano had clearly begun to accumulate significant amounts of money. Once again, however, his financial life did not run smoothly. He had to hurry back to London in February of that year to try to retrieve £232 he had lent to a man who was now on the point of death. His efforts were clearly in vain, for in May he learned that the man concerned ('that villain who owed me above £200') had died, '& that is all the Comfort I got from him since'. Not surprisingly he described London as 'this wickd. Town'. And he prayed that the Lord would 'keep me from all such Rascals as I have met with in London'.

Equiano was clearly prospering. He even lost a valued piece of jewellery in Thomas Hardy's house, writing to him requesting other lodgers to look for 'a Little Round Gold Breast Buckel, or broach, sett in, or with fine stones'. If anyone were to find it, Equiano wrote that he 'will pay them well for it'.[17] It is impossible to be precise, but the evidence suggests that he had, by 1792, acquired a sizeable amount of money along with some costly material possessions. Yet only five years earlier, he had been obliged to urge the Treasury and the Navy to pay his wages and expenses, incurred in the ill-fated Sierra Leone scheme, to the tune of £34.4s. His economic position had thus been utterly transformed. In 1787 he was begging for wages and relatively small expenses.[18] Five years later, he was in pursuit of £232 owed in what, presumably, was a business transaction. In both cases Equiano was the supplicant; asking for money which was his. It was a familiar refrain throughout his life. By 1792, however, it is clear that he had made a financial breakthrough, and that his book was generating income of a kind he could previously only have dreamt of.

We can get a clearer idea of how this came about by tracing Equiano's promotion of his book in Ireland in 1791–2. He sailed from Liverpool to Dublin in May 1791, with three editions already published and a fourth issued that year in the Irish capital. He travelled on to Cork and for the next eight months throughout Ireland: 'I was every where exceedingly well treated, by persons of all ranks. I found the people extremely hospitable, particularly in Belfast.'[19] He seemed especially at home in Belfast. His book was advertised in the Belfast *News-Letter* in December 1791 and the nature of the book, with its clear tone of Calvinist predestination and its account of Equiano's evangelical conversion, struck a sympathetic note with the reading public in the north. It also accorded with contemporary reading tastes in the region, already shaped by a chapbook tradition of cheap novels and adventure yarns. But more than that, Equiano found in northern Ireland a region where emergent industrial and manufacturing interests were sympathetic to the economic arguments which underpinned much of his message (and that of abolition in general).[20]

Throughout the eighteenth century, Ireland had been hindered by commercial regulations which restricted her trade with the American colonies and with Africa – to the great irritation of Belfast. Free trade between Ireland and the colonies was established in 1780 (in the middle of the American war). The slave trade seemed an obvious commercial opening, but when, in 1786, a group of Belfast merchants proposed to engage in that trade, local opposition forced a change of heart. The opposition was led by Thomas McCabe, a radical watchmaker and industrialist, and founder of the republican United Irishmen. McCabe's longstanding friend was Samuel Neilson, another United Irishman, a woollen draper and editor of the United Irishmen's newspaper, the *Northern Star*. The United Irishmen were democrats, closely linked to Wolfe Tone, the Irish nationalist, and not unlike the

London Corresponding Society (LCS). When Equiano arrived in Belfast, Samuel Neilson took care of him, introducing him to local booksellers and promoted Equiano's book at his own drapery business in Belfast. Long after Equiano had left, Neilson continued to promote abolition through the *Northern Star*. The newspaper was finally suppressed by the government in 1797.[21]

Equiano also found another local patron in Thomas Digges, a middle-aged American radical who had acted on behalf of American prisoners in the recent war. Suspected of being a spy, he turned, in peacetime, to industrial espionage, in which he did a lively trade from northern Ireland. He was a man who inspired conflicting passions, then and since. He was an undoubted rogue, possibly a traitor (he was accused of betraying Wolfe Tone), but he was also a charming, convivial man, democratic to his bones. He was also anti-slavery, and welcomed Equiano to Belfast with lavish praise for his autobiography.[22] Equiano was, wrote Digges, 'a principal instrument in bringing about the motion for the repeal of the Slave-Act'.[23]

In the company of such actively radical friends, able and keen to give him and his book such prominent local publicity, Equiano had little trouble selling his autobiography. He claimed, in February 1792, that he had sold 1900 copies of the book in Ireland.[24] Equiano's welcome in Belfast went deeper than mere personalities, however, for the local dissenting tradition found abolition a naturally attractive campaign. For more than a century, Irishmen had denounced London's control over Ireland as a form of slavery, the word itself peppering discussions about relations with England. In politics, in religion and more recently in trade, the Irish were dominated by an English system, and by English people, who seemed to care little for Ireland, using it solely to extend English interests and well-being. The origins of the United Irishmen, for example, found expression in the publication in 1784 of a series of letters, each beginning with a call to 'fellow slaves'. Slaves, slavery, chains – and their alternative, freedom and casting aside old bondage; all these words and their associated images were basic to the Irish debate in the years before Equiano's visit in 1791–2.

There had also been an Irish debate about the iniquities of black slavery. Abolition had taken root in Belfast, and, following the Quaker-inspired campaign in Dublin, a campaign had begun against the consumption of slave-grown sugar and rum. All this, of course, was now under the shadow of revolutionary France. July 14th was celebrated in Belfast and two issues – the rights of man, and an attack on slavery – became fused in the public mind. Among reformers in Belfast, abolition was an attractive symbol of the broader reforms they sought; for themselves, for Ireland, and for 'brothers' across the seas.[25]

Equiano's book was seized upon as a denunciation of major injustices. It was taken by the Belfast dissenting community as an appeal to extend equality, and its author was taken to the friendly bosom of some of Ireland's most radical groups. There were, of course, pro-slavery interests there, too; notably Belfast merchants and shippers grown fat on the sweat of West Indian slaves. Lines were already drawn in the region which were to stratify later into fiercely sectarian divisions. But in 1791–2 Equiano moved in Irish circles heady with the prospects of reform and of change. In Belfast the focus of debate was on Catholic emancipation. In England, the abolition campaign was drumming up unprecedented numbers of petitions against the slave trade. The peculiarities of the Irish situation provided Equiano with rich pickings. By the time he sailed from Belfast to Scotland on 29 January 1792, he had sold some 1900 copies of his book. But all reform campaigns were to be transformed, in February 1793, by the outbreak of war with revolutionary France.[26]

Wherever he travelled, Equiano carried with him testimonials from men who knew him and who were keen to smooth his entry in a new town. Again, it is remarkable how many eminent, well-placed people Equiano was able to call on to help his private campaign. At each point, his supporters urged their own friends and contacts, in other parts of the country, to help him sell his book. Dr P. Peckard of Magdalen College Cambridge urged readers of his letter of recommendation 'to beg the favour of your assistance to him in the sale of his book'. In Manchester, the leader of local abolition (and radical reform), Thomas Walker, wrote to others recommending 'the sale of the NARRATIVE of GUSTAVUS VASSA to the friends of justice and humanity'. When people saw the backing Equiano enjoyed, they too joined in. A group in Sheffield, influenced by letters from friends elsewhere, agreed 'to recommend the sale of the NARRATIVE of GUSTAVUS VASSA to the friends of humanity in the town and neighbourhood of Sheffield'. Equiano's drive developed a dynamic of its own, with each fresh group of supporters taking its cue from others. Men in Nottingham gave him their backing because 'of the respectable recommendation of several gentlemen of the first character' who had recommended Equiano, though the Nottingham group had also been persuaded 'from our own interviews with him'.[27]

Equiano used such letters to gain a toehold in each new town he visited. He could also use the abolitionist network. If he knew of an abolitionist, or an abolitionist group, he would certainly have been able to count on their support. But letters of recommendation also provided an immediate entrée. Thus, a letter from Thomas Digges in Belfast helped him when he travelled to Carrickfergus in December 1791. In the following year he arrived in Stockton with recommendations to wave before local contacts. They in their turn wrote to a friend in Durham, promoting both Equiano ('an African of distinguished merit') and his book: 'He has with him some copies for sale, and if you can conveniently assist him in the disposal thereof, you will greatly oblige.' He arrived in Hull in November 1792 clutching the written support of the Dean of Peterborough, 'and by many other very respectable characters'. A group of Hull men promptly added their names to his cause: 'we recommend him to the assistance of the friends of humanity in this town, in promoting subscriptions to an interesting Narrative of his life'. Similarly, a contact in Bath, William Langworthy, wrote a letter of recommendation in October 1793 to William Hughes in Devizes, introducing Equiano, 'the enlightened African'. Langworthy had met him through a similar letter of recommendation:

> He came recommended to me by men of distinguished talents and exemplary virtue, as an honest and benevolent man; and his conversation and manners as well as his book do more than justice to the recommendation.

Equiano's visit to Devizes was simple enough: 'His *business* in your part of the world is to promote the sale of his book.' Langworthy added, 'I am sure those who buy it will not regret that they have laid out the price of it in the purchase.' He hoped that Hughes would in his turn introduce 'this fair minded black man' to friends in Devizes.

In this way Equiano constructed a nationwide network of friends, sympathizers and contacts; people who met him, listened to him, entertained him, introduced him to others and, in their turn, helped him on his way to the next town via their own friends and contacts. He is likely also to have been given lodging in this way, and to have secured local outlets for the sale of his book. He sold it wherever possible: from the tenement where he lodged in Edinburgh, to a drapery shop in Belfast.

And so it continued for much of the early 1790s. From Perth, Dundee and Aberdeen to Glasgow, from Liverpool to Ireland, from London to the West Country, Equiano travelled indefatigably, using his network of friends and contacts, accumulating still more, advancing the cause of abolition, and always, perhaps most important, selling his autobiography.

It was a remarkable promotional tour, undertaken at his own initiative and under his own steam. Those who knew him and who spoke about him were clear that his work was important in spreading the abolitionist cause. But it was a period which was no less important in achieving what Equiano had always sought: to establish a reasonable livelihood for himself. The book at last enabled Equiano to shake off the economic insecurities which had dogged his life. It was no mere accident, no coincidence of timing. His success stemmed from his own shrewdness and hard work, and was the culmination of a lifetime's effort and ambition. It was also a unique (and curiously neglected) phenomenon (though fifty years later other ex-slaves were to achieve even greater fame in the USA).[28]

By the time of his success in Ireland, it was clear enough (if Equiano's estimates of the sales are accurate) that the book was selling well beyond the circle of subscribers. Its fame had clearly spread. There had been damaging allegations against him in the press (notably that he was West Indian and not African) which, he felt, 'had hurted the sale of my Books'.[29] Yet by early 1792 he had invitations to visit Holland and Germany, where his book had already appeared (as indeed it had in New York). But he chose to stay in London to hear the Commons debate on abolition in early April 1792.[30] Two years later, the book entered its ninth edition, the last published in Equiano's own lifetime. What happened to the *Interesting Narrative* after 1794 provides evidence of the role Equiano had played in the book's initial success between 1789 and 1794.

The key to the book's changing fortune was the dramatic change of political circumstances. In 1794 Pitt's government launched a full onslaught on radical agitation. The main targets were the Corresponding Societies, especially the LCS, and the nationwide web of radical groups which had, since late 1791, orchestrated a rising chorus of social and political complaints and radical demands. Though those societies traced their intellectual and political pedigree back to distinctively British roots, they had been shaped and influenced (in the short term at least) by events in France. The language of equality, of the rights of man and of fraternity, seemed contagious and found a sympathetic home among large numbers of the dispossessed in Britain. No less alarming to a government which saw France disintegrate into revolutionary anarchy and violence, revolutionary ideals had taken hold in the slave quarters of the Caribbean. The consequent upheavals in the French colony Haiti destroyed the slave system (and economy) there and, when the British tried to seize the colony for themselves, an entire British army was swallowed up.[31]

The popular radical societies of the early 1790s had also embraced abolition. Best expressed perhaps through Tom Paine's *Rights of Man*, that Bible of the popular radical movement, the Corresponding Societies had driven abolition much deeper into the British social sub-soil than ever before. Abolition had slipped its moorings among men of property and substance, and was now advocated by men of humbler origins.

As popular radicalism spread, and as France disintegrated, the government enacted ever more penal restrictions on all forms of radical activity, on meetings and publications. Government spies were everywhere, landlords were threatened if they rented their rooms to reform groups, and publishers were intimidated. Each twist of the reforming movement persuaded government ministers that they were dealing not with reformers, but with 'Jacobins'. In an increasingly frenzied political climate and as French armies seemed to sweep all before them, the shadow of revolutionary France transmuted domestic British demands for reform into a dangerous Jacobinical subversion.

On 12 May 1794, in an orchestrated series of raids, government officers arrested the leaders of the radical societies. At 6.30am Equiano's friend, Thomas Hardy was arrested.[32] Though the subsequent treason trials in October–November 1794 proved unsuccessful (for the government) and the reformers were acquitted, the trials had served their purpose. They had broken the back of the popular radical movement.

1794 was, then, a dangerous time to espouse reforming ideas. Even men of unimpeachable respectability turned their back on reform, remaining silent or rejecting their old ideals. Equiano's friend was on trial for his life, and all for little more than supporting reforming ideals which Pitt himself had favoured earlier.

Abolition went the way of reform, for it too was tainted with fears generated by the Revolution. When abolitionists made their case, their opponents had only to point to Haiti, with its black on white (and black on black) bloodshed, to silence the debate. Parliamentary abolition effectively died, for a decade, in the wake of the Revolution.

By 1794 Britain had sunk deep into a costly and threatening war with revolutionary France. Britain itself seemed insecure. Only the sea prevented the arrival of those confident French arms which had already planted revolutionary control and ideals across much of western Europe. In the West Indies the upheaval in Haiti threatened to spread like a slave bushfire, igniting long-simmering slave unrest clean across the region. And at home radical movements, using the language of equality, had gripped the imagination of thousands of working men. Those same men adopted a political vernacular in a range of provincial accents, a vernacular which resembled the French and which asserted the case both for parliamentary reform and an end to the slave trade. Thomas Hardy, writing to a man in Sheffield who was 'a zealous friend of the abolition of that cursed traffic, the slave Trade', assumed '*that you are a zealous friend to freedom on the broad basis of the RIGHTS OF MAN*'.

It was a simple association:

> I am fully persuaded that there is no man, who is, from principle, an advocate for the liberty of the black man, but will zealously support the rights of the white man, and *vice versa*.[33]

Indeed, the political language of the radical movement in the early 1790s had been suffused with imagery of slavery. The first address of the LCS had asserted (when referring to France) that 'we were MEN while they were SLAVES'.[34] The motif of the Corresponding Society in Melbourne, Derbyshire, showed a slaving scene on the coast of Africa (and that as late as 1797).[35] The point was best expressed by Thomas Hardy in 1792:

> the rights of man are not confined to this small island but are extended to the whole human race, black and white, high or low, rich or poor.[36]

The association between radical domestic demands and abolition was clear enough. Abolition had, quite simply, become popular. And popular politics, by 1794, seemed a dangerous force; one which needed to be brought to heel. Hence the onslaught and repression of 1794, and the rapid collapse of popular politics in that year. In 1795 hunger and distress drove men back to the corresponding societies in desperation. But the government was more than a match for the politics of hunger, and again imposed a series of repressive restrictions which broke the back of all but the most fanatical (and sometimes revolutionary) souls. The popular support for abolition disappeared.

In any case, by 1792 this cause had found a parliamentary home. There were many individuals and groups in both Houses who had been persuaded of the need for abolition. The time, however, was no longer right. For parliamentary success the abolition cause no longer needed that extra vital push from the public – the push which had derived from public agitation and mobilization in 1788–92. Parliament itself now needed to be persuaded, from within its own ranks, that the time was ripe for abolition; that British interests would not be harmed by ending the Atlantic slave trade. Thus, as the war raged, as Haiti was engulfed, it seemed best to leave abolition well alone. Abolition sentiment thus lay dormant but not forgotten, in Parliament, for more than a decade. It was hardly surprising then that Equiano's publishing success in the years 1789–94 came to an end. The last edition published in his lifetime came out in London in 1794. It was not to be reprinted for fifteen years, when it was published by a clergyman in the small Derbyshire town of Belper in 1809. The publisher noted: 'The Book has now for many years been out of print; and though it has gone through many Editions, the copies now to be met with are but few. . .' The author too had dropped into almost total anonymity. The publisher of the new edition wrote of Equiano:

> Of his life, after the publication of the last Edition of his Narrative, the Editor has not been able to procure any authentic account. It appears from what he has been able to collect, that he died, in some part of England, about seven years ago.

Both the book and the author were effectively unknown. This new (1809) publisher seemed more interested, in reissuing the book, in arguing with Equiano's theological views.[37] A number of new editions followed in other provincial towns. In Penryn near Falmouth in 1815 and 1816 (Equiano had first arrived at Falmouth in 1757), and in Halifax, where four further editions were published between 1812 and 1819 by a publisher who issued other African-American writers with an English connection. In 1814 a further edition was published in Leeds, but the *Narrative* was not reissued in London until the 1820s and even then only as a 12-page version in a twopenny tract series, 'The negro's friend', published by abolitionist sympathizers. In America, no edition was issued between 1791 and 1837.[38]

What is abundantly clear through all this is the critical role of Equiano himself. It was his efforts – travelling, promoting, speaking, networking – which sold the book in his lifetime. Of course, its sales were greatly helped by its location within the broader British abolition campaign. But it is impossible to imagine the book's commercial success in the 1790s *without* the author's own persistence and industry. In America, on the other hand, where Equiano had no hand in publishing or promoting the book, sales took an utterly different trajectory. There was but one edition – in 1791 – issued by a young publisher in New York, again using subscribers (though very few of them were eminent). With perhaps 1000 copies printed, 335 were destined for subscribers, distribution was wide – from Boston, through New York and Philadelphia (and curiously Middletown) – and the American version remained in print until 1803. It was a book which had no local impact or importance until, years later, it was adopted by abolitionists to advance their argument against North American slavery. Reprinted in 1837 as part of the anti-slavery campaign, Equiano's *Narrative* then dropped from sight for almost a century and a half. If the story of the book requires a historical explanation then its disappearance from the mid-nineteenth century is a mystery in even greater need of explanation.

The *Narrative* clearly dominated Equiano's life between 1789 and 1794. Though he hinted in later editions at some of the curiosities he saw and experienced in his early promotional travels, he did not provide the detail so common in his accounts of his foreign travel. Perhaps he thought local, British detail too prosaic, too mundane for a British readership. Perhaps, by then, his main task was over. The book was designed to tell an inspirational tale; the story of what could by achieved by an African when freed from slavery. Visits to Newcastle coal mines and to rivers in Manchester could scarcely hope to make the same impression.[39] But perhaps the most curious item of all in what was, in essence, an autobiography, was the passing reference, in the penultimate paragraph of the fifth edition onwards, to Equiano's marriage.

There is no reason to believe that the marriage was not important to Equiano. Yet it occupies a mere two-and-a-half lines of the entire book. Equiano's description of his wedding ceremony is a mere passing reference, in April 1792, and is squeezed in between listening to a parliamentary debate on abolition and a trip to Scotland to promote the *Narrative*. Of course, the book was about *abolition;* it was designed to promote the ending of the slave trade. The author's personal life was invoked only to the extent that it might help to that end. There was of course an abundance of detail about his family life in Africa. But there was nothing in his final, ninth (1794) edition about his personal life in England. Nothing about his wedding, about his domestic family life or about the birth of the first of his two daughters. Equiano's literary self-portrait was of a public, not a private man. For whatever reason (and there may have been many), Equiano chose to leave out some of the more interesting aspects of his life in a book which, after all, he had entitled *The Interesting Narrative of the Life of Olaudah Equiano*. He obviously felt that some aspects of his life were more interesting than others. Or was there more to it than that?

Notes

1 Quoted by Vincent Carretta, in his Introduction to *Interesting Narrative*, p. xiii.
2 See Reyahn King *et al.*, *Ignatius Sancho: An African Man of Letters* (London, 1997).
3 For details of the booksellers, see *Interesting Narrative*, title page; and Ian Maxted, *The London Book Trades, 1775–1800* (Exeter, 1980).
4 James Green, 'The publishing history of Olaudah Equiano's *Interesting Narrative*', *Slavery and Abolition*, vol. 16, no. 3, (1995).
5 *Interesting Narrative*, p. 355, n. 5.
6 Green, *op. cit.*, p. 362.
7 The latest example can be found in Henry Louis Gates, Jr and Nellie Y. McKay (eds), *The Norton Anthology of African American Literature* (New York, 1997).
8 *Memoirs of Thomas Hardy* (London, 1832), p. 15.
9 Vincent Carretta, 'Introduction', *Interesting Narrative*, p. xv.
10 See list in Appendix A of *Interesting Narrative*, p. 311.
11 Seymour Drescher, *Capitalism and Antislavery* (London, 1986), pp. 67–75.
12 The list of subscribers from different towns is reprinted in *Interesting Narrative*, pp. 15–28.
13 Green, *op. cit.*, p. 365.
14 *Diaries of Mrs Katherine Plymly*, 19 May–17 August 1793, Book No. 17 (1066/7), Shrewsbury Records and Research Unit, Shrewsbury Library. I thank Mark Jones for this reference.
15 Letter to Rev. G. Walker of Nottingham, 27 February 1792, Picton Autograph Collection, Liverpool City Libraries. Also reprinted in *Interesting Narrative*, pp. 345–6.
16 Letter to the General Assembly of the Church of Scotland, 26 May 1792, *Interesting Narrative*, pp. 346–7.
17 Letters of 27 February and 28 May 1792, in *ibid.*, pp. 346–8; Stephen J. Braidwood, *Black Poor and White Philanthropists* (Liverpool, 1994), p. 157.
18 *Interesting Narrative*, pp. 230–1.
19 *Ibid.*, p. 235.
20 The details of Equiano's Irish venture are described in Nini Rodgers, 'Equiano in Belfast: A Study of the anti-slavery ethos in a northern town', *Slavery and Abolition*, vol. 18, no. 2 (1997).
21 Nini Rodgers, *ibid.*, p. 75.
22 *Ibid.*, p. 77.
23 *Interesting Narrative*, p. 10.
24 Letter, 27 February 1792, *Interesting Narrative*, p. 345.
25 Rodgers, *op. cit.*, pp. 78–9.
26 *Ibid.*, pp. 84–5.
27 Letters of recommendation, *Interesting Narrative*, pp. 5–12.
28 Notably Frederick Douglass and Sojourner Truth.
29 Letter, 28 May 1792, TS 24/12/2. Also in *Interesting Narrative*, p. 347.
30 *Interesting Narrative*, p. 235.
31 In fact the British military were brought down mainly by disease. See David Geggus, *Slavery, War and Revolution* (Oxford, 1982). See also David Barry Gaspar and David Patrick Geggus (eds), *A Turbulent Time: The French Revolution in the Greater Caribbean* (Bloomington, IN, 1997).
32 *Memoirs of Thomas Hardy*, pp. 26–7. For details of the arrests see papers in PRO, T.S.11.96S.3510A.
33 *Memoirs of Thomas Hardy*, p. 15.
34 *Ibid.*, p. 27.
35 Membership Card, 1797, in P.C.1/3514, Public Record Office.
36 British Library, Add.Ms 277811, f. 9.
37 *The Interesting Narrative of the Life of Olaudah Equiano* (Belper, 1809), British Library copy, pp. iii–vi.
38 Green, *op. cit.*, pp. 366–7.
39 *Interesting Narrative*, p. 304, n. 672.

14

BLACK ENLIGHTENMENT

Equiano's autobiography was many things. It was part picaresque personal adventure story, part odyssey of a people. It was also the ultimate example of Equiano's talent at doing business. All books, of course, are inventions – shaped in structure, content and detail by the imagination of the author. And Equiano's was as inventive as any, though not in the sense that it was untrue or falsified. Equiano took the opportunity afforded by writing a book to reinvent himself, in literary form, for a reading public whose appetite for literature about Africa, the slave trade and slavery, had been whetted by the spate of tracts after 1783. He was not, of course, the only, or the first, African to do so. Sancho's *Letters* (1782) were perhaps the most obvious precedent. And Equiano's friend Cugoano had narrowly beaten him into print. Equiano, however, remains the best-known African author from those times. He has come to be seen as the key prototype writer: the founder and shaper of a literary genre which was to be followed by many others in the nineteenth century, especially in North America. But where precisely does he fit among his contemporaries? And what importance should we attach to his writing and ideas?

In 1808 when Thomas Clarkson came to write about his own role in the abolition of the slave trade, he went to great lengths to list the sequence of publications which shaped abolition sentiment from the mid-eighteenth century onwards. He fails to mention Equiano. The abolition movement's unofficial historian simply ignores Equiano's work.[1] This was the first step in a historiography of abolition which continued until recent times: an attempt to explain abolition as a British phenomenon. From 1808 onwards successive generations of commentators and historians have viewed this remarkable change in the fortunes of millions of people as a function of changing sensibility among the British people, and the emergence of their determination to shed the wickedness of Atlantic slavery. In much of that writing, Africa and Africans have remained noises off-stage, at best the innocent recipients of British sympathy and largesse. In recent years a new, more refined and complex search for abolition has dominated

PLATE 15. Portrait of Francis Williams; oil painting. A classical scholar, he attended Bishop's Stortford Grammar School and became a schoolmaster in Jamaica.

Source: V&A Picture Library.

academic debate. Yet even so, and especially in the search for economic change as the key determinant of abolition, attention has remained firmly focused on Europe and European interests.

A mere glance at Equiano – and at his African contemporaries – suggests the need for a more rounded interpretation. But where, precisely, do the Africans fit? And what can we learn from Equiano's life and work which might help us understand their role more clearly? No one could dispute the role which Africa and Africans played in the opening of the Americas. Not until the 1820s were Africans and their descendants dislodged from their role as *the* key labouring force in the Americas.[2]

Though it is easy to spot and to describe the African role in the *shaping* of the Americas, it has proved more difficult locating Africans and their New World descendants in the *undermining* of the slave systems of the Americas. Slave revolts were the most obvious, disruptive force in the loosening of the slave systems (especially in Haiti). Persistent damage was also caused by slave resistance in all its forms. Similarly, the rise of black communities and their 'civility' and 'progress', which so impressed outsiders, helped to corrode the slave empires in ways which have generally been overlooked. Slave attacks on slavery were most obvious when they were violent and bloody: in Haiti, in the great British slave upheavals of 1816, 1823 and 1831–2 and in the sporadic (but generally less violent) outbursts in North America.[3] In the short-term, such assaults were unlikely to win friends (though they clearly wore down plantocratic resistance). In the debate about slavery and abolition, outsiders were won over by *argument;* arguments which appealed to their religious sensibilities, to their sense of humanity, and to their grasp of economic self-interest or national interest. And here Equiano was important.

The drive for the ending of the slave trade was, in the first instance, a literary campaign, waged through a plethora of tracts and booklets in the last quarter of the eighteenth century. True, it was reinforced by verbal assaults – by lectures and sermons, especially in dissenting chapels – and by a rich and varied abolitionist iconography, ranging from Wedgwood's famous plaque through to paintings, prints, cartoons and artefacts of all kinds.[4] Again, Equiano's book is symptomatic because it was not merely a literary argument in the form of an autobiography, but it was prefaced, unusually, by a visual image of the author himself. Even before the reader had digested a word, he or she was confronted by the unambiguous fact that the author was African. The picture is of an African in European clothing, finely-dressed in contemporary western attire, with frills on his shirt and cuffs, wearing an elaborate waistcoat and coat or jacket. It was an image carefully chosen by Equiano himself, and it was subtly changed in subsequent editions to present a more assertive and powerful visual image of the author to the reader.[5]

It is a picture of an African clutching the Bible, conveniently opened at *Acts*, Chapter IV, verse 12:

> Neither is there salvation in any other: for there is none other name under heaven given among men, whereby we must be saved.

The message was simple but unavoidable: the author was African, he was devout and he was refined. The picture stood in stark contrast to the familiar visual images of Africans, in slave ships or slave colonies, as dehumanized beasts of burden devoid of any semblance of civility. Equiano, on the other hand, strikes the reader immediately as a civilized, religious man: recognizable, congenial and, in fact, at ease and at home with his British readership.

Equiano's book was much more than a simple autobiography; it was the journey of a soul – the story of one man's discovery of true faith. The book is peppered with theology, of Equiano's discovery of the Bible and true religion, his periodic struggles with his conscience about how best to secure salvation and how he found his true spiritual home. Time and again he quotes from the Bible. He carried a copy of the Bible wherever he travelled and he read the Bible whenever the opportunity arose. Not all his readers liked his religiosity. Mary Wollstonecraft reviewing the book in *Analytical Review* in 1789 was not impressed by Equiano's soul-searching: 'The long account of his religious sentiments and conversion to Methodism, is rather tiresome.'[6]

John Wesley, on the other hand, must have been more enthusiastic. He was reading Equiano on his deathbed.[7] Throughout the book, Equiano trails his theological coat, seeking to impress readers both with his grasp of theology (though he admits to uncertainties and doubts *en route*) and his mastery of the Bible. As if to reinforce the point, he provides copious examples of his socializing with clerics, and enjoying devout company. Both in Philadelphia and London, he was friendly with Quakers, and on his travels he sought the company of kindred souls. At times his piety clearly was an irritant, nowhere more obviously than in the company of fellow sailors, whose blasphemies caused the African such offence in return.

Equiano's book-learning was grounded in much more than the Bible. Again, he uses his familiarity with 'great books' to impress the reader. At times the quotations and references, too self-conscious and self-promotional, reflect the classic autodidact. Literary references and allusions abound. Milton is quoted in order to round off an argument about the inevitable consequences of slavery, and to describe the dangers of battle.[8] Equiano quotes (and misquotes) Homer on fear in warfare.[9] He quotes from Shakespeare and from Juvenal.[10] He uses Thomas Day's poem *The Dying Negro* (1773), itself a seminal publication in the evolution of abolition.[11] Less obviously eye-catching was the regular reference to, and reliance on, a number of earlier abolitionist publications. Equiano had clearly studied (and possibly taken notes) from the standard criticisms of slavery and the slave trade. In places his arguments derived substantially from what he read in other people's work. But this simple fact – learning from others – is hardly a criticism. Indeed, it speaks to an author who sought to harness his own experience with the related arguments and evidence of other writers in the same field.[12] At times Equiano makes mistakes: in attribution, in transcription, in quotation. By and large, however, these mistakes serve to *confirm* the authenticity and strength of his own argument. The very existence of his literary and scholarly frailties are *precisely* what we might expect in a self-taught man, anxious to impress his readership with a learning he had acquired the hard way. The fact that he occasionally stumbles, unknowingly (a wrong date here, a person in the wrong place, a phrase slightly misquoted), actually reinforces both his authenticity and the strength of his *Narrative*.

Like other self-taught men, Equiano took pride in the range and depth of his learning, and was happy repeating the virtues which others thought they saw in him. He was, in the words of one supporter, 'an enlightened African'. Another thought him 'an African of distinguished merit'. A review of his book spoke of Equiano being 'a very sensible man'.[13] What Equiano's book offered to the reading public was the work of a reasonable man of enlightened views; an African distinguished from most others by self-improvement. Hard work had enabled him to become an 'enlightened African'.

In many respects Equiano was a product of the Enlightenment. His views were clearly rooted in the late eighteenth-century debate about rights. He was interested in the rights of man. It was fitting that Equiano should join the London Corresponding Society in the early 1790s, for the ideals of the members were ones which he himself had supported for some years. The key event in the rise of popular radical ideas was the American Revolution of 1776, a major political break from the British colonial power, which hinged upon an emergent sense of democracy – with implications, of course, for slavery. The American debate created a powerful undertow in Britain itself. Arguments about rights, and about representation, were as relevant for the inhabitants, say, of Manchester as they were of Boston. The American cause had supporters in Britain, and the democratic debate wafted eastward from America like an invigorating breeze. The American Revolution set in place ideals and organizations in Britain which were to form the bedrock of a wider reforming movement in the years of peace after 1783.

The debate about rights was given a powerful push by the French Revolution, by the French Declaration of the Rights of Man, and by the publication in Britain of Tom Paine's *Rights of Man* (1791–2). We need to recall, however, that a similar debate, in a lower key, had *already* emerged around the related issues of slaves and the slave trade. As early as 1776 the MP for Hull, David Hartley, had proposed a motion in the Commons that 'the Slave-Trade was contrary to the laws of God, and the Rights of Man'.[14] The denial of slave rights was basic to the overall attack on the slave trade in abolitionist tracts after 1783.[15] The Quakers, too, were keen to talk about 'the natural rights of mankind' when denouncing the slave trade in their petitions to Parliament in the 1780s.[16] A tract of 1788 asserted simply:

1st. All men have by nature, an equal right to the enjoyment of personal liberty and security.

2nd. No man can be deprived of this right, unless it be forfeited by offences. . .[17]

Thus, even *before* the upheavals in France in 1789, the issue of human rights had been firmly attached to the arguments about slavery and the slave trade.

Equiano was clearly influenced by the earlier abolition debate. It had, after all, been conducted by men he knew, by groups he associated with, and by men he talked to. We know that he had read some of the key abolitionist tracts, and that his own writing was influenced by what he read. How could it have been otherwise? He was an intelligent, literate man hungry for learning and keen to harness the thoughts and ideas of others to his own unique personal experience, both in order to educate himself and to formulate his attack on slavery. Not surprisingly then, Equiano was attracted by the arguments about human rights, and returned to it throughout his own book.

The slave trade, he argued, 'violates that first natural right of mankind, equality and independency'.[18] When he petitioned the Queen in 1788 he expressed a hope that the slaves would soon 'be raised from the condition of brutes, to which they are at present degraded, to the rights and situation of men'.[19] In an earlier letter to the press, in February 1788, Equiano had described Atlantic slavery as a system designed to degrade Africans, and 'to deny them every right but those, and scarcely those we allow to a horse'.[20]

Equiano was not interested merely in abstract rights, but in the slaves' loss of practical rights. He was especially agitated by the legal system and by its denial of legal rights to slaves, and by the patently unjust ways the law dealt with slaves. He was able to recount a miserable list of slave sufferings and the arbitrary actions of white men on both sides of the Atlantic. *The Narrative* forms a dismal account of personal humilations: a story of sufferings which Equiano shared with millions of others, but which is the more poignant for being individual. Equiano used his stock of personal experiences to good effect, by simply reciting the callous brutalities which were the everyday stuff of slave life: enslaved, transhipped, re-enslaved, brutalized at work and in private moments, all these he experienced and saw. What concerned him most acutely, and outraged a growing band of liberally minded Britons, was the way the *system* made this possible. It was an inhumanity which was sustained not just by casual cruelty or rampant economic self-interest, but by legal systems on both sides of the Atlantic.

Equiano had seen how the law supported slavery both in London and the West Indies. On the other hand, his dealings with Granville Sharp, from the case of John Annis in 1774 onwards, had alerted him to the way English law might be used to black advantage.[21] The law was, at one and the same time, the surest foundation of Atlantic slavery and, therefore, the best way ultimately of undermining it. Here then was another aspect of the age of reason; an enlightened appreciation of the functioning of society and the urge to ensure, through the changes in the law, that both justice and happiness would be secured.

Equiano was keen to locate the maltreatment of black humanity not simply in the personal brutality and in the inhumanity of the people involved, but in the legal and social system which justified and sustained such behaviour. He had developed an almost scholarly interest in the legal processes of slavery, and quoted chapter and verse of those slave laws which were especially outrageous. He cited an Act of Barbados which specified a fine for the killing of a slave.[22] Equiano had already locked horns in print with James Tobin, planter and publicist for the slave system, about the legal status of slaves in the colonies,[23] and he paid particular attention to the changes in the slave laws in Jamaica discussed in London in 1792.[24]

What emerges from any analysis of Equiano's ideas is the degree to which he read widely,[25] and how he listened to that flow of arguments about slavery in the 1780s. He had made it his job not only to improve himself materially, but to educate himself as thoroughly and completely as possible. It is tempting to overstate his attainments of course; to see in his each and every utterance a mature and refined sophistication. Yet even if we prefer to be more cautious, it would be perverse not to be impressed by the tone of reason and enlightenment which informs Equiano's work. As his referees recognized, he was, quite simply, an enlightened African; a man of reason, able and keen to pit himself in literary debate with whichever political or literary authority came his way. In this he was understandably greatly influenced by earlier writers, by the ebb and flow of political (especially abolitionist) argument in London and Philadelphia. But even when Equiano seemed to be reciting well-known or established ideas, they had a different edge, and took on a sharpness, because they came from an African. His arguments were doubly powerful in issuing from an African. He was, again, a rare figure; an African who had both endured the horrors of Atlantic slavery and yet managed to cloak himself in the vernacular of European enlightenment.

The basic foundations of the Atlantic slave system were the economic benefits which accrued to all involved (saving, of course, the people who made it possible – the slaves). This simple fact provided the slave lobby with its strongest argument. Who would willingly throw away such material bounty, to the mother country as well as to the settler colonies, for mere insistence on humanity? It all seemed to hinge on the Africa trade, a trade described by one African merchant as, 'so beneficial to Great Britain, so essentially necessary to the very being of her colonies, that without it neither could we flourish, nor they long subsist'.[26] Yet did it *have* to be this way? Were there ways of squaring the economic circle; of forming an economic relationship with West Africa which was not driven by the search for slaves? Equiano, and other abolitionists, certainly thought so.

In the rapid and profitable growth of the African trade in the course of the eighteenth century, any economic or moral objections had simply been swept aside by the benefits of slave labour. There were, however, contrary voices which argued that Britain would be better served by developing other markets in Africa. The most prominent case had been advanced by Malachy Postlethwayt in 1757 in his book *Britain's Commercial Interest Explained and Improved*. Postlethwayt asked a number of simple questions:

> Whether so extensive and populous a country as Africa is, will not admit a far more extensive and profitable trade to Great Britain, than it yet ever has done?

Would Europeans not be better off by cultivating:

> a friendly, humane, and civilized commerce with those people, into the very centre of their extended country, than to content themselves only with skimming a trifling portion of trade upon the sea coast of Africa?

He also asked:

> Whether the greatest hindrance and obstruction to the Europeans cultivating a humane and Christian-like commerce with those populous countries, has not wholly proceeded from that unjust, inhumane, and unchristian-like traffic, called *the Slave Trade*, which is carried on by the Europeans?

The argument that the slave trade might be replaced by an even more profitable trade to Africa was later advanced by the Quaker Anthony Benezet, whose tract *Some Historical Account of Guinea* (1771) was enormously influential in edging Quakers towards arguing openly for abolition.[27] Thanks to Benezet this simple economic proposition – that Africa beckoned with its incalculable and yet undoubted bounty – quickly embedded itself in early abolitionist thought, and thence moved even further afield. Quakers distributed Benezet's tracts to all of England's major schools (Charterhouse, St Paul's, Merchant Taylors', Eton, Winchester, Harrow and Westminster) and spread them, via Friends, across the face of Britain.[28] We have already seen how the idea that Africa might be more profitably approached through open trade lay at the heart of the early discussion about the settlement of the Sierra Leone colony.

As abolitionists cast around to find persuasive detail to win over their readers, economics provided a tempting case. Africa beckoned as a market; a market of untold potential and with limitless scope for British goods and trade. Far from creating the disaster predicted by the slave lobby, ending the slave trade might prompt an *expansion* of British trade. In the words of one abolitionist tract of 1784:

> Were Africa civilized, and could we preoccupy the affections of the natives, and introduce gradually our religion, manners, and language among them, we should open a market that would fully employ our manufacturers and seamen, morally speaking, till the end of time. And while we enriched ourselves, we should contribute to their happiness.[29]

Gradually the idea of non-slave trade to Africa took hold in abolitionist circles. By the late 1780s, Thomas Clarkson was tirelessly touring the country with his collection of African produce and artefacts (see p. 155). From the major slaving ports he accumulated a range of African goods: gum and cotton from Gambia; indigo, musk and pepper from Whidah; mahogany from Calabar, and a range of coloured textiles. An ex-slave captain in Liverpool told Clarkson that the slave trade,

> by turning the attention of the inhabitants to the persons of one another for sale, hindered foreigners from discovering, and themselves from cultivating, many of the valuable productions of their own soil.[30]

Clarkson displayed these various African goods to his curious audiences across the country. When his own portrait was painted, he was surrounded by a display of his African artefacts.[31]

Clarkson pursued this theme in subsequent philanthropic and economic involvement with West Africa, notably in the reconstituted Sierra Leone scheme of 1791, which saw the transplantation of 1,000 or more blacks from Canada. Greatly helped by his brother John, a Royal Naval captain, he compiled a detailed report for the Sierra Leone Company which again painted a tantalizing image of African fruitfulness. Open trade would yield sugar, cotton, indigo, tobacco, oils, waxes, gums, spices, woods, gold and ivory. He thought vineyards (and even whaling) could be introduced, while the developments of ports would form a link to major interior African trading systems, thereby securing 'all the Riches of Africa'. In the process, Christianity would spread on the back of trade. The slave trade would be pushed aside and would decay.[32] This argument offers an interesting twist. The man whose abolitionism was prompted initially by moral and Christian outrage against the slave trade had been won over to the idea that the slave trade could be outflanked by the development of open trade between Europe and Africa.

Equiano's thought travelled much the same route. It was natural enough that the African should pick up abolitionist themes explored by others. Like many around him, he was persuaded (in words used by Benezet) that 'Guinea affords an easy living to its inhabitants with but little toil'.[33] Equiano's economic argument was intended to silence those who forsaw economic disaster with the ending of the slave trade:

> I doubt not, if a system of commerce was established in Africa, the demand for manufactures would most rapidly augment, as the native inhabitants would insensibly adopt the British fashions, manners, customs, &c. In proportion to the civilization, so will be the consumption of British manufactures.[34]

Africa offered a market, the enormity of which was hard to grasp. Its inhabitants would consume British goods on a scale which would dwarf any benefits currently enjoyed by the slave-based trading systems.

> A commercial intercourse with Africa opens an inexhaustible source of wealth to the manufacturing interests of Great Britain, and to all which the slave-trade is an objection.

It was hard even to imagine what Africa might offer:

> Population, the bowels and surface of Africa, abound in valuable and useful returns; the hidden treasures of centuries will be brought to light and into circulation. Industry, enterprise, and mining, will have their full scope, proportionably as they civilize. In a word, it lays open an endless field of commerce to the British manufacturers and merchant adventurers.

In all this, Equiano assumed that 'the manufacturing interest and the general interests are synonimous'. It was an argument which turned the slave lobby's argument on its head. Far from damaging British well-being, the end of the slave trade would enhance British trade and manufacture. 'The abolition of slavery would be in reality an universal good.'[35]

It is also worth noting that Equiano spoke about ending *slavery*. At the time, the main (indeed the sole) ambition of the abolition movement was to end the Atlantic slave trade. The hope of the Abolition Society was that the ending of the Atlantic slave trade would oblige West Indian planters to treat their slaves better. And from that vague, general amelioration a fertile and expansive black labour force would emerge, rendering slavery itself unnecessary. A free black peasantry would replace the slave labour force. Even that limited goal was, in reality, an enormous undertaking. Yet Equiano wanted to move beyond that. Of course abolitionists on the whole wanted an eventual end to slavery. But few mentioned it quite so openly or specifically. It seemed a distant dream and ambition, and it was much better (more practical and manageable) to concentrate on ending the Atlantic slave trade. Equiano seems to have had no such hesitations. And why should he?

Equiano hoped to see the manufacturing interests united in appreciating the benefits of free trade to Africa; a free trade which would undermine the slave trade. Only those directly involved in the slave trade – especially the manufacturers of 'instruments of torture used in the slave trade' would object. Equiano's aim was to weld economic interest onto the abolitionist passions already aroused by 'justice and humanity'. He suggested that if all the millions of Africans were to spend £5 a head on buying imported goods, it would create 'an immensity beyond the reach of imagination'. Were Africans to remain unmolested, and not to be enslaved and transported, the African population would increase regularly, and as it increased, demand for imported goods would grow. African produce, traded for British manufactures, would offer

> a most immense, glorious, and happy prospect – the clothing, etc. of a continent ten thousand miles in circumference, and immensely rich in productions of every denomination in return for manufactures.

It was a matter 'of no small consequence to the manufacturing towns of Great Britain'.[36]

In later editions of his work, Equiano incorporated examples of how this was already at work; of how large volumes of British goods and foodstuffs had recently been shipped to the new colony of Sierra Leone. He was especially pleased to see useful goods replacing the instruments of the slave trade, and decent food replacing the basic diet exported on the slave ships: '*flour* instead of *gunpowder – biscuits and bread* instead of *horsebeans – implements of husbandry* instead of *guns*'.[37]

Equiano and other abolitionists were keen to do more than merely redirect trade and undermine the slave trade. They also saw the growth of British markets in Africa as a means of 'civilizing' Africa itself. Commerce and Christianity would go hand in hand to drive out both economic backwardness and barbarism, which they assumed haunted the continent. It was a policy which was given the go-ahead when the slave trade was finally abolished in 1807, and which was tried in other parts of the world (in India and China, for example). It was, in effect, the origins of that distinctive cultural imperialism which so permeated much of Britain's dealings with the wider world in the course of the nineteenth century. Via Christian Africans strategically placed on the coast (as Equiano himself had wanted to be) Christianity would take root, Africa would be 'civilized', and trade to and from Britain would flourish. In the event, little progress along these lines was made until the mid-nineteenth century.[38] Yet it was an argument advanced here by the most prominent African in Britain in the last years of the eighteenth century.

Though Equiano was familiar with the literature of abolition, his learning, and experience, went much deeper than that. He was, first and foremost, a devout man, steeped in the Bible, at home with the Scriptures, and able to dip into the book for appropriate help and support when fashioning his ideas. Even when he spoke to overtly political issues (when speaking of rights, or when his ideas seemed shaped by America) he invariably placed his beliefs in a spiritual context. Equiano believed that all men were equal in the eyes of the Lord. By the time of his later editions, however, a widespread debate about equality had seeped into all corners of Britain, thanks to a heady political mix of American, French and Paineite ideas. In the reforming mind, black and white were brought together as never before. Though Equiano absorbed ideas from all angles, his world view was securely rooted in his firm theological foundations.

The climate in which Equiano expressed his ideas changed quite fundamentally in the course of the 1790s. When he published his first edition, in March 1789, the major upheavals in France were merely in prospect. By the time of the last edition in his lifetime (1794), Europe had been convulsed by revolution and war. France had descended into a violent conflict which sent a chill throughout propertied European life, French armies seemed invincible, the foundations of West Indian slavery had shuddered before the seismic waves radiating from Haiti – and British domestic radicalism had briefly blossomed and faded. The time for promoting fundamentally reforming ideas passed quickly. To speak the language of reform, to argue for basic rights, came to be seen as mouthing Jacobinical words. By 1793 the Earl of Abingdon, speaking in Parliament was convinced that

> the idea of abolishing the slave trade is connected with the levelling system and the rights of man. . . what does the abolition of the slave trade mean more or less, than liberty and equality? What more or less than the rights of man?

And to clinch his argument the good Earl pointed to Haiti: 'look at the colony of St Domingue and see what the rights of man have done there.'[39]

Even Wilberforce was denounced as a Jacobin, and even he, sadly, accepted that people had come to link 'democratical principles with the Abolition of the Slave Trade and will not hear mention of it'.[40] Equiano's ideas had, in effect, been by-passed by events. At least for the time being.

Those ideas, moulded over years of studying his Bible, had been refined in the politically charged atmosphere, first of the Sierra Leone Scheme, and then the early abolition movement. But by 1795 they had been rendered inexpedient. His close friends in the radicial societies had been scattered and ruined by the oppressive anti-Jacobin witch-hunts of 1794. Parliamentary abolitionists slid into silence, afraid that demands for an end to the slave trade would be seen as another aspect of Jacobinism. Even the staunchest of friends looked askance at the disasters and blood-letting in Haiti. Equiano's pleas for equality in the eyes of the Lord, for abolition as a stimulant to trade with Africa, and his argument that Africa, not the Americas, might be the economic cornucopia for the British economy, all may have seemed plausible and attractive in 1789. By 1795, however, they seemed unrealistic and even dangerous. The heady days of 1789–92, when Equiano eagerly criss-crossed Britain promoting his book like an abolitionist salesman, had given way to the risky gloom of 1795. As the country teetered on the edge of starvation, beleaguered by ascendant French power, abolition of the slave trade seemed a remote dream. Though Equiano may have enjoyed his new role as family man (though he never mentioned his family), his political hopes, his dreams of an end to the system which had blighted his life, seemed to have been dashed. The slave system appeared to have weathered the immediate storm. We now know that it had been fatally weakened; fractured by sustained pressure on its credibility and by successive bolts hurled at its defences by a widening phalanx of critics, and by slaves from within.

In the wave of abolitionist argument which surged around the slave system after 1783, it is impossible to attribute levels of importance to particular writers. But Equiano's role was unique, notwithstanding the influence of Sancho and Cugoano. His was a distinctive voice which captured the experience of Africa, of enslavement and freedom, expressing a lifetime's suffering and hope, and all in a devout tone designed to persuade the reader. But Equiano was much, much more than a devout African. He was clearly a man of reason, keen to advance a rational critique of the slave system, and to promote sensible alternatives which were reasoned and economically sensible. He was, in brief, a man of enlightened thought and action – as his British backers appreciated. He was, as friends in Nottingham testified, a man of 'good sense, intellectual improvements, and integrity'. He was, as an American radical wrote, 'an enlightened African'.[41]

Notes

1 Thomas Clarkson, *The History of the Rise, Progress and Accomplishment of the Abolition of the Slave Trade*, 2 vols (London, 1808), vol. I, pp. 85–125.
2 James Walvin, *Questioning Slavery* (London, 1996), p. 20.
3 *Ibid.*, Ch. 7; Michael Craton, *Testing the Chains* (Ithaca, NY, 1982).
4 J. R. Oldfield, *Popular Politics and British Anti-Slavery* (Manchester, 1995), Ch. 6.
5 For Carretta's comments on this illustration see *Interesting Narrative*, pp. 310–16.
6 Janet Todd and Marilyn Butler (eds), *The Works of Mary Wollstonecraft* (London, 1989), vol. 7, pp. 100–1.
7 *The Journal of the Rev. John Wesley*, 8 vols (London, 1916), vol. VIII, pp. 127–8.
8 *Interesting Narrative*, pp. 112; 89.
9 *Ibid.*, p. 82.
10 *Ibid.*, p. 238, n. 4; 5.
11 *Ibid.*, p. 267, n. 276.
12 Paul Edwards (ed.), *The Life of Olaudah Equiano* (London, 1988), pp. xxi–xxii.
13 See letters, *Interesting Narrative*, pp. 10–12.
14 Clarkson, *op. cit.*, p. 84.
15 For a good list of abolitionist tracts published in these years, see M. Canney and D. Knott, *Catalogue of the Goldsmiths Library*, 2 vols (London, 1970), vol. I.
16 Clarkson, *op. cit.*, p. 110.
17 *A General View of the African Slave Trade. . .* (London, 1788), p. 8.
18 *Interesting Narrative*, p. 111.
19 *Ibid.*, p. 232. But see the changes to the text in the later editions; p. 302, n. 657.
20 *Ibid.*, p. 331.
21 *Ibid.*, pp. 179–80.
22 *Ibid.*, p. 109.
23 *Ibid.*, p. 328–30. Parts of these earlier letters to the press were subsequently incorporated into the text of *The Narrative.* Compare, e.g., pp. 111; 328–30.
24 *Ibid.*, pp. 232; 302, n. 659.
25 Note his comments about 'the great part of my study and attention', *ibid.*, p. 231.
26 John Peter Demarin, *A Treatise upon the Trade from Great Britain to Africa, by an African Merchant* (London 1772), pp. 4–5.
27 Some of Postlethwayt's questions were reprinted in Anthony Benezet, *Some Historical Account of Guinea* (London, 1771), pp. 122–4. Postlethwayt had been active in the African trade and had turned his back on the slave trade, hoping instead to see the development of British markets in Africa. See D. B. Davis, *The Problem of Slavery in Western Culture* (Ithaca, NY, 1966), pp. 160–1.
28 Clarkson, *op. cit.*, pp. 122–5.
29 *An Inquiry into the Effect of Putting a Stop to the African Slave Trade* (London, 1784), pp. 14–15.
30 Clarkson, *op. cit.*, pp. 373; 379.
31 Portrait of Thomas Clarkson by Henry Room.
32 Ellen Wilson Gibson, *Thomas Clarkson* (York, 1996), p. 65.
33 Anthony Benezet, *Guinea*, p. 1.
34 *Interesting Narrative*, p. 233.
35 *Ibid.*, p. 234.
36 *Ibid.*, p. 235.
37 *Ibid.*, p. 304, n. 669.
38 P. J. Cain and A. G. Hopkins, *British Imperialism: Innovation and Expansion, 1688–1914* (London, 1993), pp. 353–6.
39 Hansard's Debates, vol. XXX (1792–4), cols 632–59.
40 R. T. and S. Wilberforce, *The Life of William Wilberforce*, 5 vols (London, 1838), vol. II, p. 18.
41 *Interesting Narrative*, pp. 9–10.

PART FIVE

AFTERWARDS

= 15 =

DECLINE,
FALL - AND
REDISCOVERY

In the middle of promoting his book, Equiano married. It is hard to know what to make of his reference to his marriage, on 7 April 1792, to Susanna Cullen. He had made no previous mention of her. Indeed, women had rarely figured in his account of his life, with the exception of passing references to his attraction to slave women in Montserrat many years before.[1] Now, out of the blue, he married. In his *Narrative*, the ceremony occupies a mere two-and-a-half lines; an event squeezed between a parliamentary debate on the slave trade and a trip north to promote his book.[2] We ought not to expect an eighteenth-century writer to speak, in the mode of a late twentieth-century author, about personal and intimate matters, yet even by the conventions of the time, Equiano's passing reference to his wife was brief and indirect. One of life's most significant events – a marriage – scarcely registered in a narrative devoted to the more pressing matters of abolitionist politics and selling books.

The wedding was noticed in the London press, but not under the name Equiano:

At Soham, co. Cambridge, Gustavus Vassa, the African, well known in England as the champion and advocate for procuring a suppression of the slave trade, to Miss Cullen, daughter of Mr C. of Ely, in same county.[3]

The parish register also records the marriage under the name Vassa.[4]

The wedding took place in the bride's home parish, and it seems that Equiano and his bride set up home there, though the husband's roving book promotion created a peripatetic life. Soon after the wedding Susanna accompanied Equiano on his promotional trip to Scotland, a fact which caught the attention of a local newspaper in May 1792:

GUSTAVUS VASSA, with his *white* wife, is at Edinburgh, where he has published a letter of thanks to the General Assembly of the Church of Scotland, for their just and humane interference upon the question of the SLAVE TRADE.[5]

The modern reader might ask: why did the newspaper feel the need to highlight the fact that Equiano's wife was white – not English or British – but white?

The couple had two daughters, Ann Mary (Maria) born 16 October 1793 and Joanna born 11 April 1795. Whatever happiness the couple enjoyed together, or after the arrival of their children, goes unrecorded – and was short-lived. Equiano's wife, Susanna was buried, aged 34, in February 1796. A little more than a year later she was joined by her first-born, Ann Mary, not yet four years old. The child is commemorated by a plaque on the wall of St Andrew's Church, Chesterton, Cambridge.

Near this Place lies Interred
ANNA MARIA VASSA
Daughter of Gustavus Vassa the African
She died July 21 1797
Aged 4 Years

Should simple village rhymes attract thine eye,
Stranger, as thoughtfully thou passest by,
Know that there lies beside this humble stone
A child of colour haply not thine own.
Her father born of Afric's sun-burnt race,
Torn from his native fields, ah, foul disgrace:
Through various toils, at length to Britain came
Espous'd, so Heaven ordain'd, an English dame,
And follow'd Christ; their hope two infants dear.
But one, a hapless Orphan, slumbers here.
To bury her the village children came,
And dropp'd choice flowers, and lisp'd her early fame:
And some that lov'd her most as if unblest
Bedew'd with tears the white wreath on their breast:
But she is gone and dwells in that abode
Where some of every clime shall joy in God.[6]

Equiano was left a widower, but he did not long survive his wife. In March 1797 Granville Sharp visited the deathbed of his African friend:

He was a sober, honest man, and I went to see him when he lay upon his deathbed, and had lost his voice so that he could only whisper.[7]

Equiano died in his early 50s in London on 31 March 1797, leaving an orphaned daughter of scarcely two. We do not know the cause of his death. At least he was able to ensure that his surviving child would have no material worries. Following his wife's death, Equiano had drafted a will, and that document provides a revealing insight both into his material circumstance, and into his attitude towards his property. Equiano described his possessions as 'Estate and property I have dearly earned by the Sweat of my Brow in some of the most remote and adverse Corners of the whole world'. To the end of his days, he could not forget the physical effort, the sweat – even perhaps the good fortune – which had enabled him to become a man of means. Some of his prosperity had obviously derived from his wife: land in Ely and a small annual annuity. He had income from at least three annuities, a lease on property in London, a substantial amount of cash ('The Sum of Three hundred pounds at present undisposed of') and various personal effects: 'Sundry Household Goods and Furniture wearing Apparel and printed Books'.

Books remained among his most prized possessions to the end of his life. From his days as a scarcely literate sailor/slave, guarding his books in a private chest on board ship, through to his final days as a man of modest means, books played a major role in Equiano's life. It was fitting that they should be, for by 1797 the bulk of his wealth seems to have derived from sales of his *Narrative*. No less characteristically, Equiano asked his executors 'to insure the Lives on which the several Annuities are granted at the Assurance Office in Bridge Street Blackfriars'. Equiano's estate was to be used for the maintenance and education of his daughters. In the event, only Joanna reached her majority, in 1816, inheriting the remainder of her late father's estate, to the tune of almost £1000.[8]

It is worth remembering that a decade before his death – in 1787 – Equiano had been forced to petition government officers for money owed to him; wages and expenses totalling less than £50. Ten years later, however, his estate had multiplied dramatically. It could have only come from marriage and/or his book. The painful irony is that he did not live to enjoy it. Equiano, his wife and their elder daughter were all dead by the summer of 1797. Even by the brutal standards of the day, a world scarred by sudden and unexpected infant mortality, by the chance death of young mothers, the fate of Equiano's family was distressingly harsh. For a man who had endured the severest of ordeals, but who had survived and prospered, the simple pleasures and comforts of domestic life were short-lived. He was, at the end, denied the happiness he had so assiduously sought.

Equiano's death was marked by *The Gentleman's Magazine* in their 'Obituary of remarkable Persons'. Again, he was named 'Mr Gustavus Vasa [*sic*], the African'. He was, the magazine claimed, 'well known to the publick by the interesting narrative of his life'.[9] Yet Equiano's fame and public standing evaporated almost instantly. When, a little more than ten years after his death, a new edition of his autobiography was issued in Belper, the publisher knew nothing about him; not even the date of his death.[10] A further edition in Penryn, Cornwall, in 1816 merely repeated the same point; no one knew what had happened to Equiano. He, like his book, had been virtually forgotten. He was a man of his times, and as the times changed, his fame evaporated.

The slave trade against which Equiano had campaigned had been abolished in 1807 and, when the French wars finished in 1815, abolitionists waited to see what the consequences of abolition had been. Eyes were focused on the West Indies to see if curbing the supply of new Africans had led to improvement in the lot of slaves on the islands. Increasing numbers of missionaries headed for the slave islands, to convert and to develop new congregations of black Christians, and the abolitionist reading public in Britain had more than enough material to read and digest. There was in fact a rising tide of new abolitionist literature, but it was quite different from the tracts of the 1780s. Then the debates had been about the slave trade, about the state of Africa, about how the ending of the Atlantic trade might affect Africa. Now, attention was focused directly on the slave quarters of the Caribbean. The evidence and arguments came from the pens of missionaries, visitors and officials returning from the Caribbean. Much of the older abolitionist literature seemed dated; addressed to a different set of questions and offered in a very different tone. There was little room for Equiano and his book.

Nor was there much interest in Equiano in North America. There, the revival of chattel slavery on the back of the buoyant cotton industry and westward expansion, created a whole new set of issues both for slave-holders and for their (largely northern) abolitionist opponents. Equiano seemed a mere curiosity, speaking, again, to issues of long ago and far away. The slave trade had ended, Africa was an increasingly distant memory, and Britain and British slavery seemed ever more remote from North American concerns. It was hard to see what help Equiano could offer to the North American fight against slavery, a fight advanced by African-Americans in their own way.[11]

There was, however, one aspect of Equiano's life which seemed useful, and was adopted in edited form for the reading public interested in US slavery. The defence of US slavery became progressively, and more aggressively, racist. Planters were not alone in believing that slaves (and blacks in general) were racially inferior, and the planters were joined by a raft of southern groups: doctors, scientists and clerics. One approach of abolitionist attack on this broad racist coalition was to select 'men of colour' who had done well for themselves. By pointing to black attainments, especially in those areas of social, economic and artistic life most admired by whites, abolitionists felt they might outflank racist support for slavery. Looking back, much of the argument (and even the approach) looks distinctively coy and naive. But it gave Equiano's words a new lease of life.

Equiano began to reappear in abstracted, edited form in collections devoted to the achievements of 'men of colour'. In the 1830s Lydia Maria Child produced her influential work *Appeal in Favour of that Class of Americans called Africans* and included some pages about Equiano. Her work was derived from an earlier commentary on Equiano (which had been issued in 1810). A similar compilation, of 1826, Abigail Mott's *Sketches and Interesting Anecdotes of Persons of Colour*, had been widely used in American (especially black) schools and this volume was refined and slimmed down for a new edition in 1829 with a fuller piece from Equiano. But it still remained a severely edited piece, with many of the key sections deleted, and was clearly aimed at promoting American abolition. To make any impact in America, Equiano had to be stripped of many of his defining experiences and qualities.[12]

It was hard even to find copies of Equiano's original book in North America by the 1830s (as had been the case in Britain twenty years earlier).[13] That was made good in 1837 with the issue of a new edition in Boston, prompted it seems by the earlier anthologies. It now became part of a revived abolitionist agitation in America, with an associated upsurge in abolitionist publications, among which were books by other Africans and African-Americans. Yet it was a false dawn. After the 1837 Boston edition, Equiano sank without trace in North America, not to be revived until the utterly transformed circumstance of the 1960s.[14]

In Britain, Equiano enjoyed a brief revival in the 1840s and 1850s in the British campaign against American slavery. Again, he had a walk-on role – included in collections of brief cameos produced by abolitionists and Quakers to illustrate what Africans might achieve if given the chance. Wilson Armistead (a northern Quaker) was especially active, compiling a series of anthologies, directed at American slavery.[15] In 1848 he published *A Tribute for the Negro being a Vindication of the Moral, Intellectual, and Religous Capabilities of the Coloured Portion of Mankind*, which contained almost 50 pages from Equiano's 1794 edition.[16]

Wherever pen portraits of eminent blacks were published, Equiano was afforded a niche in the roll-call of black distinction.[17] Anthologies of all kinds tumbled from British abolitionist presses, [18] especially from William Armistead. *A Cloud of Witness against Slavery and Oppression* was a chronological list of quotes and extracts from anti-slavery authorities.[19] In *God's Image in Ebony* (1854) twelve pages from Equiano's two-volume 1789 edition were paraphrased (in a book significantly dedicated to Harriet Beecher Stowe, author of *Uncle Tom's Cabin*).[20] But such formats for Equiano's words were far removed from the heady days of sixty years earlier, when Equiano had stomped across Britain selling his *Narrative* and establishing himself as an important political and literary figure on the abolitionist landscape. By the mid-nineteenth century he had disappeared without trace in North America, whereas in Britain his memory was kept alive only by the dogged efforts of a handful of abolitionist compilers. Equiano had in fact slipped from the collective memory; gone, and forgotten. It was as if he had not even existed.

As Equiano disappeared from public view and political consciousness, a new generation of black writers emerged, to occupy the position effectively pioneered by Equiano. The context, style and substance of the North American slave narratives were utterly different from anything we might find in Equiano. Nor is it clear that these slave, or ex-slave authors were aware in any substantive way of Equiano's earlier work. There was, however, a continuum of experience which clearly linked their voices. The most popular books – by Frederick Douglass, William Wells Brown and Harriet Jacobs, for example – told of their lives as slaves, and their escape or flight to freedom (normally in the North), to salvation (and often to God). These slave narratives became a hugely successful literary genre, selling in their tens of thousands (most spectacularly in Frederick Douglass' case) – and influencing, in the process, the writing of *Uncle Tom's Cabin*.[21] But where, in all, this was Equiano?

For more than a century, from the American Civil War onwards, Equiano remained forgotten and neglected. But that changed, quite dramatically, in the 1960s and over the following thirty years. Equiano once again became a bestselling author; having had no place in the English-speaking world for a century, he began to enjoy a spectacular renaissance. By the time of the bi-centenary of his death in 1997, Equiano's autobiography was selling more copies than in his lifetime.

Looking back now (1998) it is easy to see why Equiano became so attractive to a new generation of readers. He spoke, once more, to the experience of Africans and the descendants of Africans scattered around the Atlantic by the diaspora. He was, once again, a man of the times. In a period of emergent self-awareness among former colonial peoples, and among African-Americans yearning to secure their own human rights, Equiano had immense appeal. This is not the place to trace the history of the movements for colonial independence, and black civil rights in the USA, but in the complex drive for black freedom, broadly defined, earlier black voices clearly lent support. With the ending of World War II, colonial peoples throughout the British empire pressed their demand for freedom from British domination. During that war, the right of people in Europe and Asia to self-determination, to be able to decide their fate without the military or political domination of Nazi Germany or imperial Japan, provided an ideological spine to the protracted and bloody global struggles. But if, for example, the French or the Dutch, the Malays or the Indonesians, had a right to be free, what right did the old imperial powers have to reimpose their control?

The Americans in particular were in no mood to fight a costly war merely to shore up the remnants of old European empires. Nor were large numbers of subject peoples willing to accept the restoration of old imperialisms. Not surprisingly, then, the post-war years saw the flaring up of demands for independence and freedom around the world. Colonial freedom became, quickly and universally, one of the most potent global international issues, goaded by British resistance to the dismemberment of an empire in which they had taken such pride. There was, in the words of Denis Judd 'a lot of life still left in the old imperial lion'.[22] In retrospect, however, it is astonishing how quickly the old empires succumbed to independence, lowering their flags and retreating to their European heartlands within the space of a single generation.

One undercurrent to these changes was the intellectual and educational shift in former colonies. Young men and women searched for their own intellectual traditions, trying to set aside the European-centred instruction which had been part of the imperial presence. New schooling and university systems, new publishing ventures, went hand in hand with the flowering of independence. Initially, much of what emerged, certainly in the former British colonies, was greatly influenced by the former colonial power. Gradually, however, a new generation of writers and educators (many of whom had served their colonial masters in the last war) began to rediscover their past: to define a history, a literature, an intellectual legacy which was not simply derived from their former governors. Scholars and writers began to speak to, and write about, their own local cultures.

One important seedbed for these changes were the new universities which had been created in all corners of the former British empire. Though they inevitably took the shape and influence of their British backers, they quickly began to reformulate themselves and to respond to local, rather than to metropolitan concerns. This was especially striking in the arts and social sciences. African, Indian or West Indian students (and staff) wanted to know more about their own world and less about the world of their former governors. Scholars in and of Africa, for example, in part under pressure from students demanding an indigenous educational and intellectual diet, began to recast their work; to write about the

African past, about African literature, rather than simply transplanting British (remote and sometimes irrelevant) preoccupations. It is worth reminding ourselves of the views of Hugh Trevor-Roper, then Regius Professor of History at Oxford, on African history, expressed so crudely as late as 1965: 'the unrewarding gyrations of barbarous tribes in picturesque but irrelevant corners of the globe'.[23] It was in the process of rethinking African history that Equiano was rediscovered.

The initial breakthrough was by Thomas Hodgkin, whose *Nigerian Perspectives*, published in 1960 (the year of Nigerian independence), offered a path-breaking study of the new nation, and included a major extract from Equiano.[24] Seven years later, two very different scholars published their own versions of Equiano. Philip Curtin, perhaps the most influential pioneer of African history in the USA, edited a collection of essays and extracts from narratives of West Africans in the period of the Atlantic slave trade.[25] In a book designed to provide students with African source materials and to direct readers' attention to the African background of African-Americans, Equiano figured prominently. In that same year, 1967, Paul Edwards, a literary scholar from the University of Edinburgh, published an edited version of Equiano's *Narrative* (renamed *Equiano's Travels*). He later published a facsimile version of Equiano's original two-volume *Narrative*, and another edited version retitled *The Life of Olaudah Equiano*. Over the years Edwards' work on Equiano – a series of essays, scholarly studies and editions – helped to establish Equiano as a key figure in African, and black literature in general.

Paul Edwards had discovered Equiano in Africa. Edwards' African students, when he was teaching at University College, Sierra Leone, had demanded African literature to complement an educational diet which seemed overwhelmingly British. Prompted by his association with Chinua Achebe, and helped by his Edinburgh colleague Christopher Fyfe (himself a pioneering historian of Sierra Leone), Edwards published his edited Equiano in 1967 in the 'African Writers Series', published by Heinemann and aimed primarily at the African market.[26] All three scholars – Hodgkin, Curtin and Edwards – had come to Equiano in and from Africa. Equiano was seen as an *African* writer; a major figure in both Nigerian and, more generally, West African literary and historical culture.

It seems pure accident that both Curtin and Edwards published their work on Equiano in 1967, though both were clearly following parallel interests and came from an African point of departure. Yet there was more to the timing than mere accident. Interest in Africa and black culture was not restricted to Africa or Africanists, and a more broadly based interest in 'black studies'[27] generated intellectual (and political) interest in black writers and black history. It was a movement driven forward by the rapid social and political changes in the USA. Civil rights, voter registration, the influence – and death – of Martin Luther King, all and more generated a dynamic for change, and a demand that the black voice be heard. In the profusion of literature spawned by these changes, there was a search for a historical past which more adequately reflected black attainments and black history in general. Who better to illustrate both than Olaudah Equiano?

Since 1967 it has been hard to keep track of new versions of Equiano, and of the scholarship about Equiano. On the whole, much of it has been very *literary*. Even the latest, and most exactingly scholarly edition of the *Narrative*, edited by Vincent Carretta for Penguin, is the work of a literary scholar. But if we need evidence to confirm the importance of Equiano, Carretta's edition has sold 12, 000 copies to date.[28] Today there are untold academic courses which use Equiano's book, edited or in full, as a textbook. Unfortunately, many use pirated or mangled versions of the *Narrative*, which Equiano would have had difficulty recognizing as his own work. History and literature courses throughout the English-speaking world, but especially in North America, use Equiano as a basic text. He is, at one and the same time, an African writer, an African-American writer, the key founder of the slave narrative, the first spokesman for the Afro-British community and the most quoted survivor of the Middle Passage. In brief, both Equiano and his book are now accorded heroic status.

Equiano is more popular today than ever before. Pictures of Equiano festoon any number of dust-jackets, his face is used on posters to promote exhibitions and TV programmes. He has his own postcard issued by an English museum. Whenever slavery or black writers are mentioned, Equiano is rarely far from the centre of attention, and he is a regular topic for discussion on TV and radio. The ultimate accolade was the founding in London in 1996 of an Equiano Society, devoted to honour his memory and promote, among other things, 'the education of the public about the life and work of Olaudah Equiano' and to 'promote the education of the public about the contribution of African and Caribbean people who have made outstanding contributions to the arts, culture, and to the well-being of Britain during the past 400 years'.[29]

It is worth reminding ourselves that, a mere thirty years ago, very few people knew who Equiano was. In the course of a generation, he has gone from anonymity to international fame: a bestseller in Africa, North America and Britain. It is an astonishing transformation. A single African, who tried to reach the hearts and minds of late eighteenth-century British readers, has had an even more profound impact on both sides of the Atlantic in the late twentieth century. That he is able to speak so influentially across the years is itself a poignant reminder of the global consequences of the African diaspora, and of its ramifications down to the present day.

Notes

1 Of course he made frequent mention of his long-lost mother and of the trauma of being torn from her care in childhood.
2 *Interesting Narrative*, p. 235.
3 *The Gentleman's Magazine*, vol. 62, Part I (1792), p. 384.
4 *Interesting Narrative*, p. 304, n. 674.
5 *Ibid.*, p. 350, n. 18.
6 I owe this transcription to my late friend, Professor Paul Edwards.
7 Letter, 27 February 1811, Granville Sharp Papers. I consulted these papers when they were lodged in Hardwicke Court. They are now lodged in the Gloucester Record Office.
8 *Interesting Narrative*, pp. 354–5.
9 *The Gentleman's Magazine*, April 1797, vol. 67, p. 356.
10 *The Interesting Narrative* (Belper, 1809), p. vi.
11 See, for example, the recent account in Nell Irvin Painter, *Sojourner Truth* (New York, 1996).
12 James Green, 'The publishing history of Olaudah Equiano's *Interesting Narrative*', *Slavery and Abolition*, vol. 16, no. 3 (1995).
13 *Ibid.*, p. 372; *The Interesting Narrative* (Belper, 1809), p. vi.
14 Green, *op. cit.*, pp. 372–3.
15 *Five Hundred Thousand Strokes for Freedom. A Series of Anti-Slavery Tracts of which Half a Million are now first issued by the Friends of the Negro* (London, 1853; available for consultation in the Library Company of Philadelphia).

16 Published in Manchester (1848), pp. 192–239 (author's copy).
17 *Intellect and Capabilities of the Negro Race* (London, 1853), No. 79, Leeds Anti-Slavery Series, pp. 2–4 (Library Company of Philadelphia).
18 *A Garland of Freedom. A Collection of Poems, Chiefly Anti-Slavery*, by a Friend of the Negro (London, 1853; Library Company of Philadelphia).
19 London, 1853; Library Company of Philadelphia.
20 H. G. Adams (ed.), *God's Image in Ebony* (London, 1854; Library Company of Philadelphia).
21 Henry Louis Gates, Jr, and Nellie Y. McKay (eds), *The Norton Anthology of North American Literature* (New York, 1997), pp. 131–4.
22 Denis Judd, *Empire* (London, 1996), p. 322.
23 Quoted in Richard J. Evans, *In Defence of History* (London, 1997), p. 178.
24 Thomas Hodgkin, *Nigerian Perspective, An Historical Anthology* (London, 1960).
25 P. D. Curtin, *African Remembered* (Madison, WI, 1969). This was part of Curtin's continuing work on African history which was to culminate in his seminal book, *The Atlantic Slave Trade: A Census* (Madison, WI, 1969).
26 Paul Edwards (ed.), *Equiano's Travels* (Heinemann, 1967); *The Life of Olaudah Equiano or Gustavus Vassa the African* (Longman, 1988); facsimile version of the two-volume *Interesting Narrative* (Dawsons, London, 1969).
27 The topic 'black studies' quickly established itself as a specific area of academic life throughout the USA, though much of it was subsequently incorporated into newly defined sub-disciplines, more recently 'African-American' studies.
28 Private communication from Vincent Carretta.
29 Constitution of the Equiano Society, 29 November 1996. I am grateful to Arthur Torrington for information about this society.

GUIDE TO
FURTHER READING

For specific topics, readers should follow the references in relevant chapters. This guide offers some of the more useful work written on Equiano and his times.

The starting-point must be Equiano's *Narrative*. There are a number of competing versions available, but the only serious scholarly edition is the Penguin version edited by Vincent Carretta: Olaudah Equiano, *The Interesting Narrative and Other Writings* (London, 1995). Equiano's work in context can best be approached via Vincent Carretta (ed.), *Unchained Voices: An Anthology of Black Authors in the English-Speaking World of the Eighteenth Century* (Lexington, Kentucky, 1996).

Paul Edwards's essays on Equiano offer some of the best commentaries available. See especially:

Paul Edwards: Notes and Introduction, *Equiano's Travels* (Heinemann, London, 1967).
    Notes and Introduction, *The Interesting Narrative of Olaudah Equiano*, facsimile edn (Dawsons, London, 1969).
    Notes and Introduction, *The Life of Olaudah Equiano* (Longman, London, 1988).
    'Equiano and his Captains', in Anna Rutherford (ed.), *Commonwealth* (Aarhus, 1971).
    (with R. Shaw), 'The invisible Chi in Equiano's Interesting Narrative', *Journal of Religion in Africa*, vol. 19, no. 2 (1989).
    '"Master" and "Father" in Equiano's Interesting Narrative', *Slavery and Abolition*, vol. 11, no. 2 (1990).

Of the many other essays/commentaries/contextual pieces on Equiano, the following are especially interesting:

Acolounu, Catherine O., 'The home of Olaudah Equiano – a linguistic and anthropological survey', *Journal of Commonwealth Literature*, vol. 12, no. 1 (1987).
Andrews, William L., *To Tell a Free Story: The First Century of Afro-America Autobiography* (Urbana, 1986).
Baker, Houston A., *The Journey Back: Issues in Black Literature and Criticism* (Chicago, 1980).
— *Blues, Ideology and Afro-American Literature* (Chicago, 1984).
Costanzo, Angelo, *Surprizing Narrative; Olaudah Equiano and the Beginnings of Black Autobiography* (New York, 1987).

Dabydeen, David (ed.), *The Black Presence in English Literature* (Manchester, 1985).

Davis, Charles T. and Gates, Henry L., Jr. (eds), *The Slave's Narrative: Texts and Contexts* (New York, 1985).

Doherty, Thomas, 'Olaudah Equiano's journeys: the geography of a slave narrative', *Partisan Review*, 4 (1997).

Fryer, Peter, *Staying Power: The History of Black People in Britain* (London, 1984).

Gates, Henry L., Jr. (ed.), *Black Literature and Literary Theory* (London, 1984).

— *The Signifying Monkey: Theory of Afro-American Literary Criticism* (Oxford, 1989).

— and Nellie Y. McKay (eds), *The Norton Anthology of African American Literature* (New York, 1997).

Green, James, 'The publishing history of Olaudah Equiano's *Interesting Narrative*', *Slavery and Abolition*, vol. 16, no. 3 (1995).

Murphy, Geraldine, 'Olaudah Equiano, accidental tourist', *Eighteenth-Century Studies*, vol. 27, no. 4 (1994).

Potkay, Adam, 'Olaudah Equiano and the art of spiritual autobiography', *Eighteenth-Century Studies*, vol. 27, no. 4 (1994).

Rodgers, Nini, 'Equiano in Belfast: a study of the anti-slavery ethos in a northern town', *Slavery and Abolition*, vol. 18, no. 2 (1997).

Samuels, Wilfred D., 'The disguised voice in *The Interesting Narrative of Olaudah Equiano*', *Black American Literature Forum*, vol. 19, no. 2 (1985).

Sandiford, Keith, *Measuring the Moment: Strategies of Protest in Eighteenth-Century Afro-English Writing* (London, 1988).

INDEX